Michael Francis Brown   16 August 2009

From David, Janet, Daniel + Ceri.

MATTHEW BOULTON

A REVOLUTIONARY PLAYER

Edited by Malcolm Dick

BREWIN BOOKS

First published by
Brewin Books Ltd, 56 Alcester Road,
Studley, Warwickshire B80 7LG in 2009
www.brewinbooks.com

ISBN: 978-1-85858-441-6

A Cataloguing in Publication Record
for this title is available from the British Library.

Typeset in Baskerville
Printed in Great Britain by
Cromwell Press Group.

CONTENTS

Acknowledgements, *Malcolm Dick*   vi

Preface, *Jenny Uglow*   viii

1. Matthew Boulton: A Revolutionary Player, *Malcolm Dick*   1
2. Birmingham and the West Midlands in the eighteenth and early nineteenth centuries, *Peter Jones*   13
3. 'A new species of gentleman', *Shena Mason*   30
4. Matthew Boulton, enclosure and landed society, *David Brown*   45
5. Portraits of Matthew Boulton, *Val Loggie*   63
6. Coinage, commerce and inspired ideas: The notebooks of Matthew Boulton, *Fiona Tait*   77
7. His Excellency Count Woronzow the Russian Ambassador and the Hardware Man: The history of a friendship, *Olga Baird*   92
8. Was Matthew Boulton a steam engineer? *Jim Andrew*   107
9. Power at the Soho Manufactory and Mint, *George Demidowicz*   116
10. 'I almost wish to be a Potter': Matthew Boulton's relationship with Josiah Wedgwood, *Nicholas Goodison*   132
11. Silver and its substitutes, *Kenneth Quickenden*   153
12. Matthew Boulton and the Royal Mint, *David Symons*   170
13. Technology, Art and Design in the Work of Matthew Boulton: Coins, Medals and Tokens produced at the Soho Mint, *Sue Tungate*   185
14. 'Real Knowledge and Occult Misteries': Matthew Boulton and the Birmingham Assay Office, *Sally Baggott*   201

Notes on contributors   217

Index   220

ACKNOWLEDGEMENTS

Malcolm Dick

My interest in Matthew Boulton was stimulated when I was working on the Revolutionary Players Digitisation Project between 2002 and 2004, which resulted in the creation of a website www.revolutionaryplayers.org.uk, devoted to the history of the West Midlands during the eighteenth and nineteenth centuries. One focus was upon the men of the Lunar Society, including Matthew Boulton. Jenny Uglow's *The Lunar Men* (2002) provided an exciting and readable collective biography, which drew attention to the possibilities of investigating Boulton in greater detail. Further stimulation has been provided by students at the University of Birmingham who have been fascinated by his life and work. Boulton died in 1809 and the 200th anniversary of his death in 2009 provides an opportunity to focus upon the extraordinary range of his activities and achievements. *Matthew Boulton 1728–1809: a Revolutionary Player* uses the expertise of scholars from different historical perspectives, including social and cultural history, the history of art and technology and archaeology to explore his life and importance.

Several people and organisations have contributed to this publication. They include the authors who supplied articles promptly and responded positively to suggestions for changes. I am especially grateful to Jenny Uglow for contributing the preface. I want to record my appreciation to my colleague Dr Richard Clay, who commented upon several chapters and supported the creation of the book from conception to birth. I have benefited from his knowledge and my conversations with two other colleagues, Professors Peter Jones and Ruth Watts. Fellow members of the *Matthew Boulton 2009 Advisory Group*, chaired by Chris Rice (Head of Heritage Services, Birmingham Museums & Art Gallery) have also supported this publication. For the use of copyright material, I am grateful to Archives and Heritage in Birmingham Central Library, The Birmingham

Assay Office Charitable Trust and Birmingham Museums & Art Gallery. Dr Sally Baggott (Curator, The Birmingham Assay Office), Richard Albutt (Head of Digitisation and Outreach, Birmingham Archives and Heritage) and Tom Heaven (Picture Librarian, Birmingham Museums & Art Gallery) assisted in supplying and providing permission to use images from their respective institutions. I am very pleased that Mohsen Keiany and Simon Russell also supplied photographs for the book. Working with Brewin Books was a pleasure, and the firm has contributed its expertise by producing a first-class publication.

Readers of this book will find further information in a complementary publication, *Matthew Boulton: Selling What All the World Desires* (Yale University Press, 2009), which will accompany the Matthew Boulton bicentenary exhibition at the Gas Hall, Birmingham Museum & Art Gallery from June – September 2009. The book includes around 300 illustrations, essays on Boulton and a catalogue list of approximately 400 exhibition objects. Alongside *The Art of Making Money* exhibition at The Barber Institute, The University of Birmingham, its catalogue edited by Richard Clay and several other events in 2009 (http://matthewboulton2009.org/), the publications will enable Boulton to be better known at the end of 2009 than at the beginning of the year.

PREFACE

Jenny Uglow

For many years I have been impressed by how much the West Midlands contributed to contemporary experience and national life in the eighteenth and early nineteenth centuries. Despite the demolition of historic buildings and the changing urban landscape, much remains to remind us of this time. As well as the country houses and polite landscapes of the aristocracy and gentry, there are remnants of another world. The homes of two members of the Lunar Society of Birmingham, the house of the doctor, scientist, writer and poet Erasmus Darwin in Lichfield, and Matthew Boulton's Soho House, in the Birmingham suburb of Handsworth, have both been turned into lively museums. They provide an insight into the Midlands Enlightenment, which did so much to shape the technology, scientific understanding and creative thinking of the day. Other members of the Lunar Society were equally influential: Joseph Priestley extended the knowledge of atmospheres and electricity, Josiah Wedgwood combined his skill in chemistry and his love of art to establish the modern ceramics industry, and William Withering used careful observation to apply innovations in medicine.

Matthew Boulton (1728–1809) was central to the Midlands Enlightenment. At the Soho Manufactory he created the largest manufacturing factory complex in the world, making decorative ormolu, silverware, swords, buttons, medals and coins. Here he applied the division of labour, mass-production techniques and active marketing to make and sell local products throughout the world. In partnership with the inventor, James Watt, Boulton also developed the steam engine into an efficient pumping device and then transformed it by rotary motion into equipment which could be used to power machinery. The Soho Foundry, where these engines were made, deserves to be called the birthplace of mechanical engineering. Unlike the Soho Manufactory, which was demolished in the nineteenth century, the shell of the Soho Foundry survives, just outside Birmingham, in Smethwick. With other Lunar friends, Boulton was also sponsor of the regional canal network which established Birmingham at the centre of a silver cross of waterways. The canals enabled the landlocked town to obtain raw materials and to transport finished goods across Britain and – through the ports of Bristol, Hull, Liverpool and London – to export them to Africa, America, Asia and mainland Europe.

Boulton has left another legacy. The Central Library in Birmingham is home to the most important collection of archives relating to the industrial revolution in the world, and the Archives of Soho offer a wonderful insight into every aspect of Boulton's personal, intellectual and business life. These rich materials are being quarried by historians, and I found them invaluable when I was working on *The Lunar Men: The Friends who made the Future 1730–1810* (2002), which explores the connections between the members of the Lunar Society and examines their lives and achievements. *Matthew Boulton 1728–1809: a Revolutionary Player* presents the findings of several scholars who have explored these resources and examined the equally important images and artefacts held by Birmingham Museums & Art Gallery and the Birmingham Assay Office. I am delighted that the 200th anniversary of Boulton's death in 2009 gives us the chance to look again at his life and times, and celebrate his great achievements. Boulton was an extraordinary character – full of energy, imagination and zest for life – and, like other members of the Lunar Society, he was a man who changed the world.

x

Chapter 1

MATTHEW BOULTON:
A REVOLUTIONARY PLAYER

Malcolm Dick

2009 marks the 200th anniversary of the death of Matthew Boulton, industrialist, landowner, scientist and a contributor to transport development and the arts. This publication, *Matthew Boulton (1728–1809): a Revolutionary Player,* is produced to connect with this event and coincides with a revival of interest in his life and work. The Preface by Jenny Uglow outlines Boulton's importance as a revolutionary player in British industrialisation and the intellectual life of the Enlightenment,[1] but, as David Miller has noted, Boulton has suffered in comparison with his business partner, James Watt and pioneer of steam-engine development: 'Watt's fame', Miller claims, 'has weighed heavier with posterity.'[2] There is no substantial biographical study of Boulton, yet his senior colleagues in the Lunar Society, Watt; Erasmus Darwin, a medic, inventor, poet and educationalist; Joseph Priestley, the radical scientist, theologian and educationalist and political campaigner and Josiah Wedgwood, a developer of new techniques in ceramic manufacturing and anti-slavery campaigner have received substantial biographical attention recently.[3]

---

1   The term 'revolutionary player', which provides the title for this book, is borrowed from the Revolutionary Players website, which explores the history of the West Midlands during industrialisation in the eighteenth and nineteenth centuries: www.revolutionaryplayers.org.uk.

2   David Miller, 'Scales of Justice: Assaying Matthew Boulton's Reputation and the Partnership of Boulton & Watt', *Midland History*, vol.34, no.1, Spring 2009 (forthcoming).

3   Richard L. Hills, *James Watt*, vols.1–3 (Ashbourne: Landmark Publishing Limited, 2002, 2005, 2006); Maureen MacNeil, *Under the Banner of Science: Erasmus Darwin and his Age* (Manchester: Manchester University Press, 1987); Desmond King-Hele, *Erasmus Darwin: A Life of Unequalled Achievement* (London: Giles de la Mare, 1999); R.E. Schofield, *The Enlightenment of Joseph Priestley: A Study of his Life and Works from 1733 to 1773* (Philadelphia: Pennsylvania State University Press, 1997) and *The Enlightened Joseph Priestley: A Study of his Life and Works from 1773–1804* (Philadelphia: Pennsylvania State University Press, 2004); Robin Reilly, *Josiah Wedgwood* (London: Macmillan, 1992).

Boulton, nevertheless, has been studied. Two short reports by James Watt and his fellow Lunar man, James Keir, were written immediately after his death and provide fascinating assessments of how two of his colleagues perceived him.[4] David Miller has charted some of the first biographical accounts of Boulton in the early nineteenth century.[5] A detailed biography was written by Samuel Smiles in the mid-nineteenth century, though it was a double exploration of both Watt and Boulton. It is readable and full of primary source material, but it largely considers Boulton through his relationship with Watt and celebrates him as 'a true leader of men.'[6] Since then, Dickinson's brief and selective study has provided an overview of his life and Jennifer Tann has published a helpful overview in the Oxford Dictionary of National Biography.[7] Writing a full biography of Boulton will be an intimidating task, given the huge size of the Archives of Soho in Birmingham Central Library, which contain material about his personal life and relationships as well as his business, industrial and political activities.[8] Nevertheless, there have been a number of publications which have drawn attention to aspects of Boulton. These have included studies of his connections to other men in the Lunar Society by Robert Schofield and Jenny Uglow and his family life in Shena Mason's biography of his daughter, Anne.[9] Other works have considered his business or artistic activities, for example by Eric Robinson, Nicholas Goodison and Richard Doty.[10] There have also been studies which have explored Boulton in broader contexts: technology transfer and globalization by K. Bruland, J.R.

---

4   James Watt, *Memoir of Matthew Boulton* (Birmingham: City of Birmingham School of Printing, 1943, first printed in 1809); James Keir, *Memoir of Matthew Boulton* (Birmingham: City of Birmingham School of Printing, 1947, first printed in 1809).

5   Miller, *op. cit.*

6   Samuel Smiles, *Lives of Boulton and Watt* (London: John Murray, 1865): 487.

7   H.W. Dickinson, *Matthew Boulton* (Warwickshire: TEE Publishing, 1999, first printed in 1936); Jennifer Tann, 'Boulton, Matthew (1728–1809)' in Oxford Dictionary of National Biography, ed. H.C.G. Matthew and Brian Harrison (Oxford: OUP, 2004); online ed., ed. Lawrence Goldman, May 2007, http://www.oxforddnb.com/view/article/2983 (accessed September 25, 2007).

8   This collection of primary sources not only provides a vast record for studying Boulton but it is probably the most important single archive for the history of industrialisation in Britain in the late eighteenth and early nineteenth centuries.

9   Robert E. Schofield, *The Lunar Society of Birmingham* (Oxford: Clarendon Press, 1963); Jenny Uglow, *The Lunar Men* (London: Faber and Faber, 2002); Shena Mason, *The Hardware Man's Daughter: Matthew Boulton and his 'Dear Girl'* (Chichester: Phillimore, 2005).

10   E. Robinson, 'Eighteenth-Century Commerce and Fashion: Matthew Boulton's Marketing Techniques', *The Economic History Review*, New Series, vol.16, no.1 (1963), pp.39–60; Ken Quickenden, 'Boulton and Fothergill Silver: business plans and miscalculations', *Art History*, 3 (September 1980), pp.274–92; Nicholas Goodison, *Matthew Boulton: Ormolu* (London: Christie's, 2002); Richard G. Doty, *The Soho Mint and the Industrialisation of Money* (London: National Museum of American History in association with Spink and the British Numismatic Society, 1998).

Harris and Jennifer Tann, Enlightenment ideas by Peter Jones, consumer development by Maxine Berg and industrialisation and the education of the public by Malcolm Dick.[11]

The contributions to *Matthew Boulton (1728–1809): a Revolutionary Player,* are written by historians of social, cultural, technological and economic history as well as an archaeologist, an archivist and museum curators. They represent different academic disciplines and the expertise of professionals and are written in a scholarly, but accessible way. Together, they present a picture of the context in which Boulton lived, his family ties, aspirations, relationships and his scientific, industrial, artistic and business activities. They raise questions about what motivated Boulton, how he related to others and the ways in which he made contributions to the economic, social and cultural life of the late eighteenth and early nineteenth centuries.

Peter Jones' chapter provides an analysis of the geographical area in which Boulton operated. 'Birmingham and the West Midlands' may be an anachronistic label, if it refers to an integrated economic region in the late eighteenth and early nineteenth centuries, but the area was beginning to develop a number of shared characteristics as a collection of townships and small-scale metal and extractive industries became connected in a number of ways. One characteristic was the expansion of transport through turnpiking, improvements to river navigations and canal development. Boulton participated in developing the latter to bring raw materials to his manufactories and send finished goods to markets elsewhere in Britain and abroad. Boulton's Soho Manufactory, which was opened in 1762, and his foundry of 1795 were close to turnpiked roads and the network of route-ways which linked his works to the coal mines and iron foundries of the Black Country. The canal network, however, became more important: it provided easier and cheaper transport to bring raw materials from further away and take his products to markets elsewhere. Regional integration was also

---

11   K. Bruland, *Technology Transfer and Scandinavian Industrialisation* (New York: Berg, 1991); J.R. Harris, *Industrial Espionage and technology transfer: Britain and France in the eighteenth century*, Aldershot: Ashgate, 1998); Jennifer Tann, 'The diffusion of the stationery steam engine from Britain to India', *Indian Economic and Social History Review*, vol.29, no.2, 1992, pp.200–214 and 'Steam and Sugar: The diffusion of the stationery steam engine to the Caribbean sugar industry 1779–1840', *History of Technology*, 19, Nov. 1997, pp.63–84. Peter Jones, 'Matthew Boulton's 'Enchanted Castle': Visions of the Enlightenment in the English Midlands c.1765–1800' in Roland Mortier (ed.), *Visualisation* (Berlin: Verlag, Arno Spitz GmbH, 1999): 227–240, 'Industrial Enlightenment in Practice: Visitors to the Soho Manufactory, 1765–1820', *Midland History*, 33, no.1, Spring 2008, 68–96; *Industrial Enlightenment in Birmingham and the West Midlands, 1760–1820: Science, Technology and Culture* (Manchester: Manchester University Press, 2008); Maxine Berg, *Luxury and Pleasure in Eighteenth-Century Britain* (Oxford: Oxford University Press, 2005); Malcolm Dick, 'Discourses for the new industrial world: industrialisation and the education of the public in late eighteenth-century Britain', *History of Education*, vol.37, No.4, July 2008, pp.567–584.

influenced by the growth of towns, including the rapid development of Black Country townships such as Bilston and Tipton, the expansion of established centres such as Wolverhampton and Dudley and the continued importance, if relative stagnation, of county towns such as Worcester and Shrewsbury. One of these, Lichfield, the original home of Boulton's father and both of his wives, developed into an important cultural centre and location for Lunar Society meetings at Erasmus Darwin's house in the Cathedral Close. Birmingham became the most important urban area and centre of industrial growth. It was one of the two most rapidly growing towns in eighteenth-century Britain, together with Sheffield, and had reached a population size of about 75,000 in 1790. Birmingham attracted superlative comments from national and international visitors because of the breadth of its manufactured products, the productivity of its labour force and the inventiveness and adaptability of its people. Jones quotes Arthur Young, who, in 1791, described Birmingham as 'the first manufacturing town in the world.' From 1793 until the early 1800s, it experienced a recession, unemployment and demographic decline, but the strength of the domestic market, the growth of overseas trade and the ability of local businesses to adapt to changing circumstances ensured that the decline was temporary. One aspect of Matthew Boulton's commercial intelligence lay in his ability to create demand for the goods he made and adapt to changing markets.

Shena Mason considers Boulton as an example of Samuel Johnson's 'new species of Gentleman', but Boulton's trajectory towards becoming a gentleman was a complex process. His ancestors were originally members of the Staffordshire gentry, but they appear to have experienced a downturn in fortunes. His father, Matthew Boulton senior (1700–1759) like two of his brothers, served an apprenticeship. After moving from the family home in Lichfield to an apprenticeship in Birmingham, he established himself as one of the town's many button and buckle makers. Boulton senior, like other local manufacturers made his living by making inexpensive and decorative small metal products, the famous 'Birmingham's toys'. It was his son, Matthew, born in 1728, who transformed the family concern into a business, or rather a number of businesses with a national and international profile. How and why this happened are two of the important questions to ask about Matthew Boulton. Perhaps his early education played a part. Unfortunately we know little about his schooling except that he was educated in a local school run by a well-regarded teacher, the Revd. John Hausted. Though Boulton left in about 1745 to work with his father, he retained an appetite for knowledge, self-education and self-improvement and he read widely in the classics, art, accountancy and 'natural philosophy'. It is possible to argue, as Jones claims, that Boulton became a *savant-fabricant*, an individual who combined intellectual activity with practical skills as a manufacturer and businessman.[12]

These attributes brought him into contact with other gentlemen whose origins were more privileged and formal education was lengthier, including most of his associates in the Lunar Society. They also connected him to the scientific and technological ideas which were current in Britain, Europe and North America, links which would contribute to his success as a manufacturer and trader. His attributes probably helped him to marry well. In 1749, he wedded Mary Robinson, a distant relative and daughter of a wealthy Lichfield trader, a connection which brought him money and land. Mary died in 1759, but within a year, he had married her sister, Ann, who brought further wealth and property to Boulton. 1759 was an important year for Boulton. The death of his father shortly before his second marriage meant that Boulton became an independent manufacturer in his own right, and the wealth from his second marriage enabled him to invest in expanding his business and acquire the signs of wealth and status that a gentleman required. In 1761, he obtained the lease on heathland at Soho, Handsworth, in Staffordshire, which included a residence, Soho House. Though over the Birmingham boundary, it was only two miles from central Birmingham and therefore near his workshops. On this heath he built the huge Soho Manufactory and in 1766, he moved into Soho House, which he extended, improved and provided with high-quality furniture, scientific instruments, books and the decorative features expected in a gentleman's residence.[13] Boulton ate well and entertained lavishly and he also dressed to impress, a form of expenditure which caused his banker, Charlotte Matthews, some concern. Soho House, Soho Manufactory and the 'polite landscape' which surrounded his home became a place of visitation, not only for acquaintances, but also for aristocratic and intellectual visitors from abroad. One prominent guest, who became a close friend, was Count Woronzow, Russia's ambassador to the British court, whose relationship with Boulton is explored by Olga Baird in Chapter 7. Boulton became a gentleman, but he was proud of his role as a businessman. Mason quotes his remarks to his son, Matthew Robinson Boulton: 'I had rather be distinguished as the greatest manufacturer in Europe than as a Count of the Holy Roman Empire.'

David Brown's essay takes Shena Mason's exploration of Matthew Boulton's status and personality further, by looking at the relationship

---

12 Jones, *Industrial Enlightenment, op. cit.,* pp.116–120.
13 Soho House Museum, part of Birmingham Museums and Art Gallery provides an insight into the life of the Boulton family at Soho.

between Matthew Boulton, enclosure and landed society. Some traditionally-minded landowners showed little inclination to develop their estates. Nevertheless, others, like Boulton, saw opportunities to secure rewards from growing demands for food, industrial development or house-building their estates might offer. Brown claims that 'Boulton was typical of a growing kind of landowner, more often Whig than Tory, who was committed to the transformation of traditional rural society and the notion of improvement rather than conservatism.' He locates Boulton as an active member of the West Midlands élite and a major contributor to rural change, as well as the industrial transformation of the West Midlands. Boulton was an ardent advocate of enclosure, not only in Handsworth, but elsewhere in the West Midlands. He decried those who encroached onto the commons as potential claimants for poor relief and individuals who could prevent the efficient exploitation of a landscape for economic development. These traits identify him as someone who aspired to the wealth and status of a member of the landowning class and also wished to develop land for the economic benefits it could provide.

As well as creating wealth, Matthew Boulton was interested in using it to present his image and images of his family to the wider world. In this respect, as Val Loggie shows, he was following members of the established gentry and aristocracy. Boulton engaged a variety of artists to paint him: Tilly Kettle, J.S.C. Schaak, Johan Zoffany, James Millar, Carl Frederick von Breda, Sir William Beechey and Lemuel Francis Abbott. Some like Millar were best-known as provincial artists, but others, such as Beechey were patronised by royalty. Most of the paintings show Boulton dressed in the clothes of a gentleman, with no overt reference to his status as a manufacturer, but Breda displays him holding a medal and magnifying glass with the Soho Manufactory in the background and Beechey reveals him holding a medal or coin with a nearby mineral specimen in a glass dome. Boulton wanted his scientific and manufacturing interests to be represented in paint to an audience. Some of these images were displayed in exhibitions, copied for friends and associates or turned into prints. In a variety of ways, as Loggie shows, Boulton 'controlled the way his image was seen', not only as a gentleman, but also as an industrialist and a man with scientific interests.

Another insight into Boulton's personality and interests is provided by his notebooks. Ninety-six of these survive which cover the period from the 1750s until 1804. Fiona Tait's dissection of their contents reveals the range of his economic, scientific and personal interests at particular times. Boulton refers to his contracts, debts and foreign travel: the latter leads him to make comparisons between Britain and Holland and Britain and France (in the latter case there is an interesting comment on watches and scientific instruments). He also writes extensively about Soho House and its contents, gardening and landscape improvement, food and medicines. As might be expected, Boulton's interest in scientific knowledge and experimentation and his business interests feature heavily: the notebooks cover astronomy, metals, buttons, chemistry, gilding, buckle making, coinage and steam technology. They reveal, as Tait suggests, 'a man with an appetite for new ideas and knowledge, a drive to improve ways of working and a willingness to experiment to find the best solution.' They confirm him as *savant-fabricant*, with an interest in domestic as well as intellectual and economic matters.

Boulton's capacity for friendship is revealed by Olga Baird's chapter on his relationship with Count Semyon Woronzow, Russia's ambassador to the British court. Russian visitors to Soho were important contacts from the 1760s. Boulton had extensive trading relationships with Russia and he was keen to sell his products to the wealthy royalty and nobility in this country. Russians visited his works and acquired manufactured products from him directly. His connection with Count Woronzow began in the 1780s, but Boulton's involvement in developing the Russian Mint in the late 1790s led to closer bonds. In 1799, Woronzow brought his family to stay at Soho, probably as part of the Enlightenment education of Woronzow's son, Mikhail, to enable him to gain knowledge of the mechanical arts. Besides visits to the Soho Manufactory and Mint, Boulton also provided them with a cultural tour of the area, including a play at Birmingham's Theatre Royal and a canal trip through the caverns under Dudley Castle. Woronzow thanked Boulton profusely for six 'very happy' days. Their relationship remained close and developed into one of mutual admiration and concern with each other's welfare. Baird has discovered that about 150 personal and business letters between the two men survive from 1786 and 1807. Their correspondence may have started because of commercial interests, but it developed into a friendship between the Boulton and Woronzow families, the closest of any connection that Boulton had with Russian visitors to Soho.

Boulton's role as an engineer is considered by Jim Andrew, who looks critically at the popular perception that Matthew Boulton was a businessman who handled the commercial side of the steam-engine business, but left technical innovation to Watt, the inventor. He shows that Boulton was interested in the technical development of the steam engine and was prepared to get his hands dirty to make sure that machines worked in practice. Before Watt's arrival in Birmingham, he worked with another

Lunar man, Dr William Small, instructing technical staff and he was closely connected with the development of Watt's steam engine design in 1775, testing components and investigating temperatures and pressures. Later, in 1782, he suggested improvements to the sun and planet gears. Boulton may not have had the same degree of technical expertise as Watt, but Andrew claims that his letters show that he was able to provide Watt with information he could use. He concludes: 'Boulton could have become established as a competent steam engineer just as he showed other technical abilities in his partnerships in the toy trade, silverware and ormolu manufacturing and minting.'

George Demidowicz brings his expertise as an archaeologist to an exploration of how Boulton and his successors used and applied different forms of power at the Soho Manufactory and Mint. First, and perhaps surprisingly for those who associate Boulton with steam power alone, was the introduction of a water wheel in 1761, which was the only way of applying mechanical energy to machinery at Soho before the advent of Watt's rotative steam engine. But problems of drought, flood and the loss of water to Great Hockley Pool meant that water-driven energy provided an insufficiently reliable form of power, although it seems as if water power was used as a form of energy at Soho until the 1840s. In the 1770s, Boulton introduced a Watt pumping steam engine to recycle water which was used by the water mill and so extend its value to the Manufactory. Rotary motion came later to cut out metal blanks for coinage and, subsequently, to power a coin press. Though Boulton and Watt retired from the business in 1795–96, their sons, Matthew Robinson Boulton and James Watt junior, continued operations. The former installed two beamless engines, designed by William Murdock, in 1803–4. Matthew Robinson Boulton's successors continued developments at the site until the 1850s, but the site was demolished and finally disappeared in 1863. It was subsequently built over or destroyed by excavations for building sand. Given the lack of building plans and visual evidence for the internal layout of the Manufactory and Mint, archaeological evidence provides the most important means available for revealing the topography of the Soho manufacturing complex and how power was utilised to ensure it produced its goods.

Nicholas Goodison explores Boulton's long-standing relationship with Josiah Wedgwood, the North Staffordshire potter. This relationship began, so it seems, during their mutual involvement in the development of the Trent and Mersey Canal in the 1760s, an enterprise which befitted both of them economically. They had much in common. Both men were pioneering industrialists with an interest in producing high-quality manufactured goods for a growing domestic and international market and they shared an interest in using classical designs and references in their products. To what extent did they collaborate? The most spectacular example is their joint involvement in creating the tripod for James Stuart's 'Lanthorn of Demosthenes' at the Shugborough estate in 1770, where Boulton provided the bronzework and Wedgwood created the bowl, but, in general, their collaboration was limited. Boulton purchased cameos and useful ware from Wedgwood and they shared marketing ideas, but Wedgwood may have been concerned, at least during the early stages of their relationship, that Boulton was contemplating establishing himself as a potter. Goodison's exploration of the relationship between the two men throws light on the ways in which two manufacturing businesses connected with each other in the late eighteenth century and the breadth of Boulton's innovation and energy.

Boulton's approach to design, production and marketing are also revealed in Ken Quickenden's examination of the role that silver and the search for silver substitutes played in his business. Boulton wanted to produce high-quality silverware and his involvement in the creation of the Birmingham Assay Office in 1773 was part of this plan, but expensive silverware had a limited market and Boulton concentrated much of his energy on looking for alternatives. He investigated and experimented with various forms of plating such as French-plating, close-plating and Sheffield-plating, and using different alloys, including tutenague (copper, zinc and nickel), white metal or semi-argent (tin, antimony and copper) and platina (copper and zinc) for a range of products from candlesticks to buckles and buttons. Sheffield-plate became the most important silver substitute given its durability and lower cost, compared to other forms of plating, though it was unsuitable for the blades of knives and casting. Quickenden's clarification of the economic and technical dimensions of Boulton's search for alternatives to silver provides another example of his innovative approach as an industrialist.

David Symons takes another aspect of Boulton's search for business opportunities: his fraught relationship with the Royal Mint. By the 1770s, the Mint was failing to produce coinage in the quantity required to facilitate exchange in Britain's growing economy. Low denomination copper coins were in short supply, leading to the use of forgeries, blank disks and the production of trade tokens, which were minted by businesses and urban authorities to facilitate local trade. In the 1780s, there were calls in Parliament to remove the minting monopoly from the Royal Mint. Boulton already produced commemorative medals, so minting coins was a natural extension of his work. After gaining a contract to supply the East India Company with coins in 1786–7, he built a mint at Soho, which used steam technology to produce tokens, but it was not until a national financial crisis in 1797, leading to a reconstitution of the currency, that Boulton was able to secure a contract to manufacture copper coins for the state. The first examples were the famous cartwheel pennies, but twopences, halfpennies and farthings followed and in 1804, following another crisis, he gained a contract to strike new designs into Spanish silver dollars to relieve a shortage of domestic silver coins. Boulton's success angered the men at the Royal Mint, but eventually they had to adapt to survive, and Soho was contracted to supply new minting machinery to London in 1806. 'Throughout the story', Symons comments, 'Boulton's talent for innovation, his passion for finding solutions to problems and his ability to deliver these solutions shines through.'

Sue Tungate's essay complements David Symons' chapter, but her focus is upon the artistic and technical dimensions of the medals and coins produced by the Soho Mint, rather than legal and political aspects. She explores Boulton's interest in the creation and production of these items and his employment of designers, engravers and mechanics who implemented his ideas, many of whom came from overseas, such as Jean-Pierre Droz, Jean Baptiste Dupeyrat, Noel-Alexandre Ponthon, Conrad Heinrich Küchler, Thomas Wyon and Rambert Dumarest. Boulton aimed to perfect how designs were stamped on metal (die-stamping) and apply steam power to minting machinery, a technique he pioneered. His products were manufactured for consumers in Britain, Europe and Asia and illustrate political events, including the execution of Louis XVI and Marie Antoinette, military and naval victories, the iron manufacturer, John Wilkinson, and Britannia as an icon of Britishness. The mass production of Boulton's medals and coins provide an insight into cultural, political and economic history in the late eighteenth and early nineteenth centuries.

Sally Baggott's chapter concludes the book and analyses the intense rivalry between Birmingham and London, before Birmingham was able to secure the passage of a parliamentary act to establish a local assay office in 1773. Boulton wanted an assay office to prevent the long and costly journey that Birmingham silver had to make to Chester, to be assayed or proved. Historians have drawn attention to Boulton's skills as a parliamentary lobbyist and his skill in argument and public relations. The campaign though, reveals more than this, a contrast between old and new ways of representing approaches to manufacturing. Boulton effectively lobbied eminent parliamentarians and worked with Sheffield manufacturers who also wanted an assay office to create an alliance of provincial silverware manufacturers. He also engaged expert witnesses, such as Samuel Garbett to support Birmingham's case. The counter arguments of letters, petitions and replies provide documentation for the conflict. The London goldsmiths, who opposed the new assay offices, argued that London silversmiths represented quality and perfection against the ineptitude and backwardness of the provinces. Boulton claimed that the establishment of an assay office in Birmingham would increase competition, bring down prices, stimulate trade and boost employment. Garbett asserted that the London silversmiths were trying to protect their 'Shabby Occult Misteries' against the 'Real knowledge' of Birmingham men. Boulton won the case, but his own involvement in silver manufacturing was not very successful economically and his knowledge of silverware manufacturing and the skills of his artisans depended upon practices developed in London. Nevertheless, Baggott concludes, Boulton demonstrated his skills as an advocate for modern business practices and his abilities to make friends and influence people, attributes which 'render Boulton such a fascinating and charismatic figure to us in the present.'

The essays in this volume complement two publications which serve as catalogues for Birmingham-based exhibitions in 2009, they are Shena Mason (ed.), *Matthew Boulton: Selling What All the World Desires* (Yale University Press, 2009) and Richard Clay (ed.), *Matthew Boulton and the Art of Making Money*, (Brewin Books, 2009). They aim to add to existing knowledge and ensure that Boulton and his significance receive a broader profile. However, much about Matthew Boulton remains to be explored. We need to know more about his relationships with his workforce and the extent to which his achievements were influenced by the engineers and skilled workers he employed, as well as the most famous of his employees, William Murdock.[14] Boulton had a great aptitude for self-advertisement and we should not be seduced by his words. His contribution to the development of British urban artistic and civic culture is another dimension of his importance, as Birmingham developed a polite culture of philanthropy and social improvement, alongside its commercial and industrial expansion. Boulton was part of Birmingham's emergence as an economic global city as it exported technology and products beyond Europe to Asia, Africa, North America and the Caribbean, but it is also interesting to explore the extent to

---

14   Murdock would also benefit from a scholarly biography, but see John C. Griffiths, 'Murdock , William (1754–1839)', in *Oxford Dictionary of National Biography*, ed. H.C.G. Matthew and Brian Harrison (Oxford: OUP, 2004); online ed., ed. Lawrence Goldman, Oct 2007 http://www.oxforddnb.com/view/article/19561 (accessed 21 Jan 2009).

which Boulton gained from expertise elsewhere, by employing European craftsmen, or learning from artistic and scientific traditions overseas including China or India.

Boulton was often circumspect in revealing his opinions. Unlike several of his Lunar colleagues, Darwin, Priestley, Watt and Wedgwood, we have no record of his opinions on the slave trade or slavery, though he subscribed to Olaudah Equiano's best-selling anti-slavery autobiography, *The Interesting Narrative...*, but he also engaged in negotiations to supply steam engines to support plantations in the Caribbean.[15] Does this reveal something about Boulton? Was he someone who could live with potentially contradictory stances, did commercial considerations outweigh morality, was he motivated by the search for wealth? Boulton had considerable intelligence, energy and practical ability and he had a great capacity for friendship and affection, but he was also determined to get his own way and he was conscious of his significance as a manufacturer, as his famous statement to James Boswell reveals: 'I sell here, what all the world desires to have – POWER.'[16] Boulton was a complex man, but, as Baggott has written, he is a 'fascinating and charismatic figure to us in the present'. The essays in this volume reveal that this is the case, but they also show that his life, work and importance merit further exploration.

---

15   Letter to the Printer, 19 June 1790 in *Aris's Birmingham Gazette*, 28 June 1790; Malcolm Dick, 'Joseph Priestley, the Lunar Society and Anti-slavery' in Dick (ed.), *Joseph Priestley and Birmingham* (Studley: Brewin Books, 2005).
16   R.W. Chapman, (ed.), *James Boswell: Life of Johnson* (Oxford: OUP, 1980 Edition), p.704.

Chapter 2

BIRMINGHAM AND THE WEST MIDLANDS IN THE EIGHTEENTH AND EARLY NINETEENTH CENTURIES[1]

Peter Jones

The phrase 'Birmingham and the West Midlands' is something of an anachronism when used in the context of the life of Matthew Boulton. Whilst the expanding physical presence of Birmingham drew frequent comment from travellers in the second half of the eighteenth century, none would have recognised an entity called the West Midlands. Indeed, it can be doubted whether contemporaries would even have acknowledged an area of the country called the 'Midlands'. Neither guide books nor trade directories can shed much light on this question, although the phrase 'Birmingham and District' appears to have been in fairly widespread use by the century's end. The notion of a 'Black Country', that is to say a crude rectangle of territory bounded by Wolverhampton and Walsall to the north and Smethwick, Halesowen and Stourbridge to the south, is also an anachronism in the context of this volume since the expression cannot be traced back beyond the 1840s.[2]

Why then do we couple together 'Birmingham' and the 'West Midlands' in a single phrase? There are two possible answers, the second of which is the more persuasive. Historians, in common with geographers, like to identify regions for rhetorical purposes, that is to say as convenient frameworks within which to carry out analysis. The alternative is to use concepts which have a rather anachronistic ring to them as retrospective tools with which to

---

1   This essay is a condensed and re-worked version of a chapter in the author's: *Industrial Enlightenment: Science, Technology and Culture in Birmingham and the West Midlands, 1760–1820* (Manchester: Manchester University Press, 2008).

2   See W. Gresley, *Colton Green, a Tale of the Black Country* (London, 1847); also R.H. Trainor, *Black Country Elites: the Exercise of Authority in an Industrialised Area, 1830–1900* (Oxford: Clarendon Press, 1993), pp.1–3 and figure.

mount an investigation. This is the approach that we have adopted here. The West Midlands, it will be suggested, was a 'constructed' not a 'natural' entity, and the motive force in the building process was the dynamism of the town of Birmingham itself. By the end of the eighteenth century, Birmingham had emerged as the hub of a highly integrated regional economy.

The regional setting

The first point that needs to be borne in mind when discussing the regional context is that neither Birmingham, nor the towns that would become its satellites were fashioned according to any pre-existing administrative template. In his study of the rise of the Midlands industries, W.H.B. Court[3] described 'Birmingham and District' as a smallish area of some 200 square miles made up of parts (parts of south Staffordshire, north Warwickshire, and east Worcestershire). Birmingham town-ship grew up at the point where these three counties intersected, but he cautions that this district or mini-region was not sufficient unto itself. As an area increasingly defined by metal working, its manufacturers maintained close links with the coal and iron industries of east Shropshire (Coalbrookdale) and, to a lesser degree, with the Warwickshire coal-field situated between Nuneaton and Coventry. Apart from the county towns (Stafford, Warwick, Worcester) about which more will be said below, only Coventry offered an alternative regional focus and economic role model. But Coventry was a textile town (ribbon weaving) and by the eighteenth century was plainly living on its past. Most visitors to Birmingham and the West Midlands travelled through Coventry, if only for the reason that the main London–Holyhead road passed along its high street, yet they had little reason to linger there.

How, then, was this previously unrecognised collection of metal-working towns and villages fashioned into a region identifiable in its own terms? One approach might be to highlight a favourable natural resource endowment comprising coal, iron-ore, limestone and fireclays which established parameters for the development of an energy-rich, regional economy along the lines proposed by Tony Wrigley.[4] Explosive population growth after mid-century and the emergence of distinctively new types of towns within the orbit of Birmingham, certainly conforms to the expectations of this model. Observations made at the time provide some support for an energy-driven explanation of growth as well. Barthélemy Faujas de Saint-Fond who visited Matthew Boulton at Soho in 1784 concluded that it was the abundance of coal

---

3   W.H.B. Court, *The Rise of the Midlands Industries, 1600–1838* (Oxford: Oxford University Press, 1938), p.2.

4   E.A. Wrigley, *Continuity and Change: the Character of the Industrial Revolution* (Cambridge: Cambridge University Press, 1988), chapter 3.

which had produced the 'miracle' [5] of Birmingham, while Alessandro Volta's [6] remarks on his tour through the Black Country and Coalbrookdale a couple of years earlier can be construed in a similar vein.

Yet it should be remembered that Birmingham – at mid-century – was not on the beaten track. Travellers had to leave the main highway about ten miles west of Coventry in order to gain access to the town. Nor did it enjoy the benefits of river communication inasmuch as the Severn, whilst navigable as far as Shrewsbury, was nearly twenty miles distant. The natural endowment argument will only take us so far then, as Wrigley himself acknowledges. The spur or trigger which helped to unlock this mineral wealth and launch the region upon an extraordinary industrial trajectory must be sought elsewhere. Economic geographers argue that transportation innovations provide the key to regional growth and differentiation in the late eighteenth and early nineteenth centuries. The turn-piking of highways and the construction of canals and river navigations promoted spatial integration, facilitated the expansion of intra-regional trade and credit networks, and improved long-distance communication beyond and between regional centres. According to this scenario Birmingham actively remedied its relative isolation, therefore, and in the process a dense 'region' with a specific hardware vocation came into being.

Disentangling the causal sequence linking transport improvements to urbanisation and industrialisation is not a straightforward matter, of course. Moreover it could be objected that Birmingham, if not the still microscopic Black Country industrial villages, was already firmly set upon a pattern of growth before the introduction after the middle of the century of significant improvements to land and water transportation. Nevertheless, this argument has much to recommend it at the regional level. Turn-piking came early and vigorously to the West Midlands, and it does seem to have been a response to pre-existing heavy road usage – particularly the roads frequented by the huge eight-horse wagons used to haul industrial raw materials. Even though Birmingham required a detour, travellers had a choice of two fully turn-piked routes from London as early as 1740. The same may be said of canal building in which the activism of local manufacturers such as Matthew Boulton, Josiah Wedgwood and Samuel Garbett was very much to the fore. All three had excellent commercial motives for promoting canal construction, whether to

---

5   B. Faujas de Saint-Fond, *A Journey through England and Scotland to the Hebrides in 1784*, 2 Vols. (Glasgow: Hopkins, 1907), ii, p.346.

6   *Epistolario di Alessandro Volta. Edizione nationale sotto gli auspice dell'Istituto Lombardo di scienze et lettere e della società italiana di fisic*, 5 Vols. (Bologna, 1949–55), ii, pp.119, 469–73; also G. Pancaldi, *Volta: Science and Culture in the Age of the Enlightenment* (Princeton: Princeton University Press, 2003), pp.160–2.

facilitate the movement of raw materials or to secure access to national and international markets for their finished products.

Work on the Grand Trunk canal which was intended to link the Trent and the Mersey rivers began in 1766. Wedgwood was one of its chief backers and took care to acquire land for his new factory of Etruria in Staffordshire on the proposed route of the waterway. Not until 1777, however, did unimpeded navigation along its entire 140 mile length become possible. In the meantime Boulton and the other Birmingham manufacturers lobbied for a navigable link of more immediate value, namely one which would connect the town's industries to their fuel sources in the Black Country. In 1768 the Birmingham Canal Bill passed both houses of Parliament, thereby enabling the construction of a waterway through the Black Country to Aldersley, north of Wolverhampton, with a view to joining up with the Staffordshire and Worcestershire canal. Whilst such a link would make it possible to bring in pit coal, pig iron and other raw materials by barge rather than by overland transport, it would also provide a convenient exit route for Birmingham wares via the Stour to the Severn and on to Bristol and, in due course, northwards via the Trent and Mersey to either Hull or Liverpool. Within two years the first cargoes were already tying up at the town's brand new coal wharves, and with the completion of the Staffordshire and Worcestershire canal in 1772, the West Midlands gained its first point of access to the sea. The boost which the rapidly executed Birmingham Canal project gave to the regional economy is hard to over-estimate; likewise the Birmingham–Fazeley canal of 1783 which opened up a shorter route to the port of Hull and the markets of northern Europe.

The impact of these new arteries on the economic life of the region was immediate. William Hutton, Birmingham's first published historian and a contemporary observer, noted how they brought relief to a road network groaning under the weight of industrial traffic. Before the opening of the Birmingham Canal, 'it was common to see a train of carriages for miles, to the great destruction of the road, and annoyance of travellers.'[7] They also massively reduced transportation costs for heavy, bulky or, in Wedgwood's case, fragile goods. Wednesbury pit coal which had sold in Birmingham for about thirteen shillings per ton before the opening of the twenty-two mile cut, commanded just seven shillings in 1772 and eight shillings and four pence by the time Hutton published the third edition of *An History of Birmingham* in 1795. Matthew Boulton benefited from this canal system which he had helped to bring into being. It reduced the cost of raw materials such as coal and iron arriving from the Black Country whilst facilitating the transportation of the

---

7   W. Hutton, *An History of Birmingham* (Birmingham: Thomas Pearson, 3rd edn, 1795), p.402.

products of his Soho Manufactory to other parts of Great Britain and beyond, via the ports of Hull, Liverpool, Bristol and London. In the meantime, steady improvements to the road network reduced the quickest passenger journey times between London and Birmingham from around two, or two and a half days at mid-century to as little as fourteen hours by the summer of 1782.

It is important to emphasise that these improvements in the transportation network were regional in focus, however. As John Stobart [8] has argued specialised regional growth was not only generating highly distinctive patterns of industrialisation in this period, it was throwing into sharp relief less well endowed or less well developed parts of the country. Thanks to the turnpikes, Matthew Boulton together with his partner James Watt were able to travel to the French capital via London and Dover in six days during the late autumn of 1786, and letters from Paris to Birmingham routinely took four. Yet Boulton's journeys to oversee steam-engine erectors in Cornwall required a minimum of eight uncomfortable days on the road, and letters between Truro and Birmingham took up to fifteen. If improvements in communications combined with a highly favourable natural resource endowment provide the key explanation of how Birmingham and the Black Country were subsumed into a discrete West Midlands region, then, it is the interlocking quality of the transportation revolution that needs to be highlighted.

The testimony of trade directories is particularly useful in this respect, for they enable us to take a look *inside* the embryonic West Midlands at a given moment in time. On this evidence, the principal industrial nodes by the 1790s were Birmingham, Wolverhampton, Walsall, Bilston, Dudley and Stourbridge inasmuch as the working population of these towns generated nearly two-thirds of the region's output of iron and steel goods. These towns, moreover, were increasingly inter-connected, whether by turnpikes, canal cuts, or wagon and carrier services. By the time Pigot's directory [9] was published in 1835, Birmingham boasted 594 carriage departures to thirty-seven destinations each week, and the best served destinations were those located in its industrial hinterland to the west and the north-west. Communication *between* the towns of the Black Country had also become intensive, particularly between Wolverhampton and Dudley. Nevertheless, eighty-three percent of Wolverhampton's scheduled carrier traffic continued to move in the direction of Birmingham.

---

8   J. Stobart, *The First Industrial Region: North-West England c.1700–60* (Manchester: Manchester University Press, 2004).

9   N. Raven and J. Stobart, 'Networks and Hinterlands: Transport in the Midlands' in J. Stobart and N. Raven (eds), *Towns, Regions and Industries: Urban and Industrial Change in the Midlands, c.1700–1840* (Manchester: Manchester University Press, 2005), pp.86–7.

The Wolverhampton – Birmingham axis was the region's main industrial artery in fact. When the La Rochefoucauld brothers came to visit Dr Joseph Priestley in 1785, they reported that even at this date the fourteen-mile stretch of road resembled 'one continuous town.'[10] The French military engineer, Charles-Pierre Dupin[11] who had occasion to take the same route in 1816 but at night time, evoked an horizon lit by fire. The nailers' cottages strewn along the highway had mostly been ousted by ironworks, brickworks and forges as a result of the opening of the Birmingham Canal. It was access to this canal that had prompted James Keir to select Tipton Green as the site for his new chemical works in 1781, and in 1795 the sons of Boulton and Watt would choose Smethwick as the location for their steam-engine plant (the Soho Foundry) for the same reason. In a plateau district where ground water was often in short supply, the canal network also fostered the expansion of steam power technology inasmuch as factory owners were encouraged to set up their operations canal-side by the prospect of cheap coals *and* a ready water source for their engines. Pumping engines were a virtual prerequisite for canal development in the region in any case. One of the earliest orders for Watt's improved steam engine was placed by the proprietors of the Birmingham Canal Company. It was installed at Smethwick in 1776 in order to replenish the supply of water to the locks. All in all, around 1,500 Black Country collieries and ironworks were linked to the canal network by 1798, and by the ending of the Napoleonic Wars Birmingham could no longer be considered an out-of-the-way place. Dupin[12] reported eight major roads entering the town and a total of 348 kilometers of canal navigation within a radius of thirty-two kilometers.

If we shift the focus in order to view the regionalisation of the West Midlands from a demographic point of view, two clear patterns emerge: the explosive growth of the Black Country towns and villages, and the relative stagnation of the non-industrial 'county' towns. The south Staffordshire landscape which would form the kernel of the Black Country was in a state of transition in the second half of the eighteenth century. A habitat based on fields, rural lanes, villages and isolated farms whose coherence was still largely agricultural was being gnawed away by unmistakable signs of industrial growth, which was imposing in turn its own raison-d'être in terms of turnpikes, canal basins and tramways. Places such as Bilston, Tipton,

---

10   N. Scarfe, *Innocent Espionage: the La Rochefoucauld Brothers' Tour of England in 1785* (Woodbridge: Boydell, 1995), p.106.

11   C. Dupin, *Voyages dans la Grande-Bretagne entrepris relativement aux services publics de la Guerre, de la Marine, et des Ponts et Chaussées en 1816, 1817, 1818 et 1819*, 6 Vols in 3. (Paris: Fain, 1820–24), iv, p.22.

12   Ibid, pp.225–6.

Willenhall or West Bromwich which were scarcely more than agricultural, or at best proto-industrial, parishes until the 1770s or the 1780s, experienced a population surge as demand for basic hardwares soared and capital combined with entrepreneurship unlocked the resources of the sub-soil and put in place infrastructure improvements.

The other dimension of the story of regional integration in the West Midlands concerns the established towns. Wolverhampton, Stourbridge, Walsall and Dudley were all urban centres of some antiquity whose local economies were well placed to take advantage of the opportunities materialising in the second half of the eighteenth century. Wolverhampton's profile of demographic growth was second only to that of Birmingham. In 1801 it was comfortably the second largest urban centre in the district, having almost doubled in size since the middle of the century to attain around 12,500 inhabitants. Although the township retained an important market function throughout the period of interest to us, metalworking had been the mainstay of its economy since the 1740s, if not earlier. The growth of Stourbridge situated on the southern perimeter of the Black Country was less spectacular to be sure. But, like Wolverhampton, it had a long history – as a prosperous market town, as a centre of woollen cloth manufacture, and latterly as the principal site of the regional glass industry.

Ringing Birmingham and the Black Country to the west and the north were the 'county' towns, that is to say the long-established municipal and parliamentary boroughs which were often county seats as well. Whilst it would be overly schematic to juxtapose dynamic industrial towns and stagnant 'county' towns as though industrialisation was a precondition for urban expansion, the fact remains that places like Worcester, Lichfield, Stafford and even the more distant Shrewsbury had a gentler profile of growth in the eighteenth century. On the economic front Worcester probably had most to fear from the rise of Birmingham. Despite its advantageous position on the river Severn, the population of the town only increased by a little over a third across the century.[13] As for Lichfield, it rested on its laurels, only to see the road network reconfigured to its detriment and the canal and, in due course, the railway pass it by. Like Worcester, Lichfield concentrated instead on its status as an ecclesiastical capital and on its capacity to cater for the needs of the well-to-do. The town boasted a range of clubs and societies nurtured mostly by the families of the Anglican clergy who formed a large component of the resident élite.

---

13   See D. Whitehead, 'Georgian Worcester' (MA dissertation, University of Birmingham, 1976), p.10; A. Dyer, 'Midlands' in Clark (ed.), *The Cambridge Urban History*, ii, pp.106–7; P. Borsay, *The English Urban Renaissance: Culture and Society in the Provincial Town, 1660–1770* (Oxford: Oxford University Press, 1989), p.206.

Birmingham

The 'miracle birth' of Birmingham should not be viewed purely in eighteenth-century terms as many accounts seem to suggest. It is nonetheless true that only in the eighteenth century does it become possible to capture the town's development in any detail. Birmingham's gestation as a centre of metal working must be traced back to the sixteenth century at least, for even in Tudor times it was not a village but a middling market town. By the 1670s this market town which had long echoed to the sound of forge hammers was beginning to approach in size the leading 'county' towns of the region. Thereafter, to be sure, an extraordinarily rapid increase in its population took place – even if the precise demographic profile of the town at the start of the eighteenth century remains difficult to fathom. William Hutton's [14] computation of 15,032 for 1700 is certainly too high, since C.W. Chalklin [15] found only about 11,400 in the town's principal parish around 1720. A baseline figure of between 7,000 and 8,000 seems more likely. If this estimate can be accepted, Birmingham tripled in size during the first half of the century and tripled again between 1750 and 1791, at which point its demographic expansion was more or less curtailed for a decade. By 1775 Birmingham appears to have become the third most populous town in England (after London and Bristol), its rate of growth exceeding all rivals. Sheffield, another metal-working town, evinced a similar trajectory, albeit from a lower base. Manchester, the shock city of the nineteenth century, together with the port of Liverpool would catch up Birmingham and then surpass it around the turn of the century.

The trade directories and guide books describe the Birmingham of the third quarter of the eighteenth century as a settlement 'about two Miles in length (including the hamlets of Deritend and Bordsley)', which is 'pleasantly situated on the Side of a Hill forming nearly a half-Moon.'[16] Whilst not inexact, these statements scarcely capture the reality of a town which seems to have resembled a permanent building site from the 1750s onwards. Visitor evidence cannot be relied upon for population estimates, but it is quite eloquent on the subject of the visual changes taking place in the town. In any case, data generated for the purpose of Poor Rates assessment confirm the overall picture of dynamic urbanisation. Birmingham, we learn, consisted of 907 houses configured into fifteen streets laid out along the flank of a hill in 1660. The focal point was the river Rea (little more than a stream) and its

---

14   Hutton, *An History of Birmingham*, p.69.
15   C.W. Chalklin, *The Provincial Towns of Georgian England: a Study of the Building Process, 1740–1820* (London: Arnold, 1974), p.22.
16   *The New Birmingham Directory, and Gentleman and Tradesman's Compleat Memorandum Book: Containing a Brief Description of the Town of Birmingham* (Birmingham and London: Swinney, n.d. [1774]), p.4.

crossing-point at Deritend, thus aligning the town with the roads arriving from the south. Subsequent residential expansion would mainly take place on the higher ground of the plateau to the north. By 1700 the township embraced over 2,500 houses and twenty-eight streets, figures which had risen to 3756 and fifty-one respectively by 1731. However, the first in a series of growth spurts which would transform the built environment began in the late 1740s, and by 1781 Birmingham comprised no fewer than 133 streets and 9,536 occupied dwelling houses.[17] Jabez Fisher, a Quaker from Philadelphia who visited during the summer of 1776, reported: 'half the town is new, and they continue to build with greater rapidity than ever.'[18] The onset of conflict in America may have cooled the speculative property market for a spell: the evidence is inconclusive. Matthew Boulton's own expansion at Soho seems to have hesitated for a time. However, the decade after 1781 proved to be the most prosperous in Birmingham's eighteenth-century history, whether measured qualitatively or in terms of demographic and urban growth. Capital for urban development within the private sector was easily raised, and landlords rushed to build street after street of low rent dwellings for the migrating poor who were drawn to the town's booming workshops. Sometimes these houses were constructed on the courtyard pattern which would become a typical feature of Birmingham's urban topography in the nineteenth century. In the process, of course, open land and gardens became scarcer and the central areas of the town more tightly packed. In 1791 William Hutton calculated that the town contained 12,681 houses and 203 streets, of which seventy (and 3,745 houses) had been added over the previous decade.[19] It was noted, however, that only 1,300 of the 8,000 houses built during the previous thirty years (and only around 25 percent of the town's total stock of housing) were rated for Poor Relief.[20]

This scenario of headlong expansion on all fronts would come to a halt in the early 1790s and 1800s, though. The war with Revolutionary and Napoleonic France, 1793–1815 abruptly curtailed Birmingham's growth trajectory. Within a couple of months of the outbreak of hostilities (February 1793) well-placed sources within the town were claiming that

---

17   See Hutton, *An History of Birmingham*, p.69; Chalklin, *The Provincial Towns of Georgian England*, p.229 and *passim*; R.K. Dent, *Old and New Birmingham: a History of the Town and its People*, 2 Vols. (East Ardsley, Wakefield: The Scolar Press reprint, 1973), ii, p.293; J.A. Langford, *A Century of Birmingham Life or a Chronicle of Local Events from 1741 to 1841*, 2 Vols. (Birmingham: More & Co, 1870), i, pp.15, 198, 443, 451.

18   K. Morgan ed, *An American Quaker in the British Isles: the Travel Journal of Jabez Maud Fisher, 1775–1779*. Records of Social and Economic History, new series XVI. (Published for the British Academy by Oxford University Press, 1992), p.254.

19   Hutton, *An History of Birmingham*, p.69.

20   Dent, *Old and New Birmingham*, ii, p.293.

10,000 had been thrown out of work. Julius Hardy, a substantial master buckle maker, certainly laid-off half his work force and put the rest onto half-time working because he confided as much to his diary.[21] Yet it seems unlikely that 10,000 remained permanently unemployed (many joined the army). Nevertheless, both Wedgwood and Boulton, who were far better able to weather the commercial crisis, reported a down-turn consequent upon the war as well. The speculative building spree of the 1780s and early 1790s had probably outstripped demand by this date in any case. Moreover, it had resulted in a town of rather sombre appearance: ill-built houses of dark red brick, unpaved or poorly cobbled streets, a dearth of civic and monumental architecture, and everywhere smoke and coal dust. Adam Walker who passed through in the summer of 1791 referred charitably to Birmingham's 'smoky majesty,'[22] but most visitors and travellers were a good deal less charitable about the atmospheric pollution. The Dutch natural philosopher, Martinus van Marum,[23] travelled up from London to visit Priestley in 1790 but found the heavily-laden air so oppressive that he abandoned plans to go to Soho and retreated from the town with a hacking cough. By this date there were already some houses standing empty for want of tenants, and their numbers increased with the onset of the war and the food scarcities of the later 1790s. According to C.W. Chalklin[24] around 12 percent of the town's 15,650 dwelling houses were unoccupied by 1801, but a contemporary memorialist put the figure much higher, at near enough 3,000, observing: 'this, I believe, was the first decline Birmingham ever experienced.'[25]

The English agricultural writer, Arthur Young, visited Birmingham several times in the 1760s and 1770s, and in 1791 labelled it 'the first manufacturing town in the world.'[26] There can be no doubt that Birmingham had become the pre-eminent centre for the manufacture of metal goods by the century's end, nor that it was known as such throughout Europe and the Americas. It would keep this lead for much of the nineteenth century. In his preface to a handbook compiled in 1865 following the meeting of the British Association for the Advancement of Science in Birmingham, Samuel Timmins

---

21 Birmingham Archives and Heritage (BAH), MS 218 diary of Julius Hardy, button maker of Birmingham, 1788–93.

22 A. Walker, *Remarks Made in a Tour from London to the lakes of Westmoreland in the Summer of M,DCC,XCI* (London, 1792), p.16.

23 See R.J. Forbes, E. Lefebvre and J.G. de Bruijn (eds), *Martinus van Marum: Life and Work*, 6 Vols. (Haarlem: Tjeenk Willink & Zoon, 1969–76), iii, p.63.

24 Chalklin, *The Provincial Towns of Georgian England*, p.278.

25 See S.J. Pratt, *Harvest-Home: consisting of supplementary Gleanings, original Drama and Poems, contributions of literary Friends and select re-publications*, 3 Vols. (London: Richard Phillips, 1805), i, p.309.

26 See *Annals of Agriculture*, 16 (1791), 532.

observed that 'within a radius of thirty miles of Birmingham nearly the whole of the hardware wants of the world are practically supplied.'[27]

Whilst the generous natural resource endowment and the precocious development of an integrated regional economy contributed much to this pre-eminence, allowance must be made, too, for the extraordinarily skilful, inventive and entrepreneurial site which was the West Midlands. Process innovation seems to have been the cornerstone of Birmingham's domination in domestic and international markets. Visitors commented repeatedly on how the town's manufacturers of ornamental metal wares were forever on the look out for cost savings through stratagems such as the division of labour. Samuel Garbett who passed for an elder of the town, acknowledged this strength when he remarked to Lord Lansdowne in 1787 that 'our object is to excel in pretty appearances for little money – And in that respect we are wonderfully eminent.'[28] Even when compared with other domestic centres of metal-goods production, the region outshone its rivals. The French metallurgist and inspector of mines, Antoine-Gabriel Jars the younger,[29] attributed Birmingham's superior labour productivity when compared with that of Sheffield, to the lack of trade guilds and the greater flexibility of the work force. By the same token British visitors to Paris and other European capitals were struck by the routine and unenterprising nature of much craft activity on the Continent.

Product innovation or improvement – inventiveness – was the pendant to the singular discovery of how to mobilise by labour division the energies and skills of a workforce in a cost-effective manner. A former employee of the Patent Office, Richard Prosser,[30] assembled a remarkable record of patents granted to inhabitants of Birmingham between 1760 and 1850. With barely concealed pride, this son of Birmingham noted that Manchester (including Salford) lagged far behind the West Midlands town in the league table of technological prowess. Until this latter date no other provincial town could match Birmingham for artisanal skill and ingenuity. Prosser claimed that two Midlanders, Lewis Paul and John Wyatt, patented the first commercially viable roller spinning machine. It was subsequently taken up by Richard Arkwright and extensively employed in the cotton mills of the North-West.

27 S. Timmins, (ed.), *The Resources, Products, and Industrial History of Birmingham and the Midland Hardware District: a Series of Reports, collected by the Local Industries Committee of the British Association at Birmingham in 1865* (London: Hardwicke, 1866), p.viii.

28 BAH, 510639 Photostatic copies of letters from Samuel Garbett to Lord Lansdowne 4 Vols. 1766–1802, S. Garbett to Lord Lansdowne, Birmingham, 3 September 1787.

29 J. Chevalier, 'La Mission de Gabriel Jars dans les mines et les usines britanniques en 1764', *Transactions of the Newcomen Society*, 26 (1947–48), 63.

30 R.B. Prosser, *Birmingham Inventors and Inventions being a Contribution to the Industrial History of Birmingham* (Birmingham, 1881).

Matthew Boulton who was a past master at tapping into other men's minds, took Wyatt into his own employ and also found work in the Soho Manufactory for his two sons.

Patents were expensive to obtain and hard to defend, however, and, if anything, Prosser's evidence probably understates the scale of craft and trade inventiveness. Edward Thomason, another graduate of Soho, invented in rapid succession a self-steering fire-ship; a one sail windmill for pumping water from ponds; folding steps for carriages; an improved corkscrew; a sliding toasting-fork; a metal walking-cane incorporating a cigar lighter; and a dice-throwing machine.[31] Only the stow-away carriage steps and the improved corkscrew were patented, however, and only the latter proved to be profitable.

Another point on which visitors, and particularly overseas visitors, to Birmingham in the second half of the eighteenth century were generally agreed was the bustle of the place. The Göttingen *savant* Georg Christoph Lichtenberg, who left a memorable account of the repartition of labouring activities he saw being practised at Soho in 1775, also commented on the incessant 'hammering, pounding, rubbing and chiselling'[32] that greeted his ears and eyes on entering Birmingham. This assault on the senses prompted similar, if less favourable, remarks by John Bicknell,[33] a musicologist who passed through the town in the same year. But it was the accelerating speed of industrial life that drew comment from the 1780s onwards, as the frequency of communication by road and canal intensified. Chrétien de Malesherbes [34] was struck by the alacrity of ordinary work people as they sped about their daily tasks, and such observations became a diarists' commonplace in the years thereafter.

Quickness, and more especially quickness of response to the opportunities of the marketplace, would become the defining characteristic of Birmingham's formula for commercial success in fact. In 1781 William Hutton remarked of the buckle – one of the town's staple products – that 'this offspring of fancy, like the clouds, is ever changing. The fashion of today is thrown into the casting pot tomorrow.'[35] Adaptability, innovation and

---

31   *Sir Edward Thomason's Memoirs during Half a Century*, 2 Vols. (London, 1845), i, pp.3–4.

32   *Lichtenberg's Visits to England as Described in his Letters and Diaries*. Translated and Annotated by Margaret L. Mare and W.H. Quarrell (Oxford: Clarendon Press, 1938), p.99.

33   'BIRMINGHAM, A most noisy, unharmonious, smoaky town, where the harsh sound of the hammer and the anvil, together with the incessant clashing of pots, frying pans, and coppers, which was the only music I heard at my arrival, made me augur ill of my success at this place,' J. Bicknell, *Musical Travels through England by Joel Collier* (London, 2nd edn, 1775), pp.81–2.

34   M.C. Jacob, *Scientific Culture and the Making of the Industrial West* (New York and Oxford: Oxford University Press, 1997), p.7 and note 13.

35   Hutton, *An History of Birmingham*, p.107.

speed (in getting to market) were harnessed together to produce an industrial version of the Enlightenment practice of 'emulation'. But speed and the cost advantage conferred by the division of labour underscored all other considerations.

Birmingham's vocation as a centre for the manufacture of 'toys', that is to say ornamental and fashion goods, was scarcely pre-ordained. Rather it evolved in tandem with the expansion of England's eighteenth-century consumer economy. For perhaps the first three or four decades of the century nails, utilitarian ironmongery and edge-tools remained the principal stock-in-trade of the town, as in times past. Only by mid-century does it become clear that unskilled and semi-skilled hardware manufacture was moving to the outskirts of the town and into the Black Country. In its place came buckle and button workshops, brass founders, japanners, gun makers and jewellers. These were the trades whose products (buckles, buttons, watch chains, snuff boxes, *papier-maché* tea caddies, ornamental brass fittings, pins, pen-knives, silver-plated wares, medallions, cut-glass, etc) were known collectively as 'toys'. Edmund Burke had such products in mind when, in 1777, he referred to Birmingham as 'the great Toy Shop of Europe'.[36] Most of the merchants and manufacturers who became pre-eminent in the town during the latter part of the eighteenth century or the early nineteenth century, emanated from this milieu. Henry Clay, japanner, whose workshops employed 300 at their peak, learned his trade as an apprentice of John Baskerville in the 1740s. John Taylor began his career as a small-scale button maker and gilder before creating and then cornering the market for enamelled snuff boxes. In the process he built up a work force which may have reached 500 at its height, and would leave a considerable fortune on his demise in 1775. Matthew Boulton, the subject of this book, was drawn from a similar background, and so was Edward Thomason. Later on in life, Thomason recalled how his father's workshops could turn out 1,000 pairs of buckles a day, or 6,000 a week, when working at full stretch. Buckles were worn both by men and women as well as by children and were chiefly made of white metal to resemble silver. Depending on the vagaries of fashion they might be as large as six inches by three and a half, remembered James Bisset in his commonplace book. But the domestic market for shoe buckles collapsed towards the century's end owing to a shift in fashion towards slippers and laces.[37] Buttons, and particularly the showy but inexpensive gilded buttons, remained impervious to market fluctuations by contrast. Between 1770 and 1788 the number of button manufacturers operating in the town more than doubled.

---

36   See Dent, *Old and New Birmingham*, ii, p.258.

37   On 10 May 1790 *Aris's Birmingham Gazette* contrasted 'the manly buckle' with 'that most ridiculous of all ridiculous fashions, the *effeminate* shoe string.' Quoted in J. Money, *Experience and Identity: Birmingham and the West Midlands* (Manchester: Manchester University Press, 1977), p.262.

What drove Birmingham's industrial dynamo during these years? Economic historians have debated the role of internal and external factors and at the macroscopic level at least there appears to be little agreement as to whether the emphasis should be placed on a captive and expanding market of domestic consumers, or on a speculative market made up of overseas customers. In a period largely devoid of reliable quantitative indicators, neither home demand nor overseas trade is easy to measure. In the case of Birmingham, though, there is enough information available for us to get a sense of the direction of developments over time at the very least.

During the first half of the eighteenth century the growth of Birmingham was almost certainly powered by domestic demand for its utilitarian hardwares. But this dynamic was already starting to change in the 1750s if the testimony of John Taylor, the town's largest manufacturer, can be relied upon. In 1759 he informed a House of Commons committee that the metal 'toy' trade employed around 20,000 persons in Birmingham and the West Midlands and put into the marketplace wares to the value of £600,000 per annum. He went on to claim that over 80 percent of these ornamental goods were exported, a figure which seems excessive.[38] A little over fifty years later Thomas Attwood would testify to Parliament in a similar vein on the impact of the Orders-in-Council. However, his claim that Birmingham and district produced goods worth about two million pounds each year, of which 65 percent by value were exported, seems entirely plausible.[39] We know that the town's merchants did an extensive and profitable trade with Portugal in the 1750s because it was badly disrupted by the Lisbon earthquake of 1755, and in the mid-1760s Matthew Boulton would remark that 'more than half the letters we receive are wrote in the German language.'[40] Yet Eric Hopkins [41] who has investigated the eighteenth-century history of the West Midlands in some depth, believes that Birmingham's growth in the third quarter was still largely driven by the home market.

Be that as it may, a decisive re-gearing of the town's industrial economy seems to have been taking place in the 1780s. The leading manufacturers had already begun to concentrate on continental European markets from the mid-1770s – perhaps in response to the mounting dislocation of trade with the American colonies. John Fothergill, Boulton's first partner, had been promoting Soho wares throughout northern Europe since the late 1760s, in fact, and in

---

38   E. Hopkins, *Birmingham: the First Manufacturing Town in the World, 1760–1840* (London: Weidenfeld & Nicolson, 1989), pp.6, 16.

39   E. Hopkins, 'The Birmingham Economy during the Revolutionary and Napoleonic Wars, 1793–1815', *Midland History*, 23 (1998), 111–20.

40   Hopkins, *Birmingham: the First Manufacturing Town*, p.15.

41   Ibid, pp.15, 37, 74.

1776 he embarked on a trade mission to Saint-Petersburg. Josiah Wedgwood who kept a close eye on what Boulton was doing, also expanded into Europe. His partner Thomas Bentley made a sales trip to Paris in 1776, and by one calculation around 80 percent of the output of Etruria was heading in the direction of European (and mainly Dutch) markets by 1784.[42] Samuel Garbett whose financial difficulties at the Carron ironworks in Scotland had not prevented him from running a successful precious metals refining business in Birmingham, reckoned that his fellow manufacturers' success in penetrating European markets in the 1780s owed much to 'our Merchants resorting to every principal Town with their Patterns, & the Great Periodical fairs have been thereby reduced to insignificance for the sale of Manufactures.'[43] What he meant to say was that the principal 'toy' makers of the town had adopted the tactic of selling direct to shopkeepers via pattern books, cards or catalogues of goods which were taken from town to town by travelling salesmen. By this route Birmingham metal wares made of brass and copper, in particular, became ubiquitous throughout Europe. Bourbon France seems to have constituted the most lucrative market in these years, although entrepreneurs such as Matthew Boulton were extremely reluctant to discuss either the volume or the direction of exports to the Continent lest the French government take steps to impede their commerce. All of the 'toy' manufacturers lived in fear of trade embargoes and taxes on raw materials. When the Habsburg Emperor promulgated an edict in 1785 to restrict imported manufactured goods, its effects were felt immediately in Birmingham and, no doubt, in Sheffield and Manchester as well.

By 1790 at least a quarter of Birmingham's hardware output was heading in the direction of overseas markets – whether by official or unofficial routes. This fact helps to explain the shock experienced by the regional economy when continental Europe, in particular, became inaccessible. The boom times of the 1780s continued until 1792, or so it would seem. This was certainly the impression gained by foreign visitors, and local evidence provides confirmation. The button maker Julius Hardy prospered in 1791, having sold 25 percent more goods than the year before.[44] Yet by the autumn of 1792 the economic outlook had begun to deteriorate, and not just in the metal-ware towns. The descent of France into political revolution had generated a number of commercial opportunities, not least for Matthew Boulton, but it had also caused turbulence in credit markets and delayed remittances. A poor harvest in 1792 was depressing home demand, and war between France and the German Powers (the Habsburgs and Prussia) was disrupting overland trade routes.

---

42   M. Berg, *Luxury and Pleasure in Eighteenth-Century Britain* (Oxford: Oxford University Press, 2005), p.143.

43   BAH, 510639 S. Garbett to Lord Lansdowne, Birmingham, 5 November 1789.

44   BAH, MS 218 diary of Julius Hardy, 1788–93.

In fact the crisis that would arrest Birmingham's headlong growth only became fully apparent in April 1793 when Parliament was forced to intervene and authorise the issue of £5 million in exchequer bills to support leading merchant houses. France had declared war on Britain on 1 February and within weeks the implications of the closure of much of the Continent to the products of Birmingham and the Black Country began to register. With a little over a quarter of the town's exports habitually directed towards France, many merchants found themselves over-extended when remittances dried up. Garbett complained as early as 1 April that his sales of gold and silver to the gilding, plating and jewellery workshops had dropped by half.

The streets, he reported on 17 April, were filled with workmen and women who had been laid off. According to Garbett, 3,000 unemployed males had enlisted in the army by the third week of April. 'The situation of Trade in this Town is frightful,'[45] he reported that summer, adding that it would get much worse if a rupture with America were to take place as well.

Matthew Boulton would cope with the credit crisis of 1793 rather better than most of his fellow manufacturers, thanks in no small measure to the strength and support of his London bankers. The lean years that followed he was able to weather because of the diversification of his business and the buoyancy of the home market. The Cornish mines had partly recovered from the shock of the slump in copper and tin prices of 1787, and by the end of 1792 all of the B&W pumping engines were back in operation once more. More important, demand for rotary-motion engines from the cotton spinners of Manchester and Stockport was booming, not to mention the demand nearer to home from the colliery owners and iron founders of the Black Country. In February 1791 James Watt [46] reported an order book of twenty and a desperate shortage of skilled engine erectors. Birmingham town remained in the doldrums throughout the 1790s and even into the 1800s, however. The only local industry to positively flourish was the gun trade. The economic nadir was probably 1796–7 when the French ascendancy in Europe almost sealed off the Continent from British manufactured goods. Contemplating the stopping of remittances from France, the Netherlands, Italy and Spain in November 1796, Boulton expostulated to a correspondent that he had 'a thousand mouths, and more, to feed every week & whom I cannot request to fast till the war is over, without setting the example myself.'[47]

---

45 BAH, 510639 S. Garbett to Lord Lansdowne, Birmingham, 28 August 1793.
46 James Watt to Van Liender, Birmingham, 24 February 1791 in J.A. Verbruggen (ed.),
    *The Correspondence of Jan Daniël Huichelbos van Liender (1732–1809) with James Watt (1736–1819)
    and Boulton & Watt, supplemented by a few related Documents compiled and annotated by Jan A. Verbruggen*
    (privately printed, 2005), p.228.
47 BAH, MS 3782/12/4 [copy of] M. Boulton to E.G. Eckhardt, Soho, 7 November 1796.

The years after 1806 witnessed a slow recovery, notwithstanding Napoleon's Continental Blockade. The town's manufacturers switched their attentions to the Americas which had long been a steady market for nails, whips and fairly basic hard-wares, and by 1811 it was reported that half of Birmingham's manufacturing output was being shipped across the Atlantic. Trade into northern Europe via Holland also held up remarkably well in the circumstances. In the meantime new consumer goods industries were developing on the strength of home demand. Louis Simond [48] described how the town's glass-works were turning out expertly cut flint-glass products for the neighbourhood's *nouveau riche* customers.

These promising signs of recovery were sharply curtailed by the crisis over the Orders-in-Council, however. The determination of the British government to exercise control over neutral merchantmen sailing into French-dominated Europe produced a rift with the United Sates of America. The impact on Birmingham in 1811 was immediate, and little short of catastrophic. Many of the town's manufacturers joined forces to petition the government, and in June 1812 the Orders were repealed. But by this time the damage had been done, for the confrontation with the United States turned into outright war and another market was lost.

Matthew Boulton would not live to see the end of these conflicts in Europe and the wider western world. He died in 1809 when the war against French expansionism was approaching its nadir. Bonaparte's Continental System and naval blockades had brought commercial intercourse across the Channel and the North Sea to a virtual standstill. The Soho Manufactory would continue to turn out fashionable consumer goods for the home market and, until 1811, for the Americas, but the manufacture of *objets d'art* for a wealthy clientele had long since ceased. The fortunes of the business partnership between Matthew Boulton, James Watt and their sons now lay elsewhere – in heavy engineering carried on at the Soho Foundry in Smethwick.

Abbreviations
BAH – Birmingham Archives and Heritage, Central Library, Birmingham B3 3HQ.

---

48   L. Simond, *Voyage d'un français en Angleterre pendant les années 1810 et 1811*, 2 Vols. (Paris, 1816), i, p.128.

Chapter 3

'A NEW SPECIES OF GENTLEMAN'

Shena Mason

During the eighteenth century and on into the nineteenth, the boundaries between 'old' and 'new' money became increasingly blurred. The landed aristocracy still held sway over most of the countryside, but in some of the fast-growing towns there emerged a new breed – the wealthy and powerful manufacturer-merchants. Rough diamonds some of them may have been, but their money and influence gained them a measure of acceptance in polite society and the resources to keep up appearances, from their fashionable clothes and the food on their sophisticated tables, to the furnishings in their homes and the latest model carriages. James Boswell reported that Dr Johnson had been heard to observe that 'An English merchant is a new species of Gentleman',[1] while in Birmingham William Hutton declared that 'Gentlemen, as well as buttons, have been stamped here.'[2] Arthur Young poked fun at aspirational tenant farmers for aping their betters by buying 'piano-fortes for their parlours and post-chaises for driving their wives to assembly rooms, ... putting their servants into livery, sending their daughters to expensive boarding schools and their sons to university'.[3] The same lifestyle hunger which drove those farmers (or their wives) was shared by upwardly-mobile manufacturers, and Gillows and their competitors must have noted with satisfaction the number of medium-sized, mahogany D-end dining tables on claw-footed pedestals on their order books.

Matthew Boulton could perhaps be cited almost as a classic example of the ambition for gentrification. Born in 1728 into a Birmingham button-maker's family, he would go on to become, in James Watt's words, 'more like a

---

1   *The Life of Samuel Johnson, LL.D.* Vol.1, (1793), footnote to p.457. Boswell thought Dr Johnson had taken the idea from Sir Richard Steele's play *The Conscious Lovers* (1772), where one character observes '...we merchants are a species of gentry that have grown into the world this last century, and are as honourable, and almost as useful, as you landed folks that have always thought yourselves so much above us...'

2   William Hutton: *History of Birmingham* (1781).

3   Arthur Young, *The Farmer's Tour through the East of England* (1771), quoted in Hibbert, Christopher: *The English, A Social History* (1987), p.321.

sovereign than a private manufacturer'[4] (though Mrs Ann Watt, who was less impressed, once summed up her husband's business partner drily with the words, 'If he had millions he would find ways to spend it').[5]

Yet Matthew Boulton's life is not a straightforward rags-to-riches story. There *was* money, land and influence in Boulton's family background. He could trace his line of descent directly back to the Revd. Zachary Babington, Chancellor of Lichfield (d.1613) and Sir Richard Dyott (d.1659). Sir Richard, who was married to Dorothy Dorrington of Stafford, had been a member of King Charles I's Privy Council and had fought on the King's side at Edgehill. Subsequently he was imprisoned for his support of the King; several of his sons also served in the Royalist cause. These two distinguished old county families came together in 1655 with the marriage of Zachary Babington's great-granddaughter, Mary Babington, to Sir Richard Dyott's son, Matthew Dyott. In 1699 one of Matthew and Mary Dyott's daughters, Elizabeth (b.1670), married John Boulton, a.k.a. Bolton (d. after 1741). The Boultons' first son, born in 1700, was named Matthew after his Grandfather Dyott. This Matthew Boulton (henceforth referred to as Matthew Boulton senior) was the father of Matthew Boulton of Soho. John Boulton's trade or profession are at present unknown, but the fact that his son moved from the family home in Lichfield to Birmingham, and after an apprenticeship eventually set himself up in the button and buckle trade, suggests that possibly the family fortunes had taken a downturn at some stage – Matthew Boulton senior's siblings included a shoemaker and a peruke-maker, so the family seems to have needed to turn to trade for their living.[6]

In 1723, twenty-three-year-old Matthew Boulton senior was married at St Martin's Church in Birmingham, to Christiana Piers, said to be the daughter of Daniel Piers of Chester, of whom little is yet known.[7] The Matthew Boulton who forms the subject of this book was their third child (and the second to be called Matthew: their firstborn having died at the age of two in 1726, his grieving parents re-used the name for their next son).

By the time this second Matthew Boulton junior was born in 1728, his father's button and buckle business in Snow Hill was well-established, though not on a large scale – just one of the numerous small firms in Birmingham producing goods of this type, mainly in cut steel. As well as buckles and buttons, these goods included watch chains, chatelaines, small boxes and similar items, ornamented with a myriad steel studs faceted in the manner of gemstones to

4   Birmingham Archives and Heritage (BAH). MS 3782/13/37/111, James Watt, Memoir of Matthew Boulton, 17 September 1809.

5   BAH, MS 3219/4/5/30, Mrs Ann Watt to James Watt, 24 September 1785.

6   For sources and a detailed account of Boulton genealogy, *see* Mason, S, *The Hardware Man's Daughter* (2005), Appendix, pp.197–212.

7   BAH, Parish Register, St Martin's Church (Birmingham Archives and Heritage).

make them sparkle. Such goods were known collectively as 'Birmingham toys', and the production of these small personal accessories accounted for thousands of jobs and a valuable export trade in the town at this period. Other metals, such as silver, pinchbeck[8] and brass, were also used in the Birmingham workshops, but it is not known whether Boulton senior's business produced wares in silver at this period, no record of a registered maker's mark having been found for the elder Boulton in either Chester or London, which would have been the assay offices used by Birmingham silver producers at this period.

Little is known about Matthew Boulton junior's childhood, beyond the fact that, according to his nineteenth-century biographer Samuel Smiles, he attended a school in Deritend run by the Revd. John Hausted, whose merits as a teacher were lauded in his obituary in the local paper.[9] In about 1745 young Boulton left Hausted's tuition and began work for his father. By this time the latter was evidently employing a number of men, for many years later a former employee would write of working there as a youngster in 1737 and listening to the old men at the bench telling tales of their youth spent fighting 'in the Warrs of Queen Ann & George 1st'.[10]

Matthew Boulton's early notebooks reveal that far from his education finishing when he left school, it was just beginning. Clearly a young man driven by insatiable and wide-ranging curiosity, his reading and writing darted to and fro over an eclectic mix of disciplines, from the classics and the latest novels to fine art and accountancy, from geology to astronomy, and from medicine to physics, chemistry and biology – in fact all the sciences then covered by the term 'natural philosophy'.[11] Thus, having acquired the basics at school, Matthew Boulton became largely self-educated in the kind of subjects which a boy of more genteel birth and upbringing might have gone on to study at public school and university. Throughout his life, Boulton never lost the desire to learn, or his respect for learned people and their knowledge, or, indeed, the determination to foster a love of learning not only in his own children but in promising lads in his workforce.

At the age of twenty-one, in 1749, Matthew Boulton married for the first time. His bride was Mary Robinson, daughter of a well-to-do Lichfield mercer, Luke Robinson, who was to die in the autumn following his daughter's wedding. Mary's settlement brought money and land to the marriage. The

---

8   Pinchbeck: an alloy of copper and zinc developed in the eighteenth century by Christopher
     Pinchbeck to produce a colour resembling gold.
9   *Aris's Birmingham Gazette*, 25 August 1755.
10   BAH, MS 3782/13/8/66, John Bentley to Matthew Robinson Boulton, 1 February 1811.
11   Matthew Boulton's notebooks are found under BAH, MS 3782/12/108/1–96, covering a period from
     c.1759–1804. Some are dedicated to one subject, such as the Soho Mint, Cornish engines, etc.
     and some are general, full of personal everyday notes including shopping lists, sketches for ideas,
     and notes on scientific interests. See Chapter 6 in this volume.

couple were distantly related, for they had Babington ancestors in common. The Robinsons were an important and influential 'trade' family in Lichfield and were possessed of considerable amounts of land in the Lichfield area and beyond, some of which had come down to them from the Babington side. The Boultons themselves do not appear to have had much in the way of land at this period; the various Dyott estates had mostly gone to other branches of the Dyott family and much of the Babington land had ended up with the Robinsons. Nevertheless, the Robinsons must have been sufficiently impressed both by young Boulton's ancestry and his general manner and ambition to feel that he was an acceptable husband for their daughter. So not only had he succeeded in marrying tolerably well, he had also re-connected himself with the Babington fortunes. It is not clear where Boulton and his first wife lived. The baptisms and burials of their three children took place in Lichfield, and some early household bills are from there, but others are from Birmingham, where Boulton was working with his father.[12]

In 1759 Mary Boulton died. She was buried in the Robinson family vault at St Giles' Church, Whittington, near Lichfield, while the bell tolled for her at St Mary's Church in the city centre where the couple had married. A month after Mary's death Matthew Boulton senior also died, and his newly-widowed son took full control of the family business. On Mary's death Boulton wrote a poem to her, which he placed in her coffin (having first taken the precaution of making a copy of it).[13] This speaks of her in emotional and affectionate terms, yet only months after her death he began bombarding her younger sister, Ann Robinson of Lichfield, with love-letters. Flying in the face of family and public disapproval, Boulton and his 'lovely, dearest, sweetest charmer'[14] were married in London in June 1760,[15] ten months after Mary's death, and just a month after the death of Mary and Ann's mother, Luke's widow Dorothy Robinson. Between them Mary and Ann had brought some six thousand pounds in money plus a fair amount of land into Boulton's control; Ann's fortune (and consequently her husband's) would be further greatly increased on the death of her sole surviving and unmarried brother, Luke Robinson junior, four years after the marriage.[16]

---

12 For example, BAH, MS 3782/6/189/2, Edmund Hector (Lichfield) to MB, 5 April 1749 – 11 December 1752; MS 3782/6/190/6, John Barker (Lichfield) to MB, 17 January – 14 October 1759; MS 3782/6/190/11, William Bailye (Lichfield) to MB, 14 June 1760; MS 3782/6/190/93, Thomas Carr (Birmingham) to MB, 18 June 1756 – 25 May 1762; MS 3782/6/189/24, Daniel Ruston (Birmingham) to MB, 9 November 1757 – 17 January 1759.

13 BAH, MS 3782/12/112/72.

14 BAH, MS 3782/Mrs Ann Boulton/11, MB to Ann Robinson, March 1760.

15 Parish Register, St Mary's Church, Rotherhithe, London.

16 Will of Luke Robinson Junior, 1764. PRO, Prob.11/929. This Will, along with Luke's mother Dorothy Robinson's Will, was not proved until 1767.

The few early letters and bills which survive indicate that Boulton went to some trouble to prepare the Boulton family home on Snow Hill in suitable style for Ann, who after growing up in the comfortable Robinson family house in Bore Street, Lichfield, would have expected a smart home. But while a round of redecorating and shopping ensued for the Snow Hill house, Boulton was also engaged in a much bigger quest: the search for a site for a new, larger factory. Having rejected a few sites, in 1761 he paid £1,000 for the lease on thirteen acres of open heathland at Soho, in Handsworth[17] (the name 'Soho' is said to come, like that of its London counterpart, from a hunting cry). The area, about two miles from Birmingham town centre, was then just over the county boundary, in Staffordshire.

Here Boulton set about building the showpiece Soho Manufactory. Now at last he had the space to diversify. The range was gradually expanded to include all manner of ornamental and luxury goods, leading his friend Josiah Wedgwood to describe Boulton as 'The most complete manufacturer in metals in England'. As consumerism and a demand for fashionable goods took off, there was a growing taste for such products among the moneyed classes, both in Britain and abroad. The Soho business and its fame, together with that of its owner, grew rapidly, and fashionably-dressed nobility and gentry rolled up in their coaches in droves to see the Manufactory and its machines at work. Though he grumbled about the disruption, Boulton enjoyed playing the host, and made full use of the access it gave him to a bevy of counts, dukes, ambassadors and sundry lesser (but well-to-do and influential) gentry.

Soho House came with the land; built c.1757, it accounted for £300 of the £1,000 price-tag.[18] Initially Boulton moved his mother and one of his sisters into the house, but in 1762 they had to make way for his new business partner, John Fothergill. The next few years were largely taken up with the development of the Manufactory and the business, until by 1766 Boulton felt the need to live nearer to his work and a protesting and disgruntled Fothergill was obliged to vacate the house, and Boulton and his second wife, Ann, moved in. Their two children were born at Soho House, Anne in 1768 and Matthew Robinson Boulton in 1770. (Plate 1).

The genteel lifestyle required servants to support it, and both at Snow Hill and at Soho House there were maids and other servants. There are references to them in letters and bills which record payments for their clothing and occasional medicines. One shoe bill, covering the period from 21 June – 24 November 1760, from shoemaker Zachariah Babington (who must surely be a relation), lists shoes for 'your selfe' [i.e. Boulton], for 'your Wife',

---

17   BAH, MS 3782/12/60/265, Memoranda by Matthew Boulton, respecting his partnership with
      John Fothergill, 3 September 1765 – 20 March 1766. Headed 'Case between B&F'.
18   See note 17.

'your boy' (who is likely to have been a servant as the Boultons had no children at this time), and for 'your Black' – raising the question of whether there was in fact a black servant in the Boulton household at Snow Hill, though there is no other reference to substantiate it, and it could just refer to a servant whose name was Black, or indeed to a pair of black shoes.[19] Servants tended to be re-engaged annually and Boulton wrote to Ann in 1763, while they were still living at Snow Hill but she was visiting her brother in Lichfield, that he had engaged 'proper maids' for her and a cook, and that they needed only a manservant to make the household complete.[20] In later years at Soho House the number of indoor servants increased somewhat and included a butler, a footman, a housekeeper, a valet and a cook, as well as maids and outdoor servants including a liveried coachman and various gardeners.

Again, surviving household bills make it clear that Soho House was a stylish and up-to-date home, as befitted a top manufacturer making his mark in the world by catering for the latest demands of fashion, and entertaining a regular stream of sophisticated guests. Mrs Boulton had a fortepiano by Zumpe, then one of the best-known makers. In an engaging sequence of letters in 1767 Boulton wrote to Zumpe, explaining that his friend, Mr Dean of Hagley, had ordered two fortepianos, one for himself and one for Boulton, but not having received his, Boulton had then re-ordered directly from the maker, only to be embarrassed by the arrival of an instrument from his friend. Extricating himself blandly from the new order, Boulton assures Zumpe that he is so pleased with the fortepiano that further orders from among his friends will undoubtedly follow.[21]

As well as the 'pianoforte in the parlour', Soho House boasted gilded furniture in the drawing-room, imposing gilt-framed mirrors above carved marble chimneypieces, Wedgwood china on the dinner table and silverware produced in Boulton's own workshops. In the study and in Boulton's small library, with its library table and globes, there were the latest books, including popular fashionable novels such as Sterne's *Tristram Shandy* and Richardson's *Pamela*. His treasured scientific equipment, resplendent in polished brass and mahogany, included an orrery,[22] a thermometer, a pyrometer, a barometer, three microscopes and a telescope and a 'cammora' (presumably a camera obscura).[23] Boulton's desire to have a gentleman philosopher's retreat echoes clearly from his diaries and notebooks, where he makes lists of instruments

19 BAH, MS 3782/6/190/39. Bill. Zachariah Babington to MB, 21 June – 24 November 1760.
20 BAH, MS 3782/Mrs Ann Boulton/14, MB to Mrs AB, 1763.
21 BAH, MS 3782/12/1/10 [Letterbook 1766–68] MB to Mr Zumpe, 27 July 1767.
22 BAH, MS 3782/6/6/1047, George Donisthorpe to MB, 18 October 1763 – 9 January 1773. This bill includes, on 12 December 1765, 'To making a new Electrical Orrery' at £1.8s.0d.
23 BAH, MS 3782/12/108/7, Notebook 8, 1772, pp.14–15.

and books to buy, and sketches the kind of bookcases he wants. In one notebook he describes his ideal 'hobby horsery' in some detail:

> A round building for my Study, Library, Museum or Hobby Horsery to hold 6 handsome Book Cases with drawers in the lower parts to hold things which relate to subjects of the books wch are in ye upper parts, e:gr: a Book Case containing Chymical Books should have drawers under wch contain Metals Minerals & Fossells – between each Book Case should be a Sophi & under the Space between ye upper parts of ye Cases should be fixed such instruments as Baromotor, Thermomotor, Pyromotor, Quadrants, all sorts of Optical, Mathematical, Mechanical, Pnumatical & Philosophical instruments also Clocks of Sundry kinds both Geographical & Syderial, Lunar & Solar system & one good regulator of time. A table in ye middle of ye room & a skylight in ye middle of the domical roof wch roof may be coverd either with Sail Cloth or brown paper. Out of this round room should open a private door into a passage in which passage should open doors into Sundry convent: rooms such as Cold & Warm bath, a Labritory, a dressing & powdering room & an observatory for a transit instrumt &c.[24]

The following year he was still hankering after a museum of his own, like Mr Hunter's (John Hunter, the London surgeon whom the Boultons consulted about their daughter's orthopaedic problems,[25] and whose private museum would later become the Hunterian Museum at the Royal College of Surgeons). Noting that Hunter's museum, which he had evidently seen, was about 1620 square feet, he added 'A museum about 800 feet area wd be big enough for me'.[26] These pursuits were very much those of the eighteenth-century gentleman with perhaps rather more leisure time than Boulton had, for his museum never quite materialised in the way he had envisaged and the astronomer Alexander Aubert bought the first Soho House telescope from him in 1778, after noticing during a visit that the instrument appeared to be suffering from weather and neglect.[27] Boulton did, however, have a small 'fossilry' built to house his fossil and mineral collection somewhere in the grounds, until, much later, the rear entrance hall was altered to make a little room for it on the ground floor of Soho House.

---

24 BAH, MS3782/12/108/6, Notebook 7, 1771, pp.87–8.
25 BAH, MS3782/13/53, Erasmus Darwin to MB, 19 June 1769; MS 3782/MB/Correspondence 1758–73/195, John Hunter – William Small, 5 April 1771. Anne had been born with a slight disability, possibly a club–foot. For further discussion on this matter see Mason, *The Hardware Man's Daughter*, pp.19–23.
26 BAH, MS 3782/12/107/7, Diary 1772, p.7.
27 BAH, MS 3782/1/27/20, Alexander Aubert to MB, 25 September 1778.

Given Boulton's frequent trips to London and elsewhere on business, it is not surprising that he writes a good deal about the discomforts of travelling. More often than not, the London trips seem to have been made using the scheduled coach services between Birmingham and London. The time taken for this particular journey gradually reduced during the course of the eighteenth century, as roads, and coaches themselves, began to improve. It would have been cheaper to travel by this means than take his own coach to London, with the added need to find and pay for accommodation for the coachman and the horses, and moreover if he went to London on the stagecoach, Mrs Boulton could retain the use of the family coach in Birmingham. Boulton's notebooks and letters make it plain that he took an interest in seeing new places and new people, but nevertheless it is easy to understand why he does not appear to have relished travel for its own sake. The severe jolting from poor coach suspensions made him feel sick and gave him backache, especially as he grew older – and particularly when, as on at least one occasion, he gave up his forward-facing seat to a lady passenger. In winter the journey was cold and cramped, and the one or two nights which had to be spent en route were generally in inferior inns where the beds were damp and dirty and the food often grossly unappetising; on one occasion he wrote to Ann, 'We arrived at Warwick about one oClock [and] was put into a dirty room with dirty linen dirty knives dirty plates & stinking Butter to a stinking fowl...'[28] Journeys made using the family coach were undoubtedly more comfortable, with more privacy, room for extra blankets to fight the cold, and the opportunity to stop at will. Boulton made several long visits to Cornwall, where he and Watt had a deal of steam engine business, and on two occasions Mrs Boulton went with him although, like Annie Watt, she does not seem to have liked Cornwall. Allowing for occasional rest days en route, the journey took well over a week from Birmingham. The family coach was a top-of-the-range, high-specification vehicle but still needed regular attention from a coach mender in Birmingham in between trips, due to the shaking and jolting it received on every journey. Boulton was interested in braking and suspension systems and produced several drawings showing what he thought would be improvements to those currently in use, and Annie Watt commented in one letter to her son, Gregory, that Mr Boulton had got yet another a new coach with a new sort of springs.[29]

From household bills, it is plain to see that Boulton and his wife dressed in 'London-style' – most of their clothes and fabrics came from there, and he shopped for jewellery for her at high-class establishments which included

28　BAH, MS 3782/Mrs Ann Boulton/46, MB to Mrs AB, 23 January 1773.
29　BAH, MS 3219/7/1/26, Annie Watt to Gregory Watt, 10 November 1795.

Rundell & Bridge. From other smart London retailers he bought her lengths of satin and lace. In Paris on business in 1765 he bought silk for a gown which, he said, he would like her to have made up 'a la mode de Londre for as it's a good silk I could wish to have it well made.'[30] From London he sent her notes from time to time on what was, and what was not, being worn in the capital, once observing 'I have enquired about Ear Rings & find that they are left off amongst people of fashion except when they are in full dress & then nothing but pearls or diamants is worn,'[31] and on another occasion passing on the information that the 'in' colour for the season was burgundy.[32] As for himself, Boulton was no blend-into-the-background figure, cutting a dash in coats of red, blue or black superfine broadcloth, figured velvet waistcoats, and even a 'parrot-green mixt cloth French Frock & Breeches & a green and Gold Tissue Waistcoat', at the truly top-drawer price of £9.19s.[33] In later years, when Boulton was once again a widower, his London banker, Charlotte Matthews, strove to reign in his sartorial excesses from time to time, rebuking him gently in one letter:

> I understand your coat to be the inclosd Cloth & that *you* had fixd upon the silk pattern with *pink* in it. Now, as I wear only black, I cannot permit you to wear *pink*, but a still stronger matter is that I think the other silk pattern which I enclose is neat & handsom & at your age a similarity rather than a diversity of colors ought to be preferr'd.[34]

In an early letter to James Watt, Boulton referred to his house as the '*Hotel d'amitie sur Handsworth Heath*'[35], and as a hospitable host he kept a good table. Household bills over a long period show that various kinds of fish and seafood (predominantly salmon, cod, lobster and oysters) and meat (beef, poultry and venison) featured regularly on the menu, and the Soho House diet was also high in sugar, itself a marker of prosperity and aspirational living, with the inevitable but then unrealised consequences for the children's teeth. Anne and Matt had numerous visits to the dentist for extractions, and Anne underwent the gruelling process of a tooth transplant at least once. This was carried out by the Queen's dentist, Charles Dumergue, and involved the extraction from a fourteen-year-old girl of a healthy tooth, which was then promptly inserted into the socket of one of nineteen-year-old Anne's own

---

30   BAH, MS 3782/Mrs Ann Boulton/29, MB to Mrs AB, 8 December 1765.

31   BAH, MS 3782/Mrs Ann Boulton/49, MB to Mrs AB, 4 February 1773.

32   BAH, MS 3782/Mrs Ann Boulton/95, MB to Mrs AB, 4 April 1781.

33   BAH, MS 3782/6/192/56, Davenport & Farrant to MB, 24 December 1778.

34   BAH, MS 3782/12/67/79, Charlotte Matthews to MB, 25 July 1794.

35   BAH, MS 3219/4/66/1, Matthew Boulton (Soho) to James Watt (Glasgow), 7 February 1769.

front teeth which had been extracted at the same time.[36] The donor (or more likely one of her parents) would have been paid for the replacement tooth. It was a procedure only available to the well-to-do, done without anaesthetic of course, and with considerable risk of infection. The Dumergue family were affectionate friends of the Boultons and Anne stayed with them at their Piccadilly home when she was having dental treatment.

The staple foods were generally purchased from Birmingham suppliers, but Boulton often shopped in London for more epicurean goods suitable for a gentleman's table. Sometimes non-perishable goods such as fine wines and cognacs were sent by canal-boat, but in the main Boulton regularly sent up to Soho by the stage-coach or by Deykins' wagon, barrels of oysters, Italian specialities such as pasta, costly spices (purchased in much larger quantities than we generally buy them in today), and different kinds of tea and coffee. The wagon also brought regular consignments of mineral water from the German-born Swiss businessman, Jacob Schweppe, packed in hampers of twelve dozen half-pint bottles. Indeed so much fizzy water did the philosophers of Soho House get through that in 1802 Schweppe was moved to ask Boulton if he could find him a Birmingham agent for it.[37]

The idea of the gas-impregnated water had come from one of those 'Soho philosophers', Dr Joseph Priestley; it was Schweppe who developed it commercially. Priestley was one of the intellectuals to join the ranks of the Lunar Society when he arrived in Birmingham in 1780. This small but high-powered group of 'natural philosophers', or scientists, had had its beginnings in 1766, over a companionable dinner between Matthew Boulton and two of his friends, Dr William Small, and Dr Erasmus Darwin, at the latter's home in Lichfield. Gradually the group grew to around fourteen, taking its name from the full-moon meetings held at members' houses. Although the fourteen were never all together at once (some having died before others joined), they included, apart from Drs Small, Darwin and Priestley, the botanist and physician Dr William Withering, the chemist and metallurgist James Keir, the geologist and scientific instrument maker John Whitehurst, the potter Josiah Wedgwood, the Quaker gun-maker Samuel Galton, and the engineer James Watt, along with Richard Lovell Edgeworth, Thomas Day, the Rev. Robert Augustus Johnson, and Dr Robert Stokes. Ten of them, including Matthew Boulton, were Fellows of the Royal Society. This must have been a particularly satisfying honour for Boulton, and Whitehurst wrote to him in December 1785: 'I congratulate you on your election into the Royal Society and particularly as there was not a negative ball against you.'[38] Little is known of Johnson and

36   BAH, MS 3782/13/36/8, MB to Matthew Robinson Boulton, 29 June 1787.
37   BAH, MS 3782/12/47/239, J. Schweppe to MB, 4 August 1802.
38   BAH, MS 3782/12/81/26, John Whitehurst (London) to MB, 31 December 1785.

Stokes but the rest left their mark on history, one way or another, and between them they were also in correspondence with many other scientific minds of the period, people such as Benjamin Franklin, the botanist Sir Joseph Banks, and the astronomer Sir William Herschel (all of whom visited Boulton, either at Snow Hill or at Soho House). Lunar meetings, often at Boulton's home, provided opportunities for lively conversation, a few experiments, and a good dinner. Boulton revelled in the company of these gentlemen, many of whom had received a far longer formal education than he himself had had.[39]

Boulton also clearly enjoyed networking with the wealthy and aristocratic people with whom he regularly came into contact, either as customers for his goods or in the course of his lobbying activities for various causes (among other things he was a member of the General Hospital committee, and instrumental in the founding of Birmingham Assay Office, as well as serving, in 1794, as High Sheriff of Staffordshire). If any of them did initially look down on him as a tradesman, his irrepressible manner seems to have been able to win them over quickly, and his voluminous correspondence with assorted nobles and society figures is couched in respectful but friendly terms. People such as the fashionable hostess and intellectual Mrs Elizabeth Montagu, the 'Queen of the Bluestockings', became frequent correspondents. Mrs Montagu even helped him to choose a school for his daughter, and visited the girl there. Her London 'salons' (where the latest books written by her guests would be left casually lying around with the pages turned down at the corners to suggest where she had got to in reading them!) were a magnet for actual and would-be intellectuals, and in what may be a reference to Boulton, Richard Cumberland wrote of them in the 1780s, 'She can make a mathematician quote Pindar, a master in chancery write novels, or a Birmingham hardware man stamp rhimes as fast as buttons.'[40]

But although this particular 'Birmingham hardware man' was bent on gentrification, the desire for it did not obliterate the down-to-earth Brummie pragmatism which informed much of his working life. During the 1791 riots in Birmingham, a period of serious social unrest which resulted in several leading townsmen's homes and businesses being ransacked and burnt down, he wrote to his friend Charles Dumergue inviting him to bring the family on a visit to Soho and assuring him that 'by minding my own business I live peaceably & securely amidst the Flames, Rapine, Plunder anarchy & confusion of these Unitarians, Trinitarians, Predestinarians & tarians of all sorts.'[41]

---

39   See Jenny Uglow, *The Lunar Men* (2002), and for example, correspondence between MB to Joseph Banks, BAH, MS 3782/12/56/1–139, 1777–1806; MB to William Herschel, see note 43; MB to Benjamin Franklin MS 3782/13/53/1, 26, 32, 48, 1765–1772.

40   Richard Cumberland: *The Observer, being a collection of moral, literary and familiar essays*, Vols.1–5 published between 1786–1790.

41   BAH, MS 3782/General Correspondence/203, MB to Charles Dumergue, 18 August 1791.

Apart from such close friends as the Dumergues, guests at Soho House ranged from the likes of the Russian Ambassador, Count Woronzow, who came to stay for a week in 1799 (Boulton having hired a 'man cook' for the week to produce meals of appropriate sophistication),[42] to stars of the stage. He had helped finance the development of the Birmingham theatre on the grounds that it would help to keep well-to-do visitors in town – and spending – longer[43] (a demonstration of his instinctive understanding of what today would be called destination marketing), and so took the opportunity to invite the actress Sarah Siddons and the opera singer Elizabeth Billington to Soho when they were appearing locally; both of them seem to have expressed affection for him and are the subject of cheerful banter in correspondence from the Dumergues and other friends.

By the time Count Woronzow and his retinue arrived at Soho House in 1799, the house had undergone considerable enlargement, for in the early 1790s Boulton had embarked on a major re-design and refurbishment of his home by the nationally-known architects James and Samuel Wyatt. By this time Mrs Ann Boulton had been dead for a decade, so it was Miss Boulton and her brother who put up with the upheaval, looked at fabric and paper samples with him and chivvied the builders when he was away. The Wyatts came up with various proposals which included building a new front elevation to the old house and turning it into the central element with a large wing on either side. In the event, a new west wing, housing a much larger library, was built but Boulton's health, patience or money ran out before the remainder of the scheme could be built. The entire house was, however, redecorated and furnished in the latest style, the fashionable interior designer (and theatrical scene painter) Cornelius Dixon being brought in to transform the rooms. While it was all going on the three Boultons escaped periodically, to take the waters and recuperate at the smart spas at Cheltenham, Scarborough or Bath, though some of Boulton's visits to Cheltenham seem to have been hardly a rest-cure for he complained once of having received twenty-four letters there on one day, and told his daughter he felt so much better on days when he did not take the waters, that he was thinking of only taking the 'cure' every other day, or perhaps even every third day.[44]

The alterations at Soho House, had they been completed as planned, would have turned it into a small stately home (his friend William Herschel

42 BAH, MS 3782/12/69/161, MB to Charlotte Matthews, 7 August 1799.
43 Dartmouth MSS – Historical Manuscripts Commission, Vol.II p.259, MB to Lord Dartmouth, 22 March 1777.
44 BAH, MS 3782/14/76/45, MB to Miss Anne Boulton, 1 May 1801.

already referred to it as 'that blissful mansion'),[45] set in what was by now a sizeable park, for over the years Boulton had added considerably to the original thirteen acres. The pleasure garden (as distinct from the workaday vegetable plot) was another accoutrement of gentility, and in this respect, as in so many others, Matthew Boulton was assiduous in informing himself about current trends. His lists of books show that he read widely on the subject of landscape gardening, with works by Sir William Kent, Uvedale Price, William Mason and others on his bookshelves. Notebook and pencil in hand, he strolled round well-known gardens when opportunity arose, and paid what was clearly an inspirational visit to Painshill Park in Surrey in 1772, where he filled five pages with sketches and notes on Charles Hamilton's garden, which had been created on a similarly unpromising site to Soho.[46] Here and there he jotted ideas headed 'improve Soho'. It seems no coincidence that before long, Boulton's garden incorporated many of the features he admired so much at Painshill, in a similar style.

Boulton had taken a close interest in the garden from his earliest years at Soho House, beginning with a massive soil improvement programme to make the hungry, sandy soil more fertile, and planting large numbers of trees to create windbreaks on the high, exposed site, even before moving in there. The garden notes and surviving nurserymen's bills, along with sketches done in the 1790s by John Phillp,[47] give us some idea of how the grounds looked. In time they incorporated all the ingredients of what we have come to think of as the classic English landscaped park, but on a small scale, including a Temple of Flora, statuary, a Gothic tower, a hermitage, possibly a grotto, a small ornamental pool and below it, linked by a cascade, the large lake which had replaced the original millpool, with islands and a boathouse for Matt's little sailing boat. A neighbour obligingly built a house designed to look like a ruined castle which was visible from Soho, thus saving him the trouble of building a 'picturesk Building to look at' (which was one of the items on one of the many 'to do' lists).[48] On the grassy shores of the lake, cattle grazed. A lone Canada goose, a novelty introduction, at one time pecked disconsolately among them but possibly in time became the head of a family, for John Wyatt wrote that a mutual friend:

---

45   BAH, MS 3782/MB General Correspondence 1793/129, William Herschel to MB, July 1793.

46   BAH, MS 3782/12/108/7, Notebook, 1772.

47   John Phillp (c.1778–1815) was brought to Soho from Cornwall in 1793. A promising and artistic lad, he lived in Soho House, was apprenticed at the Soho Manufactory and received tuition in drawing from William Hollins, eventually becoming a respected member of staff who worked on designs for goods being produced in the Manufactory. Phillp was thought by some, both in his lifetime and since, to have been Boulton's illegitimate son, but no conclusive evidence has yet been found either to prove or disprove this theory.

48   BAH, MS 3782/12/108/70, Notebook, 1795.

hath a solitary Canada goose, whose mate was either killed, or lost, lately; and as he remembers you had one in the same unhappy state, he wishes out of compassion to the poor geeses that you would accept of his so that they may alleviate each others misfortunes by a reciprocal participation of their sufferings.[49]

The planting scheme for the park included hundreds of trees and shrubs, including the new and highly fashionable rhododendrons, while nearer the house there were well-filled flower beds and borders. Bills for large deliveries of mixed perennials survive, giving an idea of the planting schemes. Boulton's daughter, Anne, had developed an interest in flowers, having been taught botany by Dr William Withering, an interest and enjoyment which her father seems to have shared – in one of his notebooks at midsummer 1801 he jotted the comment 'Qr. Is it too late to sow more flowers? Next year we should plant many more flowers.'[50]

Though the garden was developed primarily to give the Boulton family pleasure, there is no doubt that it was part of the overall 'Soho image'. Another of Boulton's notebooks makes this clear, with the query: 'How shall I plant & form my Western Ground so as to be handsome to ye sight of those going to ye Manufactory?' and answers the question with: 'Make all the Entrances into Soho Dark by plantations & enter through Gothick arches made by Trees,'[51] thus echoing the ideas of Alexander Pope, who had written of 'planting trees to resemble a Gothic Cathedral'.[52] The gardens thus formed a suitably dramatic and impressive backdrop for the Manufactory. In view of the importance he clearly attached to them, it is not surprising to find Boulton at his desk in 1794, writing out a long list of the pros and cons of retaining the whole estate on its current leasehold basis *versus* buying the freehold – and concluding that if he does not buy it, in years to come houses will be built up close to his drawing room window, depriving him of the pleasant views which give him so much pleasure and diminishing the value of the estate for his descendants. He expressed it thus: 'I shall look back with more satisfaction on the days that are past, and forward with the hopes of my Descendants being opulent and respectable Manufacturers at Soho, to the Third and Fourth Generation, rather than dependent Courtiers.'[53]

---

49 BAH, MS 3782/12/85/94. John Wyatt (London) to MB, 26 July 1776.
50 BAH, MS 3782/12/108/92, Notebook 1801.
51 BAH, MS 3782/12/70, Notebook 28, 1795.
52 The reference to Pope's scheme of planting trees to resemble a Gothic cathedral is made in 'Account of an Interview between Shenstone and Thomson' [1746], quoted in Hunt, J.D. and Willis, P: *The Genius of the Place: the English Landscape Garden 1620–1820*, p.245.
53 BAH, MS 3782/12/111/150, 'Considerations upon the Propriety of buying Soho... First, as it relates to my Health & Happiness; and secondly, as it relates to my Interest.' N.d. c.1794.

That phrase, 'dependent courtiers' is significant. A dependent courtier must live his life at the beck and call of his masters or patrons, adopting a judicious veneer of deference, until his face no longer fits and he is discarded. Boulton wanted so much more than that, for himself and for his descendants. He was quick to see the potential in new ideas (such as Watt's improvements to the steam engine which led him to invite the Scot to join him in the business). Sometimes his ideas failed and cost him dear, sometimes the whole enterprise seemed to be built on shifting sands of debt, yet like a juggler he managed to keep all the balls in the air, and succeeded in constructing the gentleman's lifestyle, remaining pretty much in control of his own destiny and with the assurance born of that determination and independence. If ever a man lived up to his public image, it was Matthew Boulton. His children were brought up and educated to the genteel lifestyle, but he was anxious that his young son should keep his feet on the ground and not be overly influenced by 'puppys, Blockheads, Rakes or Impertinents'.[54] He had his own views on his place in society, as he explained to Matt, writing to the boy who was continuing his education in Germany:

> In great commercial and manufacturing countries the distinctions between one class of men and another are not so great as in remote inland villages, where agriculture is the principal employ. In such situations the distinction between the landed baron and the peasant is something similar to king and subject, and consequently the higher class is accustomed to be treated with ceremony and respect; and I think a benevolent good hearted baron is a blessing to his neighbourhood. Yet nevertheless I must own I am partial to trade, inasmuch as it extends a man's powers of doing good; and I had rather be distinguished as the greatest manufacturer in Europe than as a Count of the Holy Empire, because I suppose I pay weekly more money for ingenious labour than the first lord in England doth for common labour; and, after all, I am only a greater slave than my servants.[55]

It is this sense of purpose, above all, which makes Matthew Boulton 'a new species of Gentleman', and, more importantly, his own man.

References

Documents referenced with 'MS 3782', 'MS 3219', or 'MS 3147' are all in the Archives of Soho at Birmingham Archives and Heritage, Central Library Birmingham B3 3HQ.

---

54 BAH, MS 3782/13/36/7, MB to MRB, 8 June 1787.
55 BAH, MS 3782/13/36/27, MB to MRB, 18 December 1788.

Chapter 4

MATTHEW BOULTON, ENCLOSURE AND LANDED SOCIETY

David Brown

Matthew Boulton is best known as an industrialist and marketer of goods; next, he is remembered as a member of the Lunar Society and the group of Midland intellectuals fired by the ideas of the Enlightenment. Those whose knowledge is more detailed will know of the work of Eric Robinson and others which have demonstrated that Boulton was an expert lobbyist, but few will be aware of Boulton and his attitudes to land and society. Indeed, as a 'revolutionary player', it may well be ventured by those with Marxist leanings that Boulton should have been an inimical opponent of the landed interest and part of the up and coming bourgeois class engaged in a struggle for supremacy against the declining landed élite.[1]

Yet Boulton was intimately connected with landownership. His very position as a lobbyist meant that he had to cultivate progressive landowners to achieve his ends, perhaps as part of an emerging West Midlands community of interest between 1760 and 1800, as explored by John Money.[2] Standard biographies will reveal that while he was born into the middle class he married into land and money when he took first Mary and then Ann Robinson of Lichfield as wives. These marriages assisted his business by furnishing £28,000 of capital, but it also explains how the name 'Matthew Boulton' appears on enclosure awards in various parts of Staffordshire as a proprietor. His dependence on the Robinson inheritance is marked by his heir's middle name Matthew Robinson Boulton. Before the end of his life, Boulton became a substantial landowner in his own right by purchasing the

---

1   The standard biography is H.W. Dickinson, *Matthew Boulton* (Cambridge, 1936) which updated Samuel Smiles, *Boulton and Watt* (London, 1878). The most recent short biography is by Jennifer Tann in H.C.G. Matthew and Brian Harrison eds, *Oxford Dictionary of National Biography* (Oxford, 2004). Eric Robinson, 'Matthew Boulton and the Art of Parliamentary Lobbying' *Historical Journal* 7 (1964), pp.209–29.

2   J.D. Money, *Experience and Identity: Birmingham and the West Midlands, 1760–1800.* (Montreal, 1977).

site and environs of his factory at Handsworth from his landlord, Wyrley
Birch of Hamstead, a process facilitated by the enclosure of Handsworth
Heath under an act of 1791. This eased Boulton's entry into higher society
and the office of sheriff of the county in 1794, although he was still described
as 'engineer' in documents connected to his position. Finally his son, Matthew
Robinson Boulton, bought a substantial estate at Great Tew in Oxfordshire,
where his descendants lived until comparatively recent times.[3]

A good deal of research has shown that the Marxist view of two opposing
élites, bourgeois and aristocratic, competing at daggers drawn for social
supremacy which would be inevitably won by the former through their
growing access to capital resources, does not reflect events in Britain. People
like Boulton had at least an ambivalent relationship with the élite, using their
influence to gain the passage of beneficial legislation like acts for canals,
copyright protection and fiscal alterations. Indeed this alliance, the West
Midland interest, included Boulton in it its ranks.

Nevertheless, Boulton was a member of several important bourgeois
institutions. In the commercial world, he was heavily involved in the General
Chamber of Manufacturers, a short-lived lobby of manufacturers, intent on
promoting middle-class goals, and was Chairman of the Birmingham
Commercial Committee from 1790. His membership of the free-thinking
Lunar Society and his general social milieu composed of other middle class
intellectuals, show him to be a man of the Enlightenment where privilege by
birth or divine gift was questioned. Moreover he was born into the middle
class, the eponymous son of a successful Birmingham toymaker.[4]

The multi-faceted and complex relationship between Boulton and
landownership can be explored through the microcosm of enclosure.
Boulton's later years saw the two great waves of parliamentary enclosure, in
1760–80 and 1790–1820, which have been identified by Michael Turner, the
first characterized by enclosure of open field systems, the latter by the
transformation of commons and wastes into mixed farming land or improved
pasture. Boulton was involved in several enclosures in Staffordshire and
Warwickshire and his correspondence and actions reflect his wider attitudes
to landownership and its duties.[5]

The Boulton name occurs in four Staffordshire enclosures, Handsworth
(1791), Cheslyn Hay (1792), Needwood Forest (1801), Barton under
Needwood (1812) (where his son received an allotment) and one in

---

3   *VCH Oxfordshire* XI (Oxford,1985) p.227.
4   See for a recent investigation of the nature of the Lunar Society, Peter M. Jones, 'Living the
     Enlightenment and the French Revolution: James Watt, Matthew Boulton, and Their Sons' *The
     Historical Journal*, 42 (1) 1999, pp.157–182.
5   M. Turner, *English Parliamentary Enclosure* (Folkestone, 1980), p.70.

Warwickshire, Birmingham Heath (1801). All of these belonged to the second wave of enclosures and were typically composed largely of commons and wastes. The family's involvement in three of these enclosures was through Matthew's marriages with the Robinson family, as he had acquired land largely to the north east of Lichfield around Curborough and Barton under Needwood and a sizable property in Great Saredon to the south west of the city.[6] His involvement with the other two was indirectly a product of his marital career. Armed with capital from his marriage and his inheritance from his father, he became a leaseholder on his own account in 1762 when he took over a ninety-nine year lease of land at Soho on Handsworth Common made in 1757, where a small water-powered rolling mill had been established. Boulton was to convert this into his famous factory over the next few years. He also dabbled in the land market, but either as a speculation or to manage capital for his enterprises. For example he bought a small farm on mortgage in Yardley in 1761 and re-sold it in 1769. He certainly used his land as equity to borrow substantial sums of money, including £10,000 from Jacob Tonson. Land at this stage was clearly a vehicle to support his business; in 1772 during a trade depression, he sold his wife's Packington estate for £15,000 to Lord Donegall.[7] He acquired a small freehold farm in Handsworth about this time of perhaps twenty-two acres and was also active in reclaiming land on his leasehold; not only did he build his factory and home upon it but he was also paying tithe on barley grown on a new encroachment on the heath in 1773. As his new landlord said when he gave him first refusal on an encroachment about to be licensed to another applicant, he was 'unwilling to check your Inclination for Improvement.'[8]

Despite these early connections with landownership, it was in the 1790s that he became more intimately connected with the duties of real estate. His factory and the house at Soho were built on an encroachment authorised by the lord of Handsworth manor, Wyrley Birch of nearby Hamstead Hall. In the late eighteenth and early nineteenth centuries, the Birches were progressively liquidating most of their midland properties and eventually purchased an estate in Norfolk. Boulton was keen to acquire the freehold of the Soho property in order to secure the site of his factory (upon which he had spent £9,000 in the 1760s) and to give security for enlarging and

---

6   Birmingham Archives and Heritage (BAH), MS 3375/451030, 3 June 1806.
7   J. Uglow, *The Lunar Men: five friends whose curiosity changed the world* (London, 2002) pp.67–8; BAH, MS 3375/425438 *14 August 1761* and MS 3375/425447 *30 March 1769;* H.W. Dickinson, *Matthew Boulton* (Cambridge, 1936) pp.83 and 135 quoting Boulton to Earl of Dartmouth, 10 November 1772.
8   BAH, MS 3782/12/23/289, Rev. John Birch to M. Boulton 25 August 1773 and MS 3782/12/24/88 George Birch to M. Boulton, 4 January 1777; MS 3782/12/8, M. Boulton to the Enclosure Commissioners, 27 September 1791.

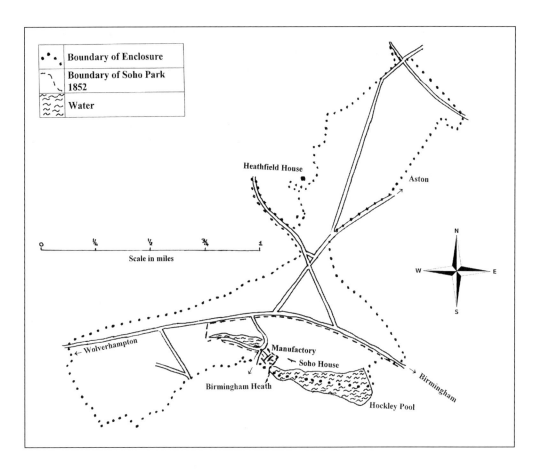

Map 4.1. Handsworth Enclosure Award 1794. Drawing by the author.

improving the mansion and its pleasure grounds to a state appropriate to a man of his means and status. The problem was that the lease from Birch was in his persona as lord of the manor, as the land was encroached from Handsworth Heath, adjoining the road from Birmingham. Moreover he wanted to 'stop up the cross roads over the heath and the whole of the Soho Bank so cultivated as to induce me to build a good house.'[9] This meant that an act of parliament to enclose Handsworth Heath and the parish's vestigial open fields was required and obtained in 1791. Boulton bought about 113 acres of land on the heath in 1794, apparently for £9,200 and started to rebuild the modest house at Soho, which he transformed into a gentleman's mansion. The extent to which he used the enclosure and subsequent allotments to create at park is shown in Map 4.1. He progressively added to

9 BAH, MS 3782/12/8, M. Boulton to G. Birch, 2 March 1790.

the estate and by the time of the tithe return around 1840, Boulton's son owned 134 acres in Handsworth and 69 acres in Birmingham.[10]

Boulton was clearly the moving force behind the process, although it was actually James Watt's desire for an enclosure to provide the site for a house for his own use that precipitated Boulton's first application to Birch to enclose. The Lord of the Manor commented in 1788 when he first discussed an enclosure, that Boulton was 'the only negotiator to me on this business' and suggested that he discuss terms with the 'freeholders who have talked with you.' Boulton was keen to purchase the site of his own encroachments but not those small plots 'where the cottages were lately pulled down' because the multiplicity of small roads there was so inconvenient.' He added that unless a general enclosure of the heath occurred he was not interested in purchasing the lease.[11]

While Birch was keen on enclosure on 'liberal terms' which many of the substantial landowners were willing to concede, it was the smaller owners whose consents were hard to obtain.[12] Eventually terms were agreed and the enclosure proceeded under an act of 1791 with Birch receiving one fifteenth including all encroachments. It should not be assumed that all interested parties consented to the action. The consents to the Handsworth enclosure are complicated as the act was also used to enclose the parish's vestigial open fields and the common at Perry Barr within Handsworth parish was not affected. At first sight, the measure seems a popular one. While freeholders of 177 acres were neutral and those holding 84 acres were opposed to the act, the land they possessed was a small proportion of the 2975 acres of land with common rights over the heath. In the open fields, owners of three acres of the land were opposed and of nine acres were neutral out of the seventy one acres involved. This fell well short of the norm of twenty to twenty-five percent of the acreage which was required to block an application. Indeed, Birch alone owned over half of the land and so only needed a few similar large owners to support him to carry the measure. This decision appears democratic; however the House of Lords Committee book also recorded the number of messuages[13] in each category. This revealed a less well-supported measure; only owners of seventy three and a half messuages out of the 103 involved supported the act – and many of those messuages were those rented

---

10   *Staffordshire Advertiser,* 26 August 1809; BAH, MS 3782/38/107 John Bishton to M. Boulton, 26 June 1793; G. Demidovicz, 'Soho House and Foundry' in A Foster, *Birmingham* (New Haven and London 2005) pp.282–6; BAH, Mss.299997; Handsworth Tithe Apportionment 1843.

11   BAH, MS 3782/1/2/33, George Birch to Boulton, 18 November 1788; BAH, MS 3782/12/8, M. Boulton to George Birch, 2 March 1790.

12   BAH, MS 3782/12/35/44, G. Birch to M. Boulton, 3 March 1790.

13   A messuage is a dwelling with the outbuildings and land associated with it.

from the large owners and the views of these tenants were not considered. In promoting the enclosure, Boulton was overlooking the interests of many of the poorer elements of the parish and endorsing the rights of property. Clearly Boulton was a very conformist kind of 'revolutionary player'.[14]

The enclosure at Handsworth propelled Boulton clearly into the landed gentry with a freehold house and park to add to the other properties held in Staffordshire. It is probably not unconnected that Boulton was nominated as sheriff of the county at the time of the act (1791) and served in the position when the award was executed (1794). The appointment to the position of sheriff was a symbol of the nominee's acceptance into landed society. It was also an expensive one, because the position required some time holding county meetings and a good deal of costly ceremonial – for example paying for the attendance of javelin men throughout the assizes. There is even a bill of expenses associated with his role as sheriff in paying tolls and hotel bills at Walsall, not the county town. His appointment as sheriff led to his acquisition of a coat of arms, of which Boulton was extremely proud. An ornamental silver tea vase with a variation of his coat of arms is to be found on display at the Soho House Museum.[15] He had already shown attitudes symptomatic of landownership in his behaviour which enclosure would only accelerate. As one of Boulton's earliest biographers, Samuel Smiles noted: 'The nature of his [Boulton's] tenure caused him to take a lively interest in the question of common lands enclosure.'[16]

Although a man of great enterprise himself, Boulton showed a hard face to the poor who were showing similar initiative in trying to earn a living through encroaching on common land rather than become a burden on the poor rate. In Boulton's view, Arthur Young's argument that enclosures of the commons was 'robbing the poor is fallacious. They have no legal title to the common land and the more of it that is cultivated, the more work and the more bread there will be for them.' When he took his lease of a portion of Handsworth Heath, it was a rabbit warren with only a warrener's cottage on its summit and, according to Boulton himself 'a few miserable huts filled with idle beggarly wretches, who by the help of the common land and a little thieving made shift to live without working.'[17] Boulton may have been

---

14   S. Shaw, *The History and Antiquities of Staffordshire* II i (London, 1801) 2 Vols., p.112 using Sherriff's survey of Hamstead and Handsworth; House of Lords Committee Book 35, 20 April 1791 p.89.

15   *The Times*, 14 November 1791; p.2 Col.C; *The Times*, 28 May 1794; p.1 Col.A; Birmingham Museum and Art Gallery Accession No, 1988M204.

16   Walsall Local Studies, MS 193; S. Smiles, Lives of Boulton and Watt (London, 1878), p.168.

17   E. Darwin, letter to Rev. Feilde of Brewood, 16 August 1768 quoted in Stebbing Shaw, *The History and Antiquities of Staffordshire* II i (1801) 112; BAH, MS 3782/12/8, M. Boulton to Lord Hawkesbury 17 April 1790.

exaggerating to emphasise his transformation of the area because along the turnpike road on the heath's northern side from Birmingham to Wolverhampton, a large number of nailers had encroached on the roadside to create gardens, small pastures and cottages with small furnaces. These formed 'one continuous village' for five or six miles between Birmingham and West Bromwich according to Arthur Young, who passed along this road in 1776.[18] Indeed the enclosure award shows numerous roadside plots which were clearly the sites of small encroachments. The downturn in the domestic nail trade which began at the same time as the American Wars of Independence (1776–83) coincided with the action of Birch as lord of the manor who in Boulton's words 'hath exterminated these very poor cottages.' Lords of the manor had an uneasy relationship with encroachers; while they paid their fines for encroaching on the commons, it was a small but useful income for the lord who would also avoid the payment of poor rates on his freehold land to support them. In addition, these improved plots would form part of any manorial allotment in the event of an enclosure and would be valued at their original unimproved value, which was clearly advantageous to the lord. Unfortunately, as the iron trade declined, presumably their ability to pay fines decreased in inverse proportion to their demands upon the poor rates. Taken together with Boulton's need for workers at his factory, the enclosure seemed to prevent any further danger of demands on the local poor rate. Boulton himself vaingloriously added that his factory had 'entirely changed' the scene with 'hundreds of clean comfortable cheerful houses' on freehold land inhabited by hands working in his factory. The irony that he was attacking people, who, like himself, had encroached on common land with manorial consent to develop industrial and agricultural plots to support themselves, seems to have escaped Boulton utterly.[19]

The enclosure however did not achieve all of Boulton's goals. Firstly there was the issue of the cottages. Boulton eventually bought some of the cottages from Birch but then found it hard to persuade the occupants to leave, the latter claiming to have freehold ownership over their plots as they had not been opened or been subject to manorial fines for over twenty one years.[20] A more serious problem for Boulton was the core reason why the other freeholders agreed to the proposal; the release of land near a growing conurbation for housing and other urban-related purposes such as accommodation for livestock. Handsworth Heath lay in an ideal situation for a middle-class suburb of Birmingham: it lay to the west of the town and so

18   *VCH Staffordshire* XVIII (Oxford, 1976), pp.38–43.
19   BAH, MS 3782/12/8, M. Boulton to Lord Hawkesbury, 17 April 1790.
20   BAH, MS 3782/12/40/289, M. Boulton to George Birch, 24 September 1795.

was relatively free from its smoke and odours because of the prevailing westerly winds of the northern hemisphere. This was doubly important in an age when the miasmatic theory of disease had strong adherence. This factor was also helped because it was well drained. The heath was on a hill whose mass could obliterate the city on its lee side and give a sunny aspect on its southern side. Finally, it was on one of the main turnpike roads from Birmingham which meant that its wealthy bourgeoisie had easy access to their counting houses and works. Such turnpike suburbs often were developed on newly enclosed heaths on the edge of growing towns: Nottingham was noted for a ring of such settlements beyond the constraining girdle of its open fields, as was London. The enclosures in the West Midlands of West Bromwich in 1801 (further along the same turnpike as Handsworth Heath) and Tettenhall in 1808 conform to this pattern and middle-class housing soon covered the former heaths.[21]

Indeed, these were some of the very reasons why Boulton decided to live here. Like some other industrialists – for example Heathcoat at Tiverton and Gott at Armley – Boulton had included a view of his works in the centre of his landed estate. However, the hill in particular gave Soho House a tranquillity much to be desired in a location so close to Birmingham. An undated invitation to dine at Soho to Mrs Dibbs remarked that 'ye quietude and fresh air of Soho will do you more good than ye smoak and Noise of Birmgm.'[22]

As a consequence, many middle-class men sought to buy sites for their villas in Handsworth and later at West Bromwich, particularly if they were concerned that the houses in the other upmarket area of Birmingham, Edgbaston, neither shared Handsworth Heath's natural advantages nor its freehold status. James Watt indeed, built his own house in 1790 on freehold land at Heathfield, but added allotments from the common until in 1794 he had enclosed about forty acres.[23] It was not such building which concerned Boulton, but the appearance of club houses for artisans in Handsworth.

Already before the act, small lots of building land on the other side of the Walsall turnpike were offered on ninety-nine year building leases and Chalkin has remarked that building clubs of artisans were in existence in Birmingham by this date. Boulton should have welcomed these institutions as examples of enterprise and industry. Groups of artisans subscribed money to buy a plot of land and to build as many houses as their collective capital

21   D. Brown, 'Enclosure and Improvement. An investigation into the motives' (PhD thesis, Wolverhampton University, 1992), pp.139–141.
22   William Salt Library SMS 478 B. Boulton to Mrs Dibbs undated.
23   S. Smiles, *Lives of Boulton and Watt* (1865) 460; more generally about Birmingham merchant's new rural homes see A Murray, *General View of the Agriculture of Warwickshire* (London, 1815), pp.28–9 and Charles Pye, *A Description of Modern Birmingham* (Birmingham, 1818).

allowed. Then a draw was held to establish which lucky members would secure a home. The winners then paid rent into the club until sufficient was raised to build more houses until all the members had a home and the club was wound up. Boulton's self interest led him to reject these local schemes. Within a year of the award, the local paper reported that sixty acres of the heath were 'already taken or purchased and intended built upon and that some of the building clubs have made a beginning upon a scale of twenty houses and gardens to an acre of land.' The paper's anonymous correspondent from Handsworth criticised this as there were already 1000 houses untenanted in Birmingham itself and many of Handsworth's own population were out of work. While the name of this clearly influential and politically aware resident is not known, it is very likely to have been Boulton who was adept at using the local media. It is also suggested by his presence at a meeting of the Handsworth vestry on the subject of how to prevent the 'evil consequences' arising from 'the great number of club and other small houses intended to be built in this parish'. It was decided unanimously that all those newcomers who may be chargeable in Handsworth should be removed by the parish officials who should also 'discourage by every legal means the building of small houses.' Birmingham's anonymous radical pamphleteer, Job Nott, was well aware of Boulton's close involvement in the decision and felt the policy was futile as it merely transferred the problem over the parish border into Birmingham. Nott wrote that 'had these resolutions been the result of the deliberations of *Country Gentlemen*, I should have felt no surprise; but when I see affixed to them the name of one of the most *justly* celebrated manufacturers in his Majesty's dominions' he was astonished. Further, Boulton was associated with the eviction of a family with smallpox and, in plans to attack the parks of the wealthy by radicals, Soho was high on the list. Moreover, for Boulton and Handsworth's other leading lights, the pressure to build houses was inexorable; in 1797 and 1798 plots and newly erected houses on building leases were rising up on the former common.[24]

This desire for the poor to be kept in their place was reflected in his attitudes on other occasions. He was a freeholder in the vicinity of Cheslyn Hay, a notorious extra-parochial waste where the poor and needy gathered to get a home and make a living from begging or selling besoms made from the gorse growing on the heath. Although there seems to be no evidence in his correspondence, of Boulton taking a lead in its enclosure, its originator,

24 *Aris's Birmingham Gazette*, 3 November 1788 p.3 Col.4; C.W. Chalklin, *The Provincial Towns of Georgian England* (1974), pp.175–8; *Aris's Birmingham Gazette*, 26 January 1795 p.3 Col.3; BAH, DRO, 86/109. Handsworth Vestry minutes, 17 December 1794; Job Nott, *An Appeal to Manufacturers on the Present State of Trade* (1795) BAH, 67417 pp.5, 8–10; Money, *Experience and Identity Birmingham and the West Midlands, 1760–1800, op. cit.*, pp.267 and 273.

John Bishton, estate agent of the Marquess of Stafford, strongly shared Boulton's views of the moral and social dangers of unenclosed heaths as shown in his passage on the subject in his *General View of the Agriculture of Shropshire*. Moreover, it is probably not coincidental that John Bishton was one of the commissioners for the Handsworth Enclosure award.[25]

Boulton himself instanced the dangers of not enclosing when in 1790 he instanced the neighbouring parish of Sutton Coldfield. This contained '10,000 acres of common land uncultivated and yet the poor rates are very high. Let this land be divided, enclosed, cultivated and rendered saleable to active, industrious and spirited men; the poor will then have plenty of work and the next generation of them will be fully reconciled to earning their bread instead of begging for it.'[26]

In this, Boulton was typical of a growing kind of landowner, more often Whig than Tory, who was committed to the transformation of traditional rural society and the notion of improvement rather than conservatism. Traditionally-minded landowners were keen to retain the status quo and, as such, showed little inclination towards the progressive development of their estates. Nevertheless, influenced by the Enlightenment and self interest in reaping the rewards of the growing demand for food as well as any industrial or housing potential their estates may offer, growing numbers of landowners were keen to promote the development of their estates. To such progressive landowners, encroachers were a dangerous crew. They were often associated with poverty and immorality and they were inefficient producers in an age when increased food production was both necessary and profitable. These two camps would occasionally come into conflict as Boulton would later discover over the issue of the proposed enclosure of Needwood Forest.

Despite his transition into the landed gentry, Boulton remained active in business with its needs to promote industry and commerce. Thus it was not long after the enclosure of Handsworth Common that its continuation in Warwickshire, the 287 acres of Birmingham Heath, came to the attention of Birmingham's leading landowners. Most of these proprietors – men like Lionel Colmore and Sir Thomas Gooch Bart. of Benacre Hall – were not really members of the local aristocracy and saw the heath simply as a potential source of profit from housing development. The one exception was John Gough of nearby Perry Barr who owned twenty percent of the land in Birmingham which had common rights over the heath. He was a substantial and wealthy landowner who was keen on profit from mortgage lending but was a private and litigious man. For example, he took a case to the Assizes

25   J. Bishton, *General View of the Agriculture of Shropshire* (Brentford, 1794), p.24.
26   BAH, MS 3782/12/8 M. Boulton to Lord Hawkesbury, 17 April 1790.

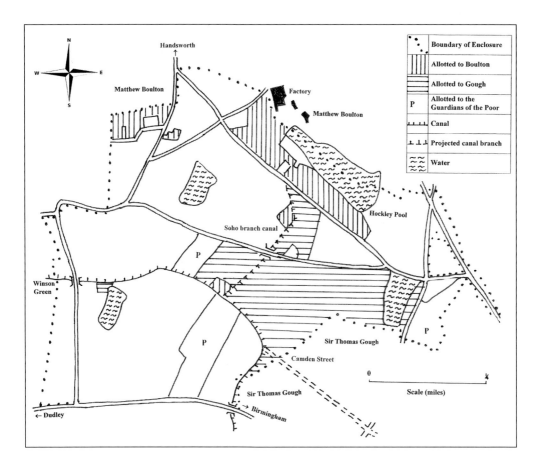

Map 4.2. Birmingham Heath Enclosure Award 1802. Drawing by the author.

against Wyrley Birch over the Perry Common enclosure of 1811 but was defeated, apparently because of his unpopularity amongst the Grand Jury. He had first proposed the enclosure of the heath in 1783 but was unsuccessful. Ten years after another attempt failed in 1788; the profitable enclosure of Handsworth Heath prompted the local landowners to promote a similar measure for Birmingham Heath which adjoined the western side of the town as shown in Map 4.2.[27]

However, many leading townspeople mounted an opposition to the bill, on account of the fact that the bill made no provision for the burgeoning poor of the town, who were now costing it £25,000 annually. This was not because the urban élite wanted to provide grazing or charity land for the

27 *Aris's Birmingham Gazette,* 21 July 1783 Journal of the House of Lords (JHL), 1798, pp.134–5; R.K. Dent and J. Hill, *Historic Staffordshire* (1975 reprint) pp.260–1; BAH, Gough Collection 196 and 364. *Staffordshire Advertiser,* 22 May 1813 p.2 Col.4 and 7 April 1827, p.3 Col.2.

poor; instead they wanted to secure part of the land to provide the site for a workhouse and other institutions and land to employ the able-bodied poor. All the proprietors agreed to such an allotment, but Gough refused to give his consent to the final bill as he wanted the right to nominate a commissioner. Despite his opposition, the bill was enacted. Boulton's generally favourable attitude to enclosure predisposed him to support the bill, especially as the heath was allegedly the resort of inhabitants to pursue cruel sports like bull baiting, but he had more practical reasons to support the proposal as he quickly made use of the enclosure to benefit his business and to extend his property.[28]

Boulton's works, originally situated because of the useful presence of water power, was remote from canals as it was on the hillside above the low-lying ground at the edge of Birmingham Heath where they were situated. He had to rely on land carriage to the Birmingham Wharf for his transport needs. As soon as the act was obtained, Boulton successfully approached the Birmingham Canal Navigation and the enclosure commissioners for permission to a cut across the heath to the Birmingham Canal Navigation's system, at his own cost, to allow the delivery of coal and dispatch of goods.[29]

In the eventual award, the Guardians of the Poor received thirty acres but this was not used for a new workhouse and other public buildings for decades. Instead, the land was used to employ the able-bodied poor in planting potatoes which in 1822 was sufficient to supply the workhouse with 600 bushels to spare. Colmore (fifty eight acres) and Gough (forty two acres) received the largest allotments as their right but Boulton received over twenty-five acres by numerous purchases of rights after the act. As Map 4.2 shows, these were situated opposite his works and beside Hockley Pool.[30]

Boulton's interest in purchasing enclosure plots led at least one seller to believe that he could be interested in urban speculation, despite Boulton's attitude towards urban development in the vicinity of his estate. When Isaac Riddell was informed of his interest in purchasing land on Birmingham Heath, he offered him his farm again and his allotment of about ten acres (actually eight) which 'most likely the commissioners would be so obliging as to let you have the allotment in almost any part that would be the most convenient and agreeable.' He believed that the farm and allotment could be let on 'building leases' especially if peace was declared. He suggested three lines of roads to open up the housing potential of the land and pointed out that the active urban developer, Sir Thomas Gooch, was planning to extend

28 *Aris's Birmingham Gazette*, 23 April 1798 p.3 c.5; JHL, 1798, pp.134–5, 13 May 1798.

29 S.R. Broadbridge, *The Birmingham Canal Navigations: Volume 1: 1768–1846* (1974), p.89.

30 BAH, Birmingham Heath Enclosure award 1802; C. Gill, *History of Birmingham* (1952), I pp.150–1 quoting report of Paul Moon James, Chairman of Birmingham Poor Law Guardians 1822.

'Camden Street' (which still survives) across his allotments. He sought to flatter Boulton by saying that where Boulton's three streets met, a column to Boulton could be erected and should be called 'Boultonia' or 'Boulton's Town'. Riddell promised that if Boulton made this initial investment, he and his friends would be glad 'to form a Building Society on a large scale providing the Ground Rent was moderated – Perhaps in the course of a few years, not only the said land but also Birmingham Heath – the chief part of Handsworth – will be nearly covered with buildings' and be called Boultonstown. He sent Boulton three copies of his plan together with a scheme to reduce the local poor rates.[31]

Boulton certainly bought Riddell's enclosure allotment but did not entertain the proposal to develop the estate. The three likeliest explanations are that Boulton did not have the capital or he did not think the proposal would have a financial return or he wanted to extend his estate and prevent the creeping urbanisation of Birmingham towards his doorstep. Given Boulton's attitude to building clubs in Handsworth, the latter is the likeliest motive and suggests something about Boulton's attitude to land. Boulton could have profited from making building leases of land around Soho but he preferred to build up a large private estate.

Boulton did recognize that landowners had a greater duty than their own narrow advantage when it came to the final enclosure with which he was personally associated – that of Needwood Forest. The enclosure of the forest had long been discussed, ever since the time of the Commonwealth, but three of the area's largest and most influential landowners, Lords Talbot, Vernon and Bagot, had vested interests in opposing the measure, apart from their conservatism, as they wished to retain their rights in the parks.

From the surviving correspondence in Boulton's records, it is clear that Boulton took an active role in promoting the enclosure among the many freeholders, although he was not a substantial owner. In fact, he was only a small proprietor – his allotment was twenty four acres – and his ally in the measure, Erasmus Darwin, thought that Boulton would be prepared to sell his allotment once the measure had been secured.[32] Boulton's support for the measure did not derive from direct financial gain from the enclosure. Boulton chaired the first meeting of the committee to promote the enclosure and certainly had the influence to secure one applicant the position of solicitor for the bill.[33] Boulton was an active propagandist for the measure. He wrote an open letter to the local newspapers outlining the main reasons

31   BAH, MS 3782/12/45/221, Isaac Riddell to M. Boulton 1 January 1800 and 15 July 1800 plans
     (NB. the name on the enclosure award as the seller of this estate was Luke not Isaac Riddell).
32   BAH, MS 3782/13/53/110, E. Darwin to M. Boulton 9 November 1800.
33   BAH, MS 3782/12/45/74 Nathaniel Edwards to M. Boulton, 12 March 1800.

for the enclosure to take place when the opposition proposed stinting the pasture. This letter clearly reflects his attitudes towards enclosure and the duties of landownership.[34]

The merchant prince began by pointing out that stinting the pasturage, in other words limiting the numbers of livestock each landowner could depasture the forest, would not prevent the problems of deer entering adjoining corn fields, nor lead to any increase in output from the land itself or 'an additional penny in the national purse'. In a phrase echoing his comments about Sutton Coldfield, he added that the land would remain 'a nursery for poachers and deer-stealers.' He also alluded to the current political and economic problems of relying on foreign imports of grain and that enclosure of appropriate commons and wastes would help the balance of payments to the extent of £5.1 million, as well as make the United Kingdom self sufficient in grain. His arguments were intended to persuade not the proprietors (of whom by November 1800 there were already nearly sufficient to carry the measure), but the powerful politicians who could easily block the measure at the committee stage in parliament.

Boulton also used his influence with various members of the aristocracy to carry the measure. He lobbied Lord Liverpool, who was Chancellor of the Duchy of Lancaster, to ensure the necessary support of the Crown for the enclosure of a royal forest. He also wrote to many others to ensure there was sufficient support at the committee stage in the House of Lords to overturn considerable opposition to the measure: twenty one opponents attended the committee to oppose it especially Lord Thurlow. As a result of his efforts at all stages of the process, the bill's solicitor wrote to Boulton and told him that 'the freeholders are in the greatest degree indebted for your exertions to forward this important measure and your last effort (to secure a large attendance of supporters at the committee stage) was not the least in importance.'[35]

Although a progressive in many ways, Boulton was able to find a strong constituency of support among sympathetic members of the aristocracy who sought to maintain their position through accommodation with those members of the middle class with deferential views. Boulton's attitudes towards the status quo are best shown by his political standpoint. Although a member of the Lunar Society and a lobbyist, Boulton is not associated with any political group as such; he was worried about the dangers of republicanism and supported the Tory administration's American policy

34   *Staffordshire Advertiser,* 4 October 1800.
35   BAH, MS 3782/12/45/389 N. Edwards to M. Boulton, 19 November 1800, MS 3782/12/46/182
     Nathaniel Edwards to M. Boulton, 1 June 1801 and MS 3782/12/46/191, Nathaniel Edwards to
     M. Boulton 18 June 1801.

during the Wars of Independence. His lobbying involved both Whigs and Tories like the Earl of Dartmouth and the Second Viscount Dudley, and his interests in politics were purely commercial. Certainly he enjoyed electoral influence at Lichfield and in North Warwickshire elections.[36] Nevertheless, unlike many fellow Lunar Society members, he did not take an active role in supporting political and social reform and opposing aristocratic privilege. Conspicuously while other local fellow members had their property destroyed or damaged during the Priestley Riots by a 'Church and King mob' of artisans whipped up to an extent by local Anglicans, Boulton's house and factory were spared. It might be argued that this was because of Boulton's purchase of flintlock muskets to defend his works, which was situated a distance outside the town. However, the rioters reached as far as Kings Norton some several miles outside the city. Boulton was an Anglican, albeit perhaps more for form than profound conviction: he owned a pew in the fashionable new church in Birmingham at St Paul's and is buried in St Mary's Church, Handsworth. His actions were precautionary and prudent in a volatile situation as was his removal of his papers to a safe place which inconvenienced the Handsworth Enclosure commissioners. His actions thereafter showed his loyalty to church and state within limitations: he established a Soho Volunteer Corps in 1798 and gave £200 to the Voluntary Contribution in Handsworth towards the defence of the country; while this was the largest in the parish, the donations of other leading manufacturers, like the £10,000 given by the future Sir Robert Peel, were conspicuously more generous. Boulton was not noted as mean man: he gave his workers a social insurance scheme, a dinner when his son came of age and was an early benefactor to Birmingham General Hospital and a guarantor of finance for the Birmingham Dispensary in 1793.[37]

It may be argued that Boulton's search for status and society had a distinctly urban rather than a landed focus. Apart from his support of Birmingham's charitable institutions, he was closely involved in attempts to improve the society and amenities of Birmingham. He was a founder and a proprietor of Birmingham's first licensed theatre and served as a street

---

36   J.D. Money, *Experience and Identity: Birmingham and the West Midlands, 1760–1800, op. cit.*, pp.101, 159, 175, 180–1, 199–202, 213–4.

37   Dorothy A. Stansfield, *Thomas Beddoes MD*, (1984), p.73; BAH, AO Letter Book Q Boulton to Enclosure Commissioners, 22 September 1791; J.P. Muirhead, *The Origins and Progress of the Mechanical Inventions of James Watt* II (London 1854) 3 Vols. pp.241–2; *Aris's Birmingham Gazette* 10 March 1798, p.3 c.2; The Industrial Revolution: A Documentary History. Series One: The Boulton & Watt Archive and the Matthew Boulton Papers from Birmingham Central Library Reel 55 Shrievalty 100–106; J.A. Langford, *A Century of Birmingham Life 1741–1841* (Birmingham 1868) 2 Vols. I 155, 157; R.K. Dent, *Old and New Birmingham* (Birmingham 1880; reprinted in 3 Vols East Adrsley 1972–3) II, p.365.

commissioner under a local improvement act in 1767. Boulton lived adjacent to his works and within a ten-minute horse ride of Birmingham. From these facts alone, it could be argued that Boulton was an urban entrepreneur whose main concerns were the middle class and Birmingham. Nevertheless, the evidence assembled here points to him being at least a transitional figure, straddling both social classes and contributing to the eventual alliance of land and industry which, symbolised by the dominance of the Conservative party from the mid 1880s onwards, has characterized Britain's peaceful transition from a landed to an urban society and one dominated by money rather than land. It is men like him who forged alliances with increasing numbers of aristocrats who averted the Marxist model of a bourgeois revolution as two classes in conflict strove to assert control.[38]

Indeed, his argument in favour of a single Birmingham theatre shows great consistency with those advanced in support of enclosure. He advocated that there should be only one theatre but it should have formal legal recognition. This would prevent competition between two theatres (how odd an idea from a great entrepreneur living at the time of Adam Smith and the advocacy of free trade) which would lead to price cutting and the attendance of the poor at the theatre with its concomitant social problems. One theatre would bring learning and culture to the town and encourage people of taste to resort there and so interaction between producers and customers would be increased. Boulton's motivation was essentially twofold: policies should encourage trade and maintain law and order. It was only an indirect benefit that Birmingham would prosper at the same time. The academic world generally has retreated from the concept of social control under the withering fire of F.M.L. Thompson, but Boulton's consistent attitudes and subsequent behaviour does strongly endorse its replacement, the idea of maintaining the moral order.[39]

At his death, Boulton behaved with some of the prudence of the businessman. While he carelessly left £120,000 for probate purposes, he had made a gift during his lifetime of a partnership in his works to his son Matthew Robinson Boulton in 1800, which avoided taxation and also prepared his son for taking over the business fully. Of course, his landed estate, like those of aristocrats, was not subject to any taxation if left to a son. Boulton's aspirations to found a landed dynasty were not shown by the trait, shown by other entrepreneurs, of buying a landed estate for his son and heir shortly before his death to avoid death duties. Nevertheless, Matthew Robinson Boulton was educated as a gentleman and considerable efforts were made to eradicate the

38 J. Uglow *The Lunar Men: five friends whose curiosity changed the world* (London, 2002), pp.170–1
     and 466.
39 F.M.L. Thompson, 'Social Control in Victorian Britain,' *Economic History Review,* 2nd ser. 34 2
     (1981), pp.188–208.

young man's tendency to drop his aitches. It is true, as Eric Robinson points out, that Boulton junior was given the appropriate education for a 'Captain of Industry' by studying mathematics, science and modern languages. Nevertheless, as Robinson admits, he was 'encouraged to be a gentleman – well... dressed, able to dance a minuet elegantly, acquainted with music, the theatre and painting.' He was also given a thorough grounding in Latin and he fell in love with a German baroness. Moreover, male Boulton descendants thereafter went to Eton.[40] In 1817 Matthew junior married the much younger daughter of his friend, the ironmaster William Wilkinson, she came, nevertheless, with a marriage settlement of £45,112 and her father had a substantial landed estate.[41] Moreover, the couple moved into a new home and estate at Great Tew in Oxfordshire, bought the year before. Although he spent most of the year at the factory for the next ten years, Matthew Robinson proceeded to extend his Oxfordshire estate and make great landscape, agricultural and building improvements. Indeed his largest addition was made *post mortem* by his trustees, who bought a huge adjoining estate for £184,000.[42] Much like his former landlords, the Birches, the Boultons left the industrial midlands for pastures new. As shown by F.M.L. Thompson, this was a well-beaten track among the aristocracy and the very prosperous middle classes. This author's own unpublished research confirms this trend. For example, the industrial West Midlands lost three of its largest resident landowners to the countryside in the nineteenth century – Lords Dudley and Dartmouth and the Birches – and Birmingham lost 27 of its wealthiest entrepreneurs who bought estates of over 1,000 acres between 1780 and 1879. More generally, of estates in existence in England and Wales in 1880, twenty-eight percent of them above a threshold of 3,000 acres/£3,000 rental (commonly seen as aristocratic estates) and thirty-eight percent of estates of between 1,000 acres/£1,000 and 2,999 acres/£2,999 (the notional boundaries of a gentry estate), had been sold to persons who derived their wealth from non-agricultural sources in the century 1780–1879.[43]

Conclusion

Matthew Boulton moved easily between the business and landed classes and his guests at Soho included aristocrats as well as political radicals. The reason was simple. Boulton's primary goals were selfish and commercial rather than

---

40   Rev. S. Parlby to M. Boulton 28 February 1785 quoted by Lynda Mugglestone, *"Talking Proper": The Rise of Accent as Social Symbol* (Oxford, 1995) pp.112–113; E Robinson, 'Training Captains of Industry' in A.E. Musson and E. Robinson eds, *Science and Technology in the Industrial Revolution* (Manchester, 1969), pp.200–215.

41   BAH, MS 3375/4552274.

42   *VCH Oxfordshire* VII (Oxford, 1962) pp.124–6; *VCH Oxfordshire* XI (Oxford, 1983), p.251.

43   F.M.L. Thompson, *Gentrification and the Enterprise Culture 1780–1980* (2001) summarises and augments his previous research on the subject.

the promotion of wholesale social and political change. Boulton, though, was motivated at times by other social and economic concerns, as his views on the enclosures of Cheslyn Hay and Needwood Forest indicate. Nevertheless, in the latter two cases, Boulton could, to an extent, afford his altruism as he had little to lose and indirectly much to gain through promoting moral order and a good food supply. In his attitudes to the poor, moreover, he shared some of the views of the country gentry, as Job Nott recognised in 1795. Many members of the middle classes wanted to make common cause with the aristocracy to maintain elements of the status quo, which they saw as being in their self interest. Boulton's attitudes served to increase the acceptability of the middle-classes to the aristocracy who were prepared to embrace industrial change and the rise of this class, provided that the former accepted the ideas of aristocratic respectability.

Moreover Boulton clearly aspired to the landed gentry as time passed: he both married into and bought land. Although he used land to support his business activities in his early days, he later served as sheriff, built a mansion in a grand park (albeit near to his works) and acquired a coat of arms. He educated his son as a gentleman and left him the means and inculcated the attitude which led to his heir buying a more substantial estate in Oxfordshire, retreating from the business in his old age and joining the aristocracy.

If Boulton was a 'revolutionary player', he was indeed one that does not fit easily into a Marxist model of social conflict, but his life does typify much about those merchant princes who played a vital role in Britain's transformation during the period called the 'Industrial Revolution'. His conservatism, landed aspirations and his willingness to reject free trade, especially where this jeopardised the status quo, does not make him an archetypal figure of the rising middle classes. Alternatively, his enterprise, his interest in business and making money and his limited entry into the landowning classes, clearly separate him from the aristocracy. Instead he belongs to a small but highly significant group of *haut bourgeoisie* who aspired to landed status and landed values. These people can be presented as 'counter-revolutionary players', as their example justified the myth of social mobility and self help. Indeed, this trend helps to answer one of the great questions of British history – why was there no political revolution in Britain when most other nations in Europe saw enormous revolutionary changes over the period? The answer is that through the influence and attitudes of both conservative members of the *haut bourgeoisie* and the progressive nature of growing numbers of the landed élite, change was accomplished both gradually and peacefully.

Chapter 5

PORTRAITS OF MATTHEW BOULTON[1]

Val Loggie

Matthew Boulton lived and worked in a period when portraiture was growing in status and popularity. Having a portrait painted was no longer the preserve of the aristocracy, it was opening out to a new group of sitters and viewers; mill owners, manufacturers and engineers; men like Boulton and his circle could now afford to commission portraits.[2] Like many of his friends Boulton had his portrait painted a number of times, by different artists, for different audiences and to be hung in different locations. Those original portraits were subsequently copied and reproduced in various formats such as miniatures and prints. It is characteristic of Boulton that he used a variety of artists to portray him, as he had encouraged numerous artists in his businesses.

The earliest known portrait of Boulton was one of a pair, painted by Tilly Kettle, the other image showing Boulton's second wife, Ann, whom he had married in 1760.[3] Kettle worked in the Midlands from 1762 to 1764 painting portraits and it is possible that Boulton was made aware of his work through sitters from the region or through Benjamin Green who produced a print after at least one of Kettle's portraits working under the name 'Pott'.[4] Green,

1 The research for this paper was undertaken as part of an AHRC funded PhD co-supervised by the University of Birmingham and Birmingham Museums and Art Gallery (BMAG). I am grateful to the staff of Birmingham Archives and Heritage (BAH), the Heinz Archive and Library at the National Portrait Gallery (NPG), Dr Alastair Brown, Dr Richard Clay, Brendan Flynn, Dr R.A. Ixer, Shena Mason, Dr Lucy Peltz, Elizabeth Spencer, Sue Tungate and Victoria Osborne for their assistance.

2 Desmond Shawe-Taylor, *The Georgians: Eighteenth-Century Portraiture and Society* (1990); Shearer West, 'Portraiture' in McCalman (ed.), *An Oxford Companion to the Romantic Age: British Culture 1776–1832* (Oxford, 1999), pp.656–658; John, Ingamells, *National Portrait Gallery Mid-Georgian Portraits 1760–1790* (2004), pp.xiii–xvi.

3 Shena Mason, *The Hardware Man's Daughter: Matthew Boulton and his 'Dear Girl'* (2005), p.4.
   The portraits are reproduced in Mason, plates 1 and 2 and Nicholas Goodison, *Matthew Boulton: Ormolu* (2002), plates 1 and 4.

4 James D. Milner, 'Tilly Kettle 1735–86', *The Walpole Society*, 1926–7 (15), pp.47–104; NPG D586 Miss Baldwin, 1760s.

originally from Halesowen, was employed by Boulton and Fothergill to produce engravings of some of their products which could be used as marketing and reference material.[5] Kettle's portraits of Boulton and his wife are half length; Boulton in a dark red coat, leans on a table. Ann Boulton wears a dark red gown trimmed with fur, pearls in her hair and around her neck. She has her right hand raised to her breast, connoting affection and mirroring her husband's pose. Painted before the Boultons moved to Soho House, the pictures would have been hung as a companion pair, perhaps either side of a fireplace in their home at Snow Hill, to be viewed by family and friends.[6] Such a domestic site of display would have been highly appropriate for portraits that recorded the spouses' fondness for one another. Indeed, the paintings depict the sitters looking away from the viewer and, as a result the portraits could have been hung in such a way that the couple would appear to look towards each other.[7]

Boulton was painted next by J.S.C. Schaak who charged £10.10s for two portraits (Plate 2).[8] It is not known who the second portrait depicted; it could have been Mrs Boulton or it could have been his partner in the hardware business, John Fothergill.[9] The half length portrait of Boulton shows a relaxed and fashionable man in a dark suit with gold frogging, apparently disturbed in the act of reading, emphasising his intellectual status. His left hand is tucked into his waistcoat, a fashionable pose in male portraits of the time.[10] If the subject of the other portrait was known it would indicate where the portraits were intended to be hung. Perhaps, if the painting represented Mrs Boulton, Schaak's pair of images would, like Kettle's, have hung in a domestic space. On the other hand, if Schaak's second image depicted Fothergill, the new pair of portraits might have hung in the Soho Manufactory being, perhaps, intended for display in the showroom that opened in 1771.[11] Shown in such a space, the portraits of

---

5　　BAH, 3782/12/60/3 John Fothergill to MB, 8 May 1762; Timothy Clayton, 'Benjamin Green', Oxford DNB online accessed 24 June 2007.

6　　Eric Robinson, 'Matthew Boulton's birthplace and his home at Snow Hill; a problem in detection', *Transactions Birmingham Archaeological Society*, Vol.75, 1957, pp.85–9.

7　　Kettle later painted their daughter Anne c.1778 when she was around ten, showing her arranging flowers in a stand, a suitable pastime for a young lady. Anne's portrait is in private collection and is reproduced in Mason *op. cit.* plate 17 and front cover.

8　　BAH, 3782/6/191/56 J.S.C. Schaak to MB, receipted 13 October 1770.

9　　A portrait of Fothergill exists in the collection of Dr Alastair Brown, reproduced in Mason *op. cit.*, plate 13. It is apparently unsigned while that of Boulton is signed by Schaak. The portraits now have different frames but either or both may have been reframed.

10　Arline Meyer, 'Re-dressing Classical Statuary: The Eighteenth-Century 'Hand-in-Waistcoat' Portrait', *The Art Bulletin*, Vol.77 No.1 March 1995, p.45–63.

11　Goodison, *op. cit.*, p.163.

business partners would have been seen by potential customers and it would have been important that, like the Boulton portrait described above, both paintings portrayed successful and confident men who understood wealth, fashion and taste.

Boulton was also painted by Johan Zoffany, perhaps in 1772 when he made an entry in his notebook of 'Zaffany the last house on ye left in Thrift Street'.[12] Originally from Germany, Zoffany moved to London in 1760 and built up a clientele which included actors, Scottish aristocrats, George III and Queen Charlotte. Queen Charlotte commissioned him to paint the Florence Gallery which he began in August 1772, so if he did paint Boulton in that year it must have been before then.[13] The painting was described by Lionel Muirhead, a descendant of Boulton as 'a hard careful likeness in a brown coat & greenish silk waistcoat [...] a small oval picture.'[14] Boulton may have been introduced to Zoffany by Joseph Banks who had arranged for Zoffany to accompany him on Cook's second voyage.[15] Boulton and Fothergill had also been involved in the preparations for this voyage, supplying a wide range of goods including varnish for Zoffany.[16]

The audience for an eighteenth-century painting could be greatly extended by its inclusion in a public exhibition, the most important of which was organised by the Royal Academy at Somerset House and was considered the major artistic event in London. Portraits were popular with the public who enjoyed the opportunity to see images of people in the news, their friends, family or themselves.[17] Visits would be made specifically to see the portraits of friends, Thomas Telford wrote to James Watt in 1802, 'I this day paid my respects to you in the exhibition room. I think Beechey has succeeded admirably well.'[18] Boulton was clearly aware of the publicity potential of inclusion in an exhibition, the architect William Chambers had exhibited a model for a candlestick and 'Various Vases, &c to be executed in ormolu by Mr Bolton, for Their Majesties' at the Royal Society in 1760.[19] The

12   BAH, 3782/12/108/7 MB notebook, p.5. The only correspondence that has been found from Zoffany is 3782/12/41/306 12 October 1796, a letter accompanying two prints.

13   Mary Webster, 'Johan Joseph Zoffany', Oxford DNB online, accessed 20 August 2008.

14   National Portrait Gallery, London (RP1532, NPG Archive), Lionel Muirhead to Cust 6 February 1909.

15   Both men subsequently withdrew from the voyage, Webster *op. cit.*

16   Papers of Sir Joseph Banks, State Library of New South Wales, Series 06.108 MB to Banks, March 1772 http://www2.sl.nsw.gov.au/banks/series_06/06_108.cfm.

17   Marcia Pointon, 'Portrait! Portrait! Portrait!' in David Solkin (ed.) *Art on the Line: The Royal Academy Exhibitions at Somerset House 1780–1863*, (2001).

18   BAH, 3219/4/44/67 Thomas Telford to JW, 3 May 1802.

19   Hilary Young, 'Sir William Chambers and John Yenn: Designs for Silver', *The Burlington Magazine*, Vol.128 No.994 January 1986, pp.31–5.

first portrait of Boulton to be shown at the Royal Academy was by Birmingham artist and family friend James Millar in 1784, the first time he had exhibited there.[20] He had painted Boulton's close friends John Baskerville and Dr William Small and possibly Boulton's nephew, Zaccheus Walker junior as a young boy in 1772.[21] Later he would paint Boulton's friend Joseph Priestley, Priestley's wife, and Francis Eginton, who had worked at Soho.[22] In Birmingham Millar was considered 'the portrait painter of the day [...] His pictures, both finished and in progress, were placed round his room so as to allow of their being seen by those who thought it worth while to gratify their curiosity.'[23] Although Millar was well regarded in Birmingham, he would still have been considered a provincial artist and a surprising choice for Boulton after London-based Schaak and Zoffany. The location of the original portrait is not known but it is possible that the portrait of Boulton by an unknown artist in the collection of the National Portrait Gallery is a nineteenth-century copy of Millar's portrait.[24] It shows Boulton in a reddish-brown jacket with a yellow waistcoat against a plain background, looking directly at the viewer.

In June 1792 John Rennie, an engineer who had worked for Boulton and Watt wrote to Boulton:

> I have often wished to be possessed of a Portrait of yourself & Mr Watt – But I have had no opportunity for some time passed of obtaining as much of your time as to have them done – In hopes of your managing matters so as to grant me that favour next time you come to London I have taken the liberty of engaging Mr Brown (who painted Mr Smeaton's portrait) to paint them wherever you will have the goodness to sit.
>
> MB [Mather Brown] lives in Cavendish Square & if you will have the goodness to let him know a fortnight before you attend I will esteem it a

20 Algernon Graves, *The Royal Academy of Arts: A complete dictionary of contributors & their work from its foundation in 1769 to 1904* (1905) entries are arranged alphabetically by artist.

21 BMAG 1940P605; BMAG files citing University of Birmingham Special Collections, Withering Collection 3.52 Receipt, 23 July 1779; WB, 'Musician & Artist Ann Walker Marries John Vincent Barber', *Birmingham Post*, 28 December 1938.

22 Ingamells *op. cit.* (see note 2) p.387; Anon, 'A Portrait of Joseph Priestley, F.R.S, by James Millar, 1789', *Notes and Records of the Royal Society of London*, Vol.2, No.1, (April 1939), pp.32–33; BMAG 1912P24.

23 *Autobiography of Samuel Lines senr,* 1862, cited in Hill and Dent, *Memorials of the Old Square* (1897), footnote p.107.

24 Lionel Muirhead believed that the NPG portrait was a nineteenth century copy, but not of the Zoffany, Ingamells *op. cit.* (see note 2), pp.64–5; letter cited in note 15. The portrait does appear to bear similarities to some of Millar's other work but comparisons are difficult if it is a copy.

favour. If I am so lucky as to be favored with your sitting shall write Mr Watt – to the same purpose.[25]

Mather Brown was an American artist who came to London in 1781 and painted the engineer John Smeaton and cotton manufacturer Richard Arkwright, both of whom were known to Boulton and Watt.[26] The response to Rennie's request was mixed. Watt replied 'I wish you to come this way [...] and we can talk about the portrait to which I am rather averse as I think it an honour I do not merit and that my countenance cannot be worth procuring.'[27] Boulton was more encouraging:

> The honour you intend me in regard to my portrait I feel as a very respectfull Compliment & therefore I wish to prevent you from putting your self to so great & unnecessary Expence—My Children are desireous of possessing a good picture of me & have induced me to consent to have one painted by Lawrence the first tiem I go to Town or when he come to Visit his Brother at Birmgm.—If this picture proves a good Likeness a Copy from it is at your Service.'[28]

The Lawrence in question was Thomas Lawrence, by then established as a portrait painter in London and enjoying the patronage of George III.[29]

In the end, Boulton did not sit for either Lawrence or Brown and the Swedish artist Carl Frederick von Breda was chosen instead (Plate 3).[30] He had moved to London in 1786, becoming a student of Sir Joshua Reynolds and was introduced to Boulton in 1791 by William Chambers and R.E. Raspe.[31] Chambers explained to Boulton in 1791:

> He is making a mixed tour, partly for pleasure & to see the Country, and partly with a view of painting portraits to defray the expenses of his journey. I take the liberty of recommending him to you, dr Sir, as the

---

25   BAH, 3147/3/296/12 John Rennie to MB, 7 June 1792.

26   Ingamells *op. cit.* (see note 2), pp.440, p.18.

27   Dickinson and Jenkins, *James Watt and the Steam Engine* (Ashbourne, 1927), pp.81–9.

28   BAH, 3782/13/49/91 MB to John Rennie, 12 June 1792.

29   Michael Levey, 'Sir Thomas Lawrence' Oxford DNB online accessed 24 June 2007.

30   Boulton never did sit for Lawrence who did paint Watt, c.1812, BMAG2007.0889 and begin a portrait of MR Boulton, BMAG1987F331 completed after Lawrence's death by Martin Archer Shee.

31   Karl Asplund, 'Carl Fredrik von Breda', *The Burlington Magazine for Connoisseurs*, Vol.83, No.489 (December 1943), pp.296–301; BAH, 3782/12/36/150 William Chambers to MB, 13 August 1791; 3782/12/36/148 Raspe to MB, 9 August 1791.

Mecenas of Birmingham, being persuaded you will have pleasure in assisting a very worthy and Ingenious Man [...][32]

Von Breda travelled to Birmingham to paint portraits of Boulton, Watt and Dr William Withering, another member of the Lunar Society in July 1792.[33] Matthew Robinson Boulton wrote to his father on 24 August 'Mr Breda left us to day, and has taken lodgings in Birmingham, but I am afraid he will meet with little encouragement there; his talents are of a too superior nature to be justly rated by the amateurs of this town.'[34] James Watt apparently provided advice on equipment as Mary Anne Galton wrote 'I remember a celebrated Swedish artist having been instructed by him [Watt] that rat's whiskers make the most pliant and elastic painting brush.'[35] After he had returned to London von Breda painted Mrs Joseph Priestley and offered to return to Birmingham in 1794, if he could be guaranteed 'the modest number of half a dozen portraits agreed upon.'[36]

The portrait of Withering was described to Boulton by his daughter Anne:

Mr Breda is painting the Drs portrait which Mrs & Miss Withering have passed sentence on by declaring it impossible it shou'd ever be a good likeness but I must say they have condemn'd it rather hastily for when they shewed it to me it was quite in an unfinished state. It is a three Quarters & the Doctor is drawn in Black, sitting in an arm chair with a flower in his hand which Matt says is intended for a Foxglove. All who have seen Mr Breda's por[traits] express themselves highly pleased [with] those manufactured at Soho, particularly with yours, which he has been often told does all but speak.[37]

Each of the portraits shows the sitter with significant attributes. Withering is holding a foxglove, the source of the heart stimulant digitalis, his great contribution to medicine. A copy of his book *Botanical Arrangement* (1787 edition) is open beside him at the page about the foxglove.[38] Watt has a

---

32 BAH, 3782/12/36/150 William Chambers to MB, 13 August 1791.

33 There are photographs in the archive of two portraits which were suggested to be of Boulton's children, Matthew and Anne by von Breda. No evidence has been found to support this and it appears to have been disproved by comparison with other portraits in 1945. 3782/21/illustrative material added by Assay Office.

34 BAH, 3782/12/57/64 MRB to MB, 24 August 1792.

35 C.C. Hankin (ed), *Life of Mary Anne Schimmelpenninck* (1858) p.34.

36 BMAG31'06; 3782/12/38/55 von Breda to MB, 27 March 1793; 3782/12/39/314 von Breda to MB, 18 November 1794.

37 BAH, 3782/13/38/7 Anne Boulton to MB, 9 September 1792.

38 T.W. Peck and K.D. Wilkinson, *William Withering of Birmingham* (1950), p.66.

drawing of a steam engine on the table in front of him. Boulton is shown three-quarter length, seated, dressed in black and looking directly at the viewer. He holds a medal and a magnifying glass with which to examine it, four mineral specimens are on the table beside him and the Soho Manufactory is in the background. Thus the image links the product, the manufacturer, the place of manufacture and possibly the raw materials in the mineral specimens.[39] Von Breda sent the portraits of Boulton and Watt to the Royal Academy exhibition of 1793,

> As the pictures intended for the exhibition at the Royal Academy are to be sent in early next week and I for many reasons am very desirous of exhibiting your Picture and Mr Watts, I must beg for your permission to send them, not questioning in the least that when my private interest can be combined with the gratification of your numerous friends, you will want no more motives for granting my request.

Once again Watt had to be convinced of the importance of allowing people to see his image. In his letter to Boulton, von Breda wrote: 'I flatter myself that Mr Watt will easily forgive me for not disturbing him with a letter on this subject and I know that, if wanted, I can have no better advocate than you.'[40]

Once a portrait had been painted it was sometimes copied or reproduced in various formats in order to make it accessible to different audiences. Marcia Pointon has argued that portraiture 'was the one genre in which copies increased rather than diminished the standing of the original' and it would be considered prestigious to have one's portrait multiplied in this way.[41] Miss Boulton ordered a miniature copy of von Breda's portrait of Boulton which was painted by Francis Gilliberg, a Swedish miniaturist recommended by von Breda. Gilliberg worked from the original portrait and as a friend of von Breda he charged a special price of seven guineas rather than ten.[42] Replica portrait miniatures were

---

39 There is not sufficient detail to determine which medal he is holding but he had made a number by this date. I am grateful to Sue Tungate for discussion on this. Ingamells *op. cit.*, p.65 suggests that one of the minerals is Blue John, which Boulton used in ormolu ornaments, Goodison, *op. cit.* (see note 3) p.47. However Ixer has stated that none are blue john, but that it not possible to identify them with any certainty, pers comm. It is possible that one shows copper ore, the raw material from which so many of Boulton's medals were made. I am grateful to Richard Clay for this point.

40 BAH, 3782/12/38/55 von Breda to MB, 27 March 1793.

41 Marcia Pointon, 'Portrait-Painting as a business enterprise in London in the 1780s', *Art History*, Vol.7 No.2, June 1984, p.195.

42 BAH, 3782/12/39/314 von Breda to MB 18 November 1794; 3782/12/39/357 Francis Axel Gilliberg to MB, 31 December 1794.

undertaken by specialist painters, often selected by the artist of the original portrait. By virtue of their size, miniatures were portable and could be carried easily when travelling. Boulton had taken a miniature portrait of his second wife, Ann, with him to London in 1773, writing home to her, 'Your picture I kiss every night its very like you'.[43] However, it was sometimes the case that a full-size copy of a painting was more appropriate than a miniature. Having failed to persuade Boulton and Watt to sit for Mather Brown, John Rennie ordered copies of von Breda's portraits.[44] Full-size copies of the portraits of Boulton and Watt were also made by von Breda for William Withering.[45] Boulton had a copy of Watt's portrait so it is possible that Watt also had a copy of Boulton's.[46] As these portraits were initiated on the request of family and friends they are likely to have hung in homes.[47]

Printing offered another method of reproducing portraits and bringing them to wider audiences. Many people collected prints, some displaying them on the wall, others storing them in portfolios in a library to be shown on special occasions.[48] In 1790, Boulton purchased from William Palmer 'A proof of Her Majesty; one each of Dr John Hunter, Dr Graham, Elliott, and Macklin; two proofs of Sir Joseph Banks and Sir William Chambers'.[49] Boulton was familiar with many aspects of the print business; he knew and worked with several people at the forefront of developing new techniques. He had employed Francis Eginton to produce early aquatints and mechanical paintings at Soho in the 1770s.[50] He invested in the firm of Francis's brother, John, who had worked for Boulton as a silver engraver; Eginton and his

43   BAH, 3782/16/1/47 MB to Mrs Ann Boulton, 2 February 1773. I am grateful to Shena Mason for this reference.

44   BAH, 3782/12/38/55 von Breda to MB, 27 March 1793. Rennie's copy of Boulton is at the Institution of Civil Engineers and his copy of Watt is at the Institution of Mechanical Engineers, Ingamells *op. cit.*, pp.65, 475.

45   BAH, 3782/12/38/169 von Breda to MB, 5 October 1793; The BMAG Boulton and Science Museum Watt were owned by descendants of Withering until 1920, BMAG files; Ingamells *op. cit.*, p.475.

46   BAH, 3782/12/39/314 von Breda to MB, 18 November 1794. The NPG copy of the Watt portrait had belonged to the Boulton family; Ingamells *op. cit.*, p.475.

47   The practice of making full-size copies has continued with other artists copying the portraits in order that institutions are able to display images of distinguished persons with whom they claim a connection. Twentieth-century copies of the portraits of Watt and Withering are known to exist. Ingamells *op. cit.* (see note 2) p.475; The Public Catalogue Foundation, *Oil Paintings in Public Ownership in Birmingham* (2008), University of Birmingham, A0229.

48   Stana Nenadic, 'Print Collecting and Popular Culture in Eighteenth-Century Scotland', *History* Vol.82 Issue 266, pp.203–222.

49   BAH, 3782/6/194/20 26 July 1790.

50   Antony Griffiths, 'Notes on Early Aquatint in England and France', *Print Quarterly*, IV, 3 1987, pp.256–270.

partner, Jee began making picture frames but moved on to prints.[51] He also worked with Benjamin Green who was one of the first printmakers to use the soft ground etching technique.[52]

Von Breda asked permission to publish a print after his portrait of Boulton and in 1796 appointed S.W. Reynolds, 'an engraver of eminent Talent, who has already engraved several of my Pictures, as for instance Sir Joshua Reynolds, the Turkish Embasador, My Lord Eglinton, Miss Langton etc.'[53] This was to be a mezzotint, a form which was quick and relatively cheap to produce and could reproduce the tonal effect of paintings.[54] The publication of a print some years after the original painting carried the risk that initial interest may have died away; the ideal time to produce a print was when the painting was exhibited. Von Breda was aware of this and apologised for the delay in arranging the work:

> I trust the original picture and the Aprobation it met with will not yet be obliterated in the memory of your Numerous friends who may wish to become subscribers. In about a fortnight I mean to wait on you at Soho and I shall then request your advice how this publication might be render'd more generally known at Birmingham – In the meantime I have been thinking that a list for taking down names of subscribers in the hands of some of your more Intimate friends would render the formality of Proposals unnecessary. The eventual Risk of this undertaking will at any rate furnish my pride with some means to make my name accompany yours.[55]

Ten days later he wrote that the print was finished and ready for publication, proof copies to be sold at twelve shillings and prints at seven and six.[56] Ultimately, Von Breda returned to Sweden, giving up all financial interest in the print and it was published by Reynolds alone.[57]

---

51 Archives of Soho, *Guide to Persons and Firms*, Eginton and Jee.

52 See note 5; Griffiths *op. cit.*

53 BAH, 3782/12/41/50 von Breda to MB, 10 February 1796.

54 They were created by roughening the entire surface of the plate so it would print a deep black and then smoothing out areas of that rough surface so it would hold less ink and print as grey. White highlights were created by rubbing the plate smooth.

55 BAH, 3782/12/41/50 von Breda to MB, 10 February 1796.

56 Proof copies were the early impressions taken from the plate, sometimes before the lettering had been added; they played to the desire of collectors for special copies and could command a higher price. Early impressions are generally of better quality, particularly with mezzotint as the plate wore very quickly. Antony Griffiths, *Prints and Printmaking: An Introduction to the history and techniques* (2004), p.149.

57 BAH, 3782/12/41/72 von Breda to MB, 20 February 1796; 3782/12/41/176 von Breda to MB, 21 May 1796.

Boulton was painted subsequently by Sir William Beechey (Plate 4), a painter of much higher status than von Breda; he had been exhibiting at the R.A. since 1776 and was a favourite painter of the royal family. On 26 September 1798 Beechey, his wife and son accompanied Boulton from Cheltenham to Soho where they stayed for about a month. Boulton sat for Beechey in his London studio on 17 November, attending a concert arranged by Lady Beechey the following day.[58] Boulton's ability to attract the friendship of such an important figure was an indication of his own status.[59] In this portrait Boulton was again depicted seated, holding a coin or medal and a magnifying glass, however, this time there was a mineral specimen under a glass dome in an alcove behind him. His products are connoted by the medal but there is no direct reference to the manufacturing process or to the place of manufacture as there is in von Breda's earlier portrait. The mineral specimen in the glass dome depicted by Beechey suggests the sitter's scientific interests, implying that Boulton is manufacturer whose knowledge of science informs and is applied to his business. Both medal and magnifying glass are displayed to the viewer more prominently in this painting but it is still not possible to identify an individual medal. Again, Boulton is dressed in black, looking directly at the audience, inviting them to admire the medal too. Beechey's portrait was exhibited at the R.A. in 1799 with the title 'Mr Boulton Of Soho, Staffordshire'.[60]

Like the von Breda, Beechey's portrait of Boulton was reproduced in a variety of formats. Lady Beechey painted a miniature head and shoulders portrait of Boulton, copied from her husband's portrait. She exhibited 'Mr and Miss Boulton' at the R.A. in 1799.[61] William Grimaldi, a leading miniaturist of the day asked permission to undertake a copy. He completed this and sent it to Soho for inspection suggesting that Beechey highly approved of it and that if 'yourself or family wish to take it the price will be thirty Guineas exclusive of the frame which is three pounds.'[62] Grimaldi probably did not help this speculative sales pitch by addressing his letter to Sir George Boulton. In October he wrote again, this time to Sir John Boulton expressing concern that he had not heard anything and that the miniature may not have arrived.[63] Some alterations were requested and undertaken with the aid of a sketch from life which became a smaller

58   BAH, 3782/12/107/26 MB diary 1798.
59   On Boulton's death Beechey was among those who received mourning rings, a mark of their friendship, BAH, 3782/13/8/61 Sir William Beechey to MRB, 12 December 1809.
60   Graves *op. cit.*
61   Ingamells *op. cit.*, p.64; NPG 1595; Graves *op. cit.*
62   BAH, 3782/12/44/301 William Grimaldi to Sir George Boulton, September 1799.
63   BAH, 3782/12/44/333 William Grimaldi to Sir John Boulton, 17 October 1799.

miniature priced at fifteen guineas. The letter accompanying this sketch for inspection was addressed to Matthew Boulton Esqr and added that it had met with the approval of Boulton's friend and banker Charlotte Matthews.[64] One of the miniatures, probably the larger, was exhibited at the Royal Academy in 1800.[65]

Beechey's portrait of Boulton was also published in print form, organised and paid for by Matthew Robinson Boulton as a present for his father.[66] It was a line engraving, a technique where parallel lines and cross-hatching were used to build up the picture. It was more prestigious than mezzotint as it took longer to execute, required more skill and was, therefore, more expensive. It also had the advantage that many more impressions could be produced before the plate wore. William Sharp, the engraver employed, was considered one of the most accomplished at the technique.[67] His pencil drawing after the painting, with grid lines drawn over it to help with transfer of the image to the copper plate, is in the British Museum.[68] Both Boulton and his son drew up lists of people they wanted to give copies, including friends, artists and business associates.[69] The print met with approval, Sir Joseph Banks suggesting in 1808 that Sharp should engrave his portrait by Thomas Phillips as he had 'engraved Boulton & John Hunter admirably.'[70] Sharp felt unable to undertake the distribution of the print himself and asked Boulton's London agent Richard Chippendall to do so, supplying details of prints taken (three hundred proofs and one hundred and thirty-nine prints) which highlights the potential lack of exclusivity of expensive proof prints. The plate was to be packed up and sent to Soho so, if Sharp wanted any to sell, he was to get them from Chippindall's stock.[71] This print was titled 'Matthew Boulton Esq. F.R.S. & F.S.A.' where the Reynolds mezzotint after von Breda had been entitled simply 'Matthew Boulton Esq.' This change in caption

64 BAH, 3782/12/44/406 William Grimaldi to Matthew Boulton Esqr, 10 December 1799; Ingamells *op. cit.*, p.66.

65 Graves *op. cit.* The miniatures are listed in Grimaldi's accounts as James Boulton. Rev. A. Grimaldi, *A Catalogue Chronological and Descriptive of Paintings, Drawings & Engravings by and After William Grimaldi, RA, Paris* (privately printed 1837), p.19.

66 BAH, 3782/13/9/103 Charles Dumergue to MRB, 17 June 1799; 3782/13/15/32 W. Sharp to MRB, 25 November 1800.

67 David Bindman, 'Prints' in McCalman (ed.) *op. cit.*

68 British Museum 1853,1210.492.

69 BAH, 3782/12/107/29 MB diary 1801 pp.10–11; 3782/13/37/30 'List of prints which MR Boulton to have sent down [...]' 12 January 1802.

70 Patricia Fara, 'The Royal Society's Portrait of Joseph Banks', *Notes and Records of the Royal Society of London*, Vol.51, No.2 (July 1997) p.206.

71 BAH, 3782/13/41/114 MRB to Richard Chippindall, 3 February 1802. Sending the plate to Soho meant the number of copies made could be controlled. It was described as 'now destroyed' by Lionel Muirhead in a letter of 20 December 1907, BMAG files.

emphasised Boulton's Fellowship of the Royal Society and Society of Arts, indicating again that he was both a man of science and a man of art, and accepted by the London-based cultural 'establishment'.

Soon after Boulton's death his son ordered two copies of the portrait from Beechey, one for James Watt and one for Miss Boulton. Beechey 'lost no time in making the copies, which are just finished and though they are the work of my own hand, and what I think will be call'd good Pictures yet I cannot come up to the original which was painted from life.'[72] Later he explained that 'I made Miss Boulton's copy of a Kit Kat size to give something of an attitude and subject – it in some measure answers the purpose of the large Picture without occupying much space'.[73]

Boulton's nephew Zaccheus Walker junior agreed that the copies were not as good as the original, 'These 2 copies must surely have been executed by Sir William's youngest pupils as a Task they are such poor specimens of the fine Original.'[74] Beechey had painted Watt in 1801, exhibiting the painting at the RA in 1802 as 'Mr Watt of Soho, Staffordshire'. Although painted at different times these portraits of Boulton and Watt were considered to be a pair and they were hung as such at Aston Hall, the home of James Watt junior from 1818 to 1848.[75] Maria Edgeworth saw them there in 1820; 'Mr Watt has fitted up half of it so as to make it superbly comfortable: fine hall, breakfast room, Flemish pictures, Boulton and Watt at either end.'[76]

Boulton was also painted by Lemuel Francis Abbott (Plate 5). He had painted a number of Boulton's friends and associates, the architect Samuel Wyatt, the astronomer William Herschel, the mezzotint artist Valentine Green and ironmaster John Wilkinson.[77] Abbott was certified insane in 1801, apparently having been a lunatic since 1798. In January 1802 Boulton received a letter from William Rhodes acting on behalf of Abbott's wife who had been appointed to administer his estate owing to his lunacy. Rhodes asked for payment as the portrait was now ready to be delivered and the premises in Caroline Street where it was had to be vacated. Abbott's ill health and subsequent death in December 1802 were probably the reasons that this portrait was not exhibited or published in the form of

---

72   3782/13/8/61 Sir William Beechey to MRB, 12 December 1809. W. Roberts, *Sir William Beechey RA* (1907) p.266. The copy made for Watt is BMAG2003.007.044.

73   Kit Kat size was 36 x 28 inches, named after the Kit Kat Club, Shawe-Taylor *op. cit.*, p.10; 3782/13/8/62 Sir William Beechey to MRB, 11 January 1810.

74   3782/8/47/31. Copy letter. Zaccheus Walker Jr. to MRB, 18 December 1811.

75   Mason *op. cit.*, p.159.

76   Quoted in Sotheby's, *The James Watt Sale; Art & Science*, London, 20 March 2003, p.42.

77   John Martin Robinson, *The Wyatts: An Architectural Dynasty* (Oxford, 1979), plate 15; NPG98; NPG1260; NPG3785.

prints.[78] This painting shows Boulton with his hands folded over one of his green notebooks with white metal clasps, still to be found in the Archives of Soho.[79] This example is inscribed 'Mint', once again signifying his preoccupation with his mint and its output above all the other products that emerged from Soho. It shows a relaxed and confident man, looking into the distance wearing a dark jacket, cream waistcoat and pink underwaistcoat.[80] Perhaps this choice of clothing revealed the real Boulton more than the sombre black of the von Breda and the Beechey; Charlotte Matthews wrote to him in 1794,

> I understand your [waist]coat to be the inclosed cloth, and that *you* had fix'd upon the silk pattern with the *pink* in it. Now, as *I* wear *only* black [she had been widowed in 1792], I cannot permit you to wear *pink*, [...] at your age a similarity rather than a diversity of colors ought to be preferr'd.[81]

Abbott's portrait was described by Boulton's biographer Dickinson as the 'most virile', in contrast to the Beechey, which he thought showed a man 'past his prime and the artist's representation of him as a benevolent old gentleman, while true at the time it was painted, does not convey the character of the man of action whom these pages has revealed.'[82] In fact Dickinson did not know the date of the Abbott and misdated the Beechey; these two portraits were actually painted within a few years of each other and are perhaps better understood as showing different aspects of their sitter's character.

This essay has examined the painted and printed portraits of Matthew Boulton which were produced during his lifetime and the ways in which those portraits were used and copied. It has not considered the three dimensional images; the wax portraits by Peter Rouw, van Waeynberghe and

---

78 A.C. Sewter, 'Some new Facts about Lemuel Francis Abbott', *The Connoisseur*, 135, 1955, pp.178–183; 3782/12/47/31 William Rhodes to MB, 29 January 1802. The painting itself is not dated and its traditional dating of 1801 is based on this letter and the assumption that the painting was completed not long before it was written. There is some doubt about this, Sewter argues that Abbott was not able to paint after 1798 although other paintings are also dated post-1798 and he continued to exhibit at the RA until 1800. Ingamells *op. cit.*, p.65 dates it as 1797–1801. Birmingham Assay Office also have a copy of this portrait but as there is no associated paperwork and as it is hung high in a stairwell it is not possible to determine when it was made.

79 3782/12/108 MB Notebooks.

80 An underwaistcoat was worn under the waistcoat with a collar designed to be seen, C. Willet and Phillis Cunnington, *Handbook of English Costume in the Eighteenth Century* (1957), p.208.

81 3782/12/68/79 Charlotte Matthews to MB, 25 July 1794.

82 H.W. Dickinson, *Matthew Boulton* (1937, Cambridge), p.198.

Isaac Gosset, the paste medallion by Sarah Brown, sculpture, medals, or the prints and drawings made after those three dimensional images.[83] Neither has it explored the prints for magazines nor those published after Boulton's death. However, this essay has highlighted the variety of the painted images of Boulton and the audiences for which they were intended. A degree of control was exercised over the production, dissemination and display of such images. Boulton selected the artists for whom he sat, sometimes accepting recommendations from friends and colleagues; he allowed the resulting images to be exhibited; he agreed to or organised their production as prints; he was involved in the distribution of those prints. In short, Matthew Boulton actively controlled the way his image was seen.

References
MS 3782 and 3219 refer to the Matthew Boulton Papers and James Watt Papers in the Archives of Soho at Birmingham Central Library.

---

83   Ingamells *op. cit.*, pp.64–7; Robert James Eidlitz, *Medallic Portraits of Matthew Boulton and James Watt*, (New York, 1928).

Chapter 6

COINAGE, COMMERCE AND INSPIRED IDEAS: THE NOTEBOOKS OF MATTHEW BOULTON

Fiona Tait

On 4 March 1787, Matthew Boulton wrote to his son Matthew with instructions on how to organise his finances and his correspondence, recommending that he keep a notebook:[1]

> I recommend it to you to keep such a pocket Book as I do wch is on one side ruled into 7 horozontal divisions for the 7 days of the week & on the other side into one set of columns of L S D for Money received & another for money spent or paid. I will send you an example by young Toney who sets out in a day or two to France.
>
> I note down in every day anything remarkable that hath occurd or where I have visited & I recommend that you note down on the space of such day of the month as you write any letter the address of such letter, Exampl (Feb 25 wrote to my Father)

In the eighteenth century, notebooks or memorandum books served a useful purpose as a portable aide-memoire and means of organising thoughts and information. Ninety-six of the notebooks kept by Matthew Boulton survive. The earliest is from the 1750s, when Boulton was in his twenties, working for his father, a metal toymaker in Birmingham. The last is from 1804, when Boulton was seventy-six, five years before his death in 1809. There are no notebooks from Boulton's childhood years; none for 1760–64, when Boulton was busy with the Manufactory; and none for his last few years, 1805–1809. Otherwise, the dates covered span the years of his life.

---

1 Birmingham Archives and Heritage (BAH), MS 3782/13/36/4.

The physical appearance of the volumes differs over the years. Most of the volumes are small – pocket size – but there are a few larger hardback ones. About a third have a hard green leather cover, with metal clasps, and another third are thin with a card cover; others have a brown leather or suede cover. Not all are fully used. The writing is in both ink and pencil, sometimes ink over pencil, and there are also sketches, in both pencil and ink, in some of the volumes. Many drawings are of machinery, but there is an interesting portrait head of a man on a folded paper stuck down with sealing wax, in notebook fifteen, and one of Nelson's head in notebook ninety-five. Most of the volumes are dated on the front and several often run concurrently, for different topics. There are five in use from 1801 for example: two on steam engines, one on the garden at Soho, one on economy and food, and one for experiments.

The notebooks are but a small part of the collection known as the papers of Matthew Boulton & Family. These records comprise a substantial archive of business and personal papers, which are owned by the Assay Office Charitable Trust and are held on permanent loan by Birmingham Archives & Heritage [ref: MS 3782]. The surviving records are substantial and reflect the variety of businesses in which Matthew Boulton was involved, his wide circle of friends and business acquaintances, the creation of his house and estate, and his personal pursuits – travel, chemistry, social activities and so on. There are also records of the businesses and estates administered by his son Matthew Robinson Boulton, some personal records of his daughter Ann and of Matthew Robinson Boulton's wife and children. The covering dates of all these records are 1737 to the twentieth century and they fill approximately 107 metres of shelving. In format, they appear as volumes, letters and papers, parchment legal documents, pattern books, printed items, architectural drawings, diaries and notebooks.

Matthew Boulton's businesses included the manufacture of toys, buttons, buckles, silver, ormolu, steam engines and coinage; his partners at various times were John Fothergill, John Scale, James Smith, James Watt, James Watt Jr. and his own son, Matthew Robinson Boulton. In 1799, Boulton records in a notebook, 'Trades in which I have totally given up & no interest in', and lists these as the manufacture of gilt, plated, pearl and metal buttons, inlaid steel buttons, steel watch chains, hilts, buttons and other steel toys, tortoiseshell pieces, gilt watch chains, toys and trinkets, japanned wares and ormolu clocks, vases and ornaments.[2] Steam engines and coinage had taken over.

The surviving household records are very detailed and include in the letters, bills and receipts, much information on servants, the household economy and the construction of the estate and gardens. There is also

---

2   BAH, MS 3782/12/108/83, p.27.

information on Boulton's social activities: music, books, art, his involvement in various civic enterprises such as the General Hospital, the Theatre Royal and the Birmingham Canal Navigations, and his position as a landowner in Handsworth, Staffordshire and elsewhere.

It is not certain from whom Boulton purchased his notebooks. There are household bills which show that Boulton bought stationery and books from Thomas Aris and Richard Bailey in the 1750s, from Thomas Pearson and Thomas Aris in the 1760s, from James Sketchley and J. Johnson in the 1770s, and from James Phillips in the 1780s. However, no bill has so far been found which is specifically for notebooks.

The majority of the notebooks were marked when in the custody of Birmingham Assay Office with one of three headings: 'General', 'Engines & Mining' or 'Coinage'. Of original markings on the notebooks, however, the year is the main distinguishing mark. There are three notebooks with the title 'Garden'; a few marked 'Coinage' or 'Mint', others are titled 'Buckles', 'Canals', 'Drawings of Mills', 'Iron'. One is marked 'Corn & Meal', and appears to be research on the subject of milling, costs, flour etc. in 1783, when Boulton & Watt took shares in the Albion Flour Mill at Blackfriars, London.

Many of the notebooks are about steam engine orders, performances, experiments, profits made from the use of the engines, etc. About a third of the notebooks are on coinage matters, Boulton's main business from the 1790s. In some notebooks, the subject range is very wide, and there are memoranda on travel, domestic issues, businesses, addresses, accounts and diagrams. It is impossible to give a full description of all of the notebooks in this limited space. I shall therefore illustrate some of the more important and interesting ideas covered in the notebooks, which reveal the range of economic, scientific and personal interests which preoccupied Matthew Boulton during his life.

Thoughts

Boulton sometimes converses with himself on paper, to clarify difficult situations. For example, when weighing up the debts which beset his partner John Fothergill, Boulton wrote in his notebook for 1773:[3]

> Thoughts on B: F [Boulton & Fothergill]
> B examine ye Books & see how much we owe that might be paid
> See how much was my stock at the time I subscribed to ye Navitn [Navigation] & what was F &
> what it was when I borrow Galtons Money & what each are now

---

3   BAH, MS 3782/12/108/9, pp.24–25.

What am I realy worth now
What hath F got pr cent pr annum or last since I joynd him & what I

A list of all bad debts from ye beginning
Make out in writing a Catologue of all his accusations & answer them one by one
a man to talk of Bankrupcy at a time when I was worth
& he worth is damnable

F agreed in the beginning to advance 1000 more than me
see if he did read over the whole of Fothg's Letters wch are in my possession & all that came from him when abroad & wch are in the Counting houses & see what he said about Ebbinghaus & other things

In 1800, his notebook mentions:[4] 'Remarks on Birmingham Memorial on [Russian] Mint. If MB had improperly employd any of the powers given to him there might have been some grounds for the Birmingham Memorial but there is not the least as I have not exported anything contrary to Law except Screw presses....'
In his 1784 notebook, he writes:[5]

> Make out a table of prices of all things used at the Mines such as
> Timber
> Ropes
> Blacksmith's work
> Ironmongery & all Bawdens [?]
> Bricks, Tyles, Stone, Lime, building
> Stationary
> Chandlery
> Mercury
> All articles delivered to ye Mines should be weighd or measured or counted by the receiver & the Bills should be examind & marked off by somebody & wrote upon examind (AB)

In 1792, Boulton reflects on his situation:[6]

> Whilst I have had the Misfortune to have been pulld back by various things I wish I could say the Albion Mill was the worst & I wish I could say

4   BAH, MS 3782/12/108/86, pp.36–38.
5   BAH, MS 3782/12/108/41, p.45.
6   BAH, MS 3782/12/108/61, p.17.

that the great Loss I sustained by Govt. misleading me was the only one I am conscious of having acted honestly honourably & Generously by Mrs F. & her Family & I must own I am hurt at the stand she hath now taken & the footing the Loan is now put upon.

Travel

The notebooks he used to record his travels show his lively and interested observations of practices and customs elsewhere, often viewed with an eye to further business opportunities. In 1779, he visited Holland. After a rough journey in the packet boat, Boulton describes Rotterdam, where the cleanness and neatness of everything much impressed him.[7]

> Through most of ye Streets are larg Canals filld with Shiping on each side is a row of green Trees mostly limes & then a very neat pavement either of Bricks or Stone for Coaches or hand 2 Wheel Carts & next ye houses is a footpath Every House seems new painted the Windows Clean & as many live up on ye 2d floor they fix on each side of the Windows without side a looking glass abt 1 foot Sqr upon a joynt so that it may be placed at any angle by wch they may within see who & what passes either one way or ye other in ye Street.[8]
> I afterward waited upon Sr Joseph [York] & conversed some Hours & shewd him 2 of our pictures. I think I should send him one. I saw there some Glass that was Gilt as fine & Solid as a looking glass is silverd & there were paintings upon the Glass in varnish Coulers so that the Ground was Gold. These were framed in Gilt frames & had 2 branches so that they servd for Sconces.[9]

His notebook shows that he also went to the Hague, Leiden and Harlem and met with Mr Van Liender and Mr Eckhardt, whom Boulton & Watt supplied with steam engines, and there are pages of notes about canals and the use of engines to lower the water level to prevent flooding.

In August 1780, Boulton visited Cornwall. While most of the visit concerned steam engines for mines, on 27 August 1780, Boulton, Mr Wilson, Mr Darwin and Mr Henderson went to Carnmath, and:

> took the Telescope & by its assistance we counted distinctly 50 Ships off Falmouth & saw in the Harbour as much greater number all wch. We supposed to be the homeward bound West India fleet. On the

---

7   BAH, MS 3782/12/108/17.
8   BAH, MS 3782/12/108/17, p.8.
9   BAH, MS 3782/12/108/17, p.15–16.

preceding day was seen off Falmouth the Russian Fleet near the foot of Carnmath we saw Westly preaching to above 4000 people whose singing seemed to reach to & be reverberated from ye Clouds. There we met Harry Papps who wth. Mr Wilson & self went & drank Tea with old Hornblower.[10]

Matthew Boulton visited Ireland with Samuel Garbett Jr. in 1783. His notebook describes the journey through Wales to the coast 'when we turned off the Wrexham road the Country became most exceedingly romantic & sublime high Hills & lofty mountains coverd with smiling Cots and Gentlemens Houses........ A most beautiful ride thro a Country of Hills, dales and fertile Lawns', then a visit to the Anglesey copper mines at Parys. Here he remarked on the inhabitants: 'got to the half way house or Gwyndw where we took a Hack Chaise & 4 Horses to the Anglesea mines at Paris mountain saw the people of the island assembled at a Large fair – Women dressed in Bleue Cloaks & Coloured Handkerchiefs round their Heads & necks and Black beaver Hats....'. The notebook then gives a detailed description of Boulton's journey in Ireland, particularly to Mr Letouche's estate, Cronborne Mine and Ballamartha Mine and there are two pages of place names and comparative mileages, in English and Irish miles.[11]

Boulton's visit to Paris in late 1786, early 1787 produced some interesting observations. The pages of his notebook have headings such as: 'Learnt in France' and 'Public meetings and schools for the promotion of human knowledge and arts'. There are notes on cotton spinning, the Marly Water Works, French weights, etc.

Within the notebook is a page headed *'France'*, with a list divided into two columns, (a partial transcript follows):[12]

Worse than England	Better than England
Inns: Brick Chamber floors sans Carpet – No Tea – send out for Coffee wch they drink in poronger	Beautifull & Elegant Watches & some very good ones
High bed sans counterpain & all bad arranged	Rings Snuff Boxes watch chains, & all sorts of Toys
Bad tables plates & pottery & no knives	Finer Silk & Velvet Cloths
Horrable bad Chiases & Horses bad Harniss & bad postillions	Science too much Cultivated & the practise too little

---

10   BAH, MS 3782/12/108/24, p.10.
11   BAH, MS 3782/12/108/38, pp.7–8
12   BAH, MS 3782/12/108/49, pp.36–37.

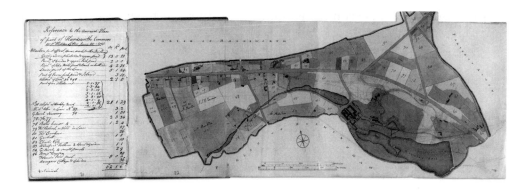

Fig. 6.1. Plan of part of Handsworth Common, from Matthew Boulton's notebook, 1793. BAH, MS 3782/12/108/68, p.32.

Better in England than in France:
Optical & Mathematical & philosophical Instrum[en]ts
Com[mo]n people live better
Neatness Cleanliness & ye conveniences of com[mo]n Life
Coaches Chaises & all Carriages

Soho House and garden, and property

The notebooks provide glimpses of Boulton's plans for the development of his house and estate at Soho, in Handsworth, Birmingham. (See Plate 1).

In a notebook covering 1768–1775, Matthew Boulton describes the study he would like, with an observatory attached:[13]

> a Round building for my Study, Library, Museum or Hobby Horsery to hold 6 handsome Book Cases with drawers in the lower Parts to hold things which relate to subjects of the Books which are in ye upper parts e:g: a Book Case containing Chymical Books should have drawers under which contain Metals Minerals & fossells — between each Book Case should be a Sophi & under the Space between ye upper parts of ye Cases should be fixed such instruments as Barometer, Thermometer, Pyrometer, Quadrant all sorts of Optical, Mathematical, Mechanical pneumatical & Philosophical instruments also Clocks of sundry kinds both Geographical Syderial, Lunar & Solor System & one good regulator of time. A table in ye middle of ye room & a Sky light in ye middle of the doomical roof which roof may be Coverd either with Sail Cloth or brown paper out of this round room should open a private door into a passage

---

13   BAH, MS 3782/12/108/5, p.88.

in which passage should open doors into sundry conven[ien]t rooms such as Cold & Warm bath, a Labritory a dressing & powdering room & an observitory for a transit instrument [a telescope used to plot the position of stars] etc.

In his 1772 notebook, there are also several pages about Boulton's interest in astronomy, including a page headed 'Observetory'. This is described as 'a round building wth an Iron toothed Wheel upon ye Wall plate to turn ye top round ye top may be cov[ere]d wth brown paper or tin foyl.' Other pages include a list of Boulton's astronomical instruments, and new ones ordered:

> I have
> 3 Microscopes, Telliscope 4 feet, Spying Glass, 3 Wedges Glass, Diagonal Mirror, Thermometer, Barometer, Pyrometer.
> Ordered
> A Cammera, Hadlys Quadrant, Pluveometer, Concave Mirrour, Convex Do.[14]

On another page is a note to 'Improve Soho' (by planting trees and making a circular walk round the estate), and a sketch of a building which may possibly be Boulton's observatory.[15]

There are three notebooks specifically devoted to garden matters. The first, dated 1795 has pencil and ink sketches of the front elevation of Soho House at the beginning of the notebook. There are several pages listing tasks, most of which have been crossed through, presumably to indicate completion. Boulton also lists 'Views from or of Soho', and writes, 'Surround my Farm & Works by a Garland of Flowers on one side & by an aquious Mirror on ye other'; 'Plant in Octr next 1795'; 'Q[ue]r[ie]s for Saml Wyatt: Where shall I build my Hot or Green House?'[16]

The notebook for 1797–1801 also has lists of various tasks, some crossed through. The list on the first page begins: 'Transplant a walnut tree', and ends 'plant Trees by the Southern Sphinx'.[17] Another notebook devoted to the garden at Soho is dated 1801. The first ten pages are taken up by a memorandum headed: 'Directions & Observations to the Gardener. Jan. 4 – 1801'. Headings on various other pages include: '1781. April. To Water ye New Warwickshire plantation', with a pencil sketch of a steam engine; 'Rents to Collect directly June 26 1802'; 'Sep[tembe]r 8 Plant Trees on the South end

14   BAH, MS 3782/12/108/7, pp.14–15.
15   BAH, MS 3782/12/108/7, p.18.
16   BAH, MS 3782/12/108/70.
17   BAH, MS 3782/12/108/75.

of my lawn so as to hide Edward's building, Key Hill Cottages, Birmingham Houses & all other unpleasant objects'.[18]

There are just a few references to work at Soho House. There is a record of the use of coals at Soho House in 1775–1776.[19] The 1787 notebook has details of the well and pump at Soho House, with mention of the size of Boulton's bath.[20]

An entry in 1801 mentions security in the house, the adding of locks and bolts to windows and doors.[21]

Two notebooks which have entries concerning Boulton's property ownership have surprises. At the centre of the notebook for 1793–1803, there is a pull out map, in watercolour, of part of Handsworth common, the lands surrounding Soho. (Fig. 6.1). The map is divided into sections representing land owned by different people, and there is a key to it.[22] The notebook for 1800 has in the middle a diagram of Boulton's warehouse at Snow Hill, showing it's relation to the canal, with an accompanying key, listing all the surrounding buildings.[23]

Business interests and products

As might be expected, Boulton used his notebooks to keep all kinds of ideas and information about his business interests. One or two have detailed descriptions of processes of manufacture. The notebook dated 1768–1775 begins: 'Vases. Materials of wch. Vases may be made'. There are notes on different metals, gilding, buttons, buckles, ormolu, with prices of metals, recipes, and experiments. At the end of the notebook there are several pages of lists under the title: 'January 1st 1769 – Materials used at Soho & then Compositions & Arts'. There follows a list of items produced at Soho and all the different materials used to make them.[24]

Another notebook, covering similar dates also has 'A List of the Articles Manufactured at Soho', (1771). A large part of this volume is made up of price lists for individual items with (?) pattern numbers and cost, such as men's steel chains, women's steel chains, steel trinkets, glass trinkets, platina buckles, plated candlesticks, chapes, etc.[25] In the book titled 'Gilt Buttons 1790', there are headings such as: 'To lay a good foundation for making

---

18   BAH, MS 3782/12/108/92.
19   BAH, MS 3782/12/108/11, p.24.
20   BAH, MS 3782/12/108/50, p.40.
21   BAH, MS 3782/12/108/92, pp.50–54.
22   BAH, MS 3782/12/108/68.
23   BAH, MS 3782/12/108/85, p.25.
24   BAH, MS 3782/12/108/5, p.129.
25   BAH, MS 3782/12/108/6.

blanks for fine Gilt Buttons'; 'properties & Improvements for a good <u>Stamp</u> & HAMMER'; and 'Gold to be allowed for different strengths or qualities of gilding as follows'. One paper enclosed in this volume reads: 'Buttons of any shape may be exactly measured by grinding the tops with narrow tin foil then cutting it off even with the edges and opening it flat.'[26] There is another notebook, titled *"Button Gilding"* and dated *"December 1799"*, which contains observations and experiments relating to buttons, especially to the gilding process. There are notes on Boulton's experiments using nitrous acid, and a list of chemistry texts.[27]

A notebook about buckle making, dated 1793, is equally informative. There are headings such as: ornaments for riveting on the tops of buckles, to calculate spring silver buckles, studs, springs, thickness of prepared metals, operations in making latchets, to make leather water-proof, to make another varnish for leather. On page 83, Boulton has written: 'Improvments made by MB in Buckl[es] Better Steel, Scaled & Rolld fine without Grinding, Bobing in the Mill, Systimised the Sizes & forms of Buckles, Better patterns & better Dies, Better Hooks to Springs' etc.[28]

The steam engine business occupied a major part of Boulton's time. The number of notebooks with details of steam engines required, and calculations for the efficiency of engines, particularly those in Cornwall, are possibly connected to the fact that Boulton and Watt received substantial income from the savings in fuel made as a result of using their engines. Hence there are notebooks which have been specially printed to record information on the performance of engines. For example, the volume dated 1774–1778, has tables printed in both black and red ink, and on the inside front cover a note which reads: 'The figure wrote with red ink, at the bottom of each page, signifies the page in the Big Calculations book, in which that engine is inserted.' Many of the notes in this volume are actually in the hand of James Watt.[29] Another notebook, dated 1778, has on the cover: Calculations & Performance of Cornish Engines,[30] and a further notebook has 'Monthly Performances of Cornish Engines. Jan[ua]ry 1778 – Jan[ua]ry 1782'. The information recorded there includes figures for the number of piston strokes, depth in fathoms, diameter of pump in inches, load in pounds, consumption of cylinder, total savings, and Boulton & Watt's third share.[31]

---

26   BAH, MS 3782/12/108/56.
27   BAH, MS 3782/12/108/82.
28   BAH, MS 3782/12/108/66.
29   BAH, MS 3782/12/108/10.
30   BAH, MS 3782/12/108/14.
31   BAH, MS 3782/12/108/16.

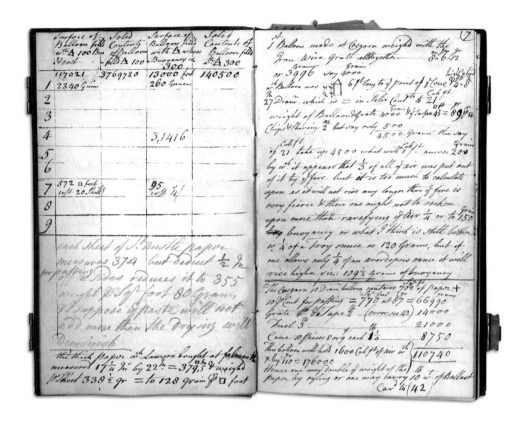

Fig. 6.2. Matthew Boulton's notes on making a balloon with wire and paper while staying in Cornwall, 1784. Birmingham Archives and Heritage.

Experiments

Other notebooks are packed with information concerning engine orders and performances and experiments to improve performance. For example, one notebook, 1780–1786, has on the cover 'Boylers – 1780'. There are dated entries of experiments concerning boilers and notes and diagrams about individual boilers, most for Cornish engines etc. Dolcoath, Ale & Cakes, and 'Wheal Chance – Trial of boyler by William Murdoch'.[32]

Boulton's enthusiasm for science and experiments, especially with chemistry, is clear from his notes. He had his own laboratory at Soho house and his friends in the Lunar Society would have encouraged his activities. The first notebook (1751–1759) includes an entry on how to give a revolving motion to a spindle, with a drawing to explain; also 'An experiment made by MB and Doctor S. [Small] upon steam', observations

32   BAH, MS 3782/12/108/23.

on the temperatures of the different bath rooms at Buxton, 1759, and a recipe for invisible ink, 'To write in a secret manner'.[33] In the notebook for 1765 is a recipe for some sort of dye: 'if ye Sauce is not red enough put in some dragon's Blood or if not yellow enough put in some more Saffron', and a page headed 'To See & Learn', which includes 'see some Black Lead pencils made' and 'how to French plate' and 'to seek a Chamber in wch ye Flowers of Brimston ar Condenced'.[34]

One volume, dated 1772–1775, has information on many experiments, including chemical ones (concentrated acid of nitre, ways of precipitating silver), various specific gravities, experiments with dipping platina buttons, the use of different oils in lamps. At the end of the book there are some pencil sketches as well as notes about olive buttons and the use of a stud grinder.[35] Another book has on the cover: 'Experiments on Carronades' (these were small cannon, developed at Carron in Scotland). The notes concern experiments made 1779–1781, and there are calculations and descriptive notes such as: 'Experiments made at the New Battery at Leith with a hundred pounder Carronade, weighing about 50 cwt and of six calibers in length, the first of October 1781'.[36] In 1780, Boulton was recording experiments with water gauges,[37] and in 1787, observations and experiments on silvering. There is also an entry: 'To make a liquor for proving if there is any Sugar of Lead in Wine'.[38]

Coinage

Matthew Boulton developed new methods of minting coins using the steam engine and improvements gathered from various sources to produce better and consistent quality of coin. He took out Letters Patent for his process in 1790. Eventually, in 1797, he was licensed to provide the Treasury with copper coinage. Soho Foundry supplied minting machinery to many countries – India, Mexico, Denmark, Portugal – and two of Boulton's notebooks have information on the mint provided to St Petersburg in 1799.

One volume contains: 'An Estimate of ye Expense in Erecting a Compleat Mint for Russia without ye Rolling Mill',[39] (and also directions on how 'To Blanch Black Dirty Dollars'!) In another notebook (1797), where 'Names of

---

33   BAH, MS 3782/12/108/1.
34   BAH, MS 3782/12/108/3, p.7.
35   BAH, MS 3782/12/108/8.
36   BAH, MS 3782/12/108/19.
37   BAH, MS 3782/12/108/18, pp.49–50.
38   BAH, MS 3782/12/108/50, p.37.
39   BAH, MS 3782/12/108/81.

Russian Workmen' is a heading, Boulton also includes 'Memorandums of things which I ought not to neglect', under which is written: 'Make each a present of fleecy Hosary'.[40]

The notebooks with information about coinage include a wealth of detail about metals, weights, exchange rates, physical manufacturing processes, with lists of tools and drawings of various machines and dies. In a notebook for 1789, the heading on p.17 is: 'Octr. 16 – 1789 Advantages of my Coining Mill', and Boulton gives a dozen reasons why it is the best, starting with:[41]

> It will coin faster, with greater ease, with fewer persons, less expence & more beautyfull than any Coining Machine ever made.
>
> One of my Coining Machines will work much faster by ye attendance of one Boy than any other press can by any number of Men
>
> Can stop by the power of a Child in an instant & set going again as quick
>
> Can work night & day say 24 hours without fateague by having 2 sets of Men or boys as all the force is given by a Steam Engine
>
> the press keeps an exact account of the number of pieces struck & can't deceive
>
> not so liable to break the dies
>
> It strikes each piece quite round, all of equal Diameter & exactly concentrick with the Edge which cannot be done <u>quick</u> by any other Machine ever used

And so on.

Boulton's concerns did not finish with the minting of coins. In a notebook of 1798, he describes a possible method of secure storage:[42]

> Q. If a Boat could not be so constructed as to prevent thieves from breaking in & stealing out Boxes of [silver] in the night
>
> 1. The boat should have a Covering Locked Bolted & Barrd wth Iron
> 2. It should have a Guard of 4 Musqueteers & Bayonets
> 3. It should be used in long Days only say in May June July or Augt
> 4. There should be a fierce Dog
> 5. & some loud Speaking trumpet or Horn
> 6. the Boxes should be Cubes with[ou]t handles & very Strong

---

40 BAH, MS 3782/12/108/76, p.3.
41 BAH, MS 3782/12/108/54, pp.17–18.
42 BAH, MS 3782/12/108/81, p.74.

Food, medicines and agriculture

The notebooks provide a unique insight into daily life at the time. Boulton's first notebook has notes on the subject of eggs:

> The Rt Honbl the Earl of Hopetoun informs me that from many years experience he finds new laid Eggs to be a very wholesome & more Nutritious food than almost anything else in use so that he thinks two with Salt & Bread only are Sufficient for a Meal & that hath been his constant Breakfast for many Years but he finds that if they have been laid 24 Hours they loose of their fine flavour & subtil—— something wch transpires through the Shell so that as soon as they are laid they are immediately thrown into Clean water wch prevents its escape or if you put a thin coat of suit [soot] over the Shell it preserves them very well.

Boulton continues to discuss how and how long eggs should be boiled, looking at different temperatures and thermometers.[43]

There are occasionally recipes for various medicines. In 1792, the notebook begins with a prescription from Dr Fordyce for Boulton to take 'when any paroxysm comes on from the Kidneys', consisting of linseed tea, sweetened with sugar and a little lemon.[44] Boulton was interested in agriculture as well as industry, and particularly in ways of producing food cheaply and efficiently. His notebook titled 'Agriculture 1793' contains information on the agricultural uses of a steam engine, from threshing corn, pulverising chalk and limestone, to raising water; a recipe for 'Birmingham Soup'; notes on manure, which he had arranged to obtain from the Birmingham Barracks 'at 6d pr horse pr week'; and 'Mr Wyatt's Receipt for making Bread'.[45]

Conclusion

Matthew Robinson Boulton (1770–1842) did, as his father had advised, keep notebooks. His surviving volumes total forty-one, covering the dates 1795–1839. Many of these are used from both ends: one being labelled 'Current' and the other 'Permanent'. They record both business and domestic memoranda; appointments, addresses, accounts, details of travel etc. Approximately a third of the notebooks, from 1821–1839, are marked 'Soho', and mostly concern business at the Manufactory or the Mint.

The notebooks of his father, Matthew Boulton, suggest a man with an appetite for new ideas and knowledge, a drive to improve ways of working

---

43   BAH, MS 3782/12/108/1, p.21.
44   BAH, MS 3782/12/108/61, p.1.
45   BAH, MS 3782/12/108/68.

and a willingness to experiment to find the best solution. Boulton emerges as a man of confidence, self reflection and a sense of humour. One notebook (1797–98) includes this toast for civil engineers:[46] 'dam[n] the canals, Sink ye Coal pits, Blast ye Minerals, Consume ye Manufactures & disperse ye Commerce of Gr[ea]t Britain'.

References
All the references are to documents held in Birmingham Archives and Heritage, Central Library, Birmingham B3 3HQ.

---

46   BAH, MS 3782/12/108/74, p.25.

Chapter 7

HIS EXCELLENCY COUNT WORONZOW THE RUSSIAN AMBASSADOR AND THE HARDWARE MAN: THE HISTORY OF A FRIENDSHIP

Olga Baird

Matthew Boulton promoted his Soho Manufactory and its products as soon as it was built in 1762. Within a few years, even before establishing the partnership with James Watt, Soho became a 'must see' for travellers. Foreign guests usually came to Soho with introductory letters from their embassy. In his turn, Matthew Boulton was keen on expanding business with the continent, and the most practical way was to do it through embassies. During the Soho history of Matthew Boulton's life (1762–1809), five ambassadors represented Russia in England. Alexander Woronzow (1741–1805) served at the beginning of this period, his brother Semyon (1744–1832) at the end.

The first links between the Russian Embassy and Soho were established by the successor of Alexander Woronzow, Alexei Semyonovich Moussin-Pushkin (1730–1817), who was accredited from 1765 to 1779 with two short gaps. He appears to have been one of the earliest of Boulton's Russian contacts. Moussin-Pushkin started to steer his countrymen towards Birmingham as early as August 1767, when Boulton wrote: 'I have French and Spaniards today; and tomorrow I shall have Germans, Russians and Norwegians.'[1] In 1770, Moussin-Pushkin himself came to Soho in order to acquire pieces for the Empress Catherine,[2] and later Boulton wrote: 'I am very much obliged to Your Excellency for the honour you intended me and done to our manufacture in causing it to be visited by some Princes and Nobles from Russia.'[3] Boulton was welcome at Moussin-

---

1   H.W. Dickinson, *Matthew Boulton* (Warwickshire, 1999), p.72.
2   Sir Nicholas Goodison, *Matthew Boulton: Ormolu* (London, 1999), p.97.
3   E. Letterbook, p.319. MB to Moussin-Pushkin, 1771.

Pushkin's London residence, and their correspondence shows well-established, if rather formal relations between Soho and the Russian Embassy.

Count Semyon Romanovich Woronzow became the most famous Russian Ambassador to England. Along with his brother and two sisters, he was a member of an ancient and influential family which belonged at the top of the Russian aristocracy. His uncle was Vice-Chancellor of the Russian Empire in the time of the Empress Elizabeth, and his elder sister, Elizabeth (1739–1792), became the mistress of Peter III, which gave the Vice-Chancellor almost unlimited power. Semyon Woronzow was loyal to the legitimate Emperor and did not support Catherine II, who for years considered him a dangerous man. The post of ambassador, at first in Venice, and then in England, was some kind of a truce offered by the Empress. Woronzow moved from Venice to London at the most difficult time of his life having just lost his young wife and finding himself a widower with two small children, Mikhail (1782–1856) and Ekaterina (1784–1856). (Fig. 7.1). He never married again, and, following the pedagogical ideas of the time, he brought up his children himself and compiled extensive programmes for their education. He held office for twenty-one years, tirelessly working to cement Anglo-Russian relations.

Woronzow closely collaborated with the chaplain to the Russian Embassy Yakov Smirnov (James Smirnove), who arrived in London in 1776 and became chaplain in 1780. Smirnove held his post for sixty years, until his death in 1840. A.G. Cross described him as 'stability in an era of great change, always at hand and ready to help Russians and Englishmen alike, the supplier of countless letters of recommendation and introduction.'[4] Smirnove first visited Soho in July 1782 being introduced to Boulton and Fothergill by a Godfrey Thornton.[5] He often fulfilled the duties of the Ambassador's secretary, and it was probably Smirnove who drew Soho to Semyon Woronzow's attention when he took up his post in 1785.

Fig. 7.1. Portrait of Count Semyon Woronzow with his children by Ludwig Guttenbrunn. Oil on board c.1795. Pavlovsk Palace, Russian Federation.

4   A.G. Cross, 'Yakov Smirnov, A Russian Priest of Many Parts' in *Oxford Slavonic Papers*, 1975, New Series, Vol.VIII, pp.37–52.

5   Birmingham Archives and Heritage (BAH), MS 3147/3/383/10. G. Thornton to Boulton & Fothergill, July 1782.

The relations between Woronzow and Matthew Boulton began slowly. The first known letter from the Ambassador to Matthew Boulton of July 1786 introduced 'Prince Golitsyn and his travelling companion who in their excursions through England intend to visit Birmingham'[6] in a rather formal way. The Russian Mint business which begun in 1796, brought them together, and helped to discover in each other the qualities that both of them respected: patriotism and a deep concern for the prosperity of their countries, the recognition of public duties and responsibilities, persistency, and self-esteem. Both were widowers with two children to bring up and they were seriously engaged in issues of education and upbringing, although, as Boulton's children were significantly older, at different times. Their correspondence of 1786–1807 consists of about 150 letters, both business and private, and demonstrates the development of their relationship from polite formalities, through mutual respect and appreciation, to genuine friendship.

Coming to London, Boulton always visited the Russian Embassy and the Count's residence in Richmond and soon became well known to Woronzow's children. Their relations were already rather informal, when on 24 January 1798, James Smirnove wrote:

> An Englishman's word, they say, is his Bond. Upon this Plea, it is, I dare say, my dear Sir, that the young Countess says you must send her a half-penny to compleat the Set which she received of you, except a half-penny, which she says you promised to send her from Birmingham – and the young Count says you have likewise made a Promise to send him a penny, which is to hold card markers in it. They have made an enquiry about it very often & I promised them to remind you of the Promise. Pray excuse the trouble I am giving you. – but I really have no heart to refuse any thing to our young and amiable Countess whom I am very fond of for many engaging qualities.[7]

In August 1799, Count Woronzow, his children, Ekaterina's governess Miss Jardine, and James Smirnove came to Soho, which had just been modernised and redecorated, and spent six days there (Plate 1). Shena Mason associates this spectacular visit with Boulton and Watt's negotiations for the Russian Mint[8] but it is more likely that it was a tour which formed a part of the education of Mikhail Woronzow who was just coming of age. Educational programmes of the Age of Enlightenment paid great attention to

6   BAH, MS 3782/12/31/90. Woronzow to MB, 24 June 1786.
7   BAH, MS 3782/13/107/Folder 4. Smirnove to MB, 24 January 1798.
8   Shena Mason. *The Hardware's Man Daughter* (Chichester, 2005), p.114.

mechanical, agricultural, and other manual skills. They were inspired by the ideas of Jean-Jacques Rousseau, who saw the mechanical arts as a means of bringing together people of different social classes and of working towards eliminating cultural prejudices.[9] In addition, Count Woronzow, analysing the ideas and events of the French Revolution, believed that it might soon be repeated in Russia. Thus the Russian ambassador taught his son to be a craftsman, so that he might earn his living, and occupy a worthy place in his country after a revolution. Mikhail was taught joinery which became one of his favourite occupations. Matthew Boulton, in his turn, although looking at mechanical skills from the point of view of their usefulness in his business, wrote to his son, Matthew Robinson: 'A knowledge of mechanicks, mathematicks, chymistry, mechanick arts, and commerce, joined to the character of an honest man, is what I am very anxious you should possess.'[10]

Their travel to Birmingham, their stay and entertainment at Soho and the mutual feelings of the guests and their hosts are vividly described in their correspondence. On the 22 July James Smirnove informed Boulton: 'We hope to have the honour of seeing you on Sunday or Monday next. Our company will consist of the Count, his son and daughter, Miss Jardine the Governess, their maid, Count's valet-de-chambre, two footmen and your very humble servant...'[11] Matthew Boulton offered his guests a visit to the Birmingham Theatre Royal, and Smirnov wrote back:

> Your letter of the 24th July has given our ladies very great pleasure at the idea of seeing your Theatre. The Count has accepted your invitation to the play on Monday evening and means to thank you for it personally. We set out tomorrow morning and mean to sleep at Buckingham; on Sunday we see the Stow gardens and probably dine at the Marquis of Buckingham and, if possible, make a stage or two nearer to you. If not, we shall set out early on Monday to be with you to go to the play after having dined somewhere on the road.[12]

Matthew Boulton's letter to Charlotte Matthew, in which he described their arrival and stay, is full of his immediate excitement and agitation, pleasure and pride, and humorous comments:

---

9 J. Pannabecker. 'Rousseau in the Heritage of Technology Education', in *Journal of Technology Education*, Vol.6, No.2 (Spring 1995). http://scholar.lib.vt.edu/ejournals/JTE/v6n2/pannabecker (accessed 27 June 2008).
10 BAH, MS 3782/13/36/34. MB to MRB, 3 August 1789.
11 BAH, MS 3782/12/44 /229. Smirnove to MB, 22 July 1799.
12 BAH, MS 3782/12/44/235. Smirnove to MB, 26 July 1799.

I will now give you a very short sketch of my Imperial Visit. On Monday in the afternoon son Excellence Monsieur le Comte de Woronzoff, General en Chef de Son Majeste l'Emperor de toutes les Russies, Son Envoye extraordinaire et Ministre plenipotentiaire pres la Cour de S M Britannique et Chevalier des differents orderes arrivé a Soho with his charming daughter & his amiable son, also mademoiselle Jardine, the Rev. Mr Smirnove, Monsieur Valet & two other domesticks. The whole party, with my 2 Misses & Self went to the theatre & saw Kemble play Hamlet with which they were very pleased.[13]

They had indeed reason to be pleased, as London theatres were closed for summer, and Drury Lane actors performed at Birmingham's Theatre Royal. The Soho party saw the great John Philip Kemble, and enjoyed 'Hamlet' so much, that on Wednesday they went to the theatre again, to see David Garrick's and George Colman's 'The Clandestine Marriage' with Tom King as Lord Ogleby, followed by 'Blue Beard' with 'all its scenery very well got up.' It seems that this second theatrical event was even more exciting that the first, as in collaboration with William Macready, the theatre manager, Boulton prepared a special surprise for the Count: when at 7 o'clock they entered their box, 'the military band struck up God Save the King, for the Count is passionately fond of His Majesty.'[14] Russian heroes of the day also were not forgotten: at the end of the play forty singers appeared on the stage and sung an especially composed song about Suworow and Emperor Paul I.[15] Indeed, Paul I who succeeded Catherine the Great on her death in 1796, recalled Field-Marshal Suworow to the army, and Russia joined the war against revolutionary France. In 1799 Suworow triumphantly carried out his Italian campaign against the French. Woronzow reported to St Petersburg that Suworow 'was the idol of the English nation, and his health is drunk every day in houses, taverns and cottages.'[16] At Soho Mint, the medal 'Alexander Suworow Italiae Liberator' was struck (See Fig. 13.3). The author of the patriotic song hardly knew that Suworow was much disliked by Paul, or that relations between the Emperor and his ambassador were not smooth or easy. However, these prosaic details did not spoil the evening:

---

13   BAH, MS 3782/12/69/161. MB to Charlotte Matthews, 7 August 1799.

14   BAH, MS 3782/12/69/161. MB to Charlotte Matthews, 7 August 1799.

15   The author of the song is unknown. It may have been Boulton himself, as he composed verses on occasion.

16   P. Longworth. *The Art of Victory. The Life and Achievements of Generalissimo Suvorov* (London, 1965), p.264.

The Count was devastated by delight & turned to shake hands with me every moment saying he was sure this was my doing but which he considered as the highest & most acceptable Compliment that could be made him. It also pleased the house & was encored and joined in the Chorus by the audience.[17]

After the performance ended, the party went out, accompanied by Mr Macready lighting them the way, and the Count 'handed out to his coronetted Coach Miss de Luc.'

After two days of seeing Soho Mint and other Birmingham manufactures, Boulton arranged another surprise: a 'secret' boat expedition as far as Dudley Cave, full of industrial sightseeing and accompanied by music. A boat with orchestra was sent forward out of sight, and 'as soon as the Count & Co was seated in the Cabin he sayd, hark I hear the musick, the windows were opened & the swell increased as we drew near. He at length exclaimed that it is delightfull & I am confident this is my dear friend's plan.'

They sailed into the Soho Foundry, then saw steam engines in action at Brades, and finally 'adjourned to Mr Hunt's house' for dinner. 'The band played in the hall whilst we dined & after dinner had some Loyal songs with Paul and Suworow.' After dinner, they:

> again entered our boats & by the assistance of musick we increased the apparent population of the County immensely... we at length entered the regions of darkness which I dispelled by 100 torches which I had provided. New and Immense Caverns opend as we proceeded, thorough which we often espied through openings the inhabitants of the Earth looking down upon us. The band of Musick playing all the time & beautifully echoed from the Salons of Erebus.[18]

Shena Mason justly associates Boulton's musical idea with Handel's *Water Music*,[19] although he also might have heard about St Petersburg 'Neva Serenades', summer musical performances on the Neva, which were introduced in the 1750s and quickly became immensely popular. In the 1760s, a contemporary described such music: 'I hear Grigory Orlov going in his boat down the river. Behind him – a train of court boats, and in front of him – a boat with forty lads making music which I have never heard in my life.'[20] Remembering Woronzow's diplomatic period in Venice, it also might be associated with Venetian musical traditions.

---

17 BAH, MS 3782/12/69/161. MB to Charlotte Matthews, 7 August 1799.

18 Ibid.

19 Shena Mason. *op. cit.*, p.115.

20 Yury Kruzhnov. *Russkaia Rogovaia Kapella*. //www.horncapella.ru. (accessed 25 July 2008).

This visit was followed by a rather hectic correspondence. While Boulton was writing from Birmingham to Charlotte Matthew, Count Woronzow was describing their experience to his Italian friend, Prince Fabrizio Ruffo Castelcicala (1763–1832)[21] who wrote back from Palermo: 'Your letter from the 5th August gave me the greatest pleasure by the details of your trip to the interior of England and to the marvellous manufactory of Messrs Boulton and Watt. You are lucky, my friend, to be able to admire this masterpiece of art and genius.'[22] James Smirnove thanked Boulton:

> most sincerely for the innumerable marks of friendship, kindness and particular attention, which I among the rest have experienced under your hospitable Roof. The Count and the Ladies are still in extasy about Soho, we have been talking of you and drinking your health everywhere ever since. – You and Suworow are our two heroes at the table, we are toasting you both continually...
>
> My respects to Miss Boulton, Miss De Luc, and Miss Keene. If I was not so old, nor married, I would be greatly tempted to send my love to them...[23]

Yury Lotman notes that the Russian idea of a noble upbringing included the necessity of good manners, which meant simplicity in communication. The ability to be 'one of them' in an aristocratic salon, or with peasants at a village market, or with children, and to communicate without pretension and effort in an unaffected and natural way, was a specific feature of the everyday behaviour of a cultivated Russian aristocrat.[24] In this context the Woronzows display a perfect example of these manners: the governess of the Count's daughter is treated as the daughter's friend and she and a Russian priest are equal members of the party. They dine with the Marquis of Buckingham, but they do not mind a dinner somewhere on the road; they are used to famous London theatres and Italian opera, but the prospect of a performance in Birmingham (although very good indeed!) also gives them a great pleasure. The Count enjoys marks of attention, but does not take them for granted, and expresses his delight in a very spontaneous and informal way. Aristocratic origin and the high position of the 'son Excellence Monsieur le Comte de

21 One of the closest friends of Woronzow and on two occasions he was an envoy of Naples in London.

22 Arkhiv kniaza Vorontsova. Vol.27, p.290. In French.

23 BAH, MS 3782/12/44/250. Smirnove to MB, 14 August 1799. Cross wrote that J. Smirnove's wife died about 1790 (By the Banks of the Thames, p.52). This letter establishes the date as 'in or after 1799'.

24 Yury Lotman. Dekabrist v povsednevnoi zhisni: Bytovoe povedenie kak istoriko-psikhologicheskaia kharakteristika (A Decembrist in day-to-day life: a common behaviour as a historic-psychological characteristic), in Bazanov V, Vatzuro V. (ed.) *Literaturnoe nasledie dekabristov*, (Leningrad: Nauka,1975), pp.25–74.

Woronzoff' did not prevent him from expressing his genuine gratitude to the
hardware man, and also to his daughter and her female companions:

> My dear and respectable friend, it is impossible for me to express (as
> I told you before) how very thankful I am for the friendship and the
> confidence you shew to me. I am flattered and honoured by it, and I may
> say that I deserve it by what I feel for you. – The Hospitality with which
> you have received & treated us during the very happy 6 days that we have
> spent in so cheerful manner at the House of the most worthy of men and
> in the most agreeable society has completely spoilt the remainder of our
> journey. The great and beautiful things conceived and executed by men
> of sublime genius, the amiable society where entertainment was always
> accompanied by interesting instruction – all this is finished for us.
>   We now shall only see fine parks, gardens and houses which are also
> to be found in all countries. I beg you to present my respects to Miss
> Boulton, and Miss de Luc, and Miss Keen. – My daughter and her friend
> are writing to Soho, and have expressed without doubts their gratitude.
> The Rev. Mr Smirnove presents their respect to the worthy patriot who
> has so well received us, and to the 3 ladies. I am and shall be all my life
> your entirely devoted admirer and sincere friend.[25]

A few days later, Boulton sent to Woronzow words of a 'loyal song' from
the Theatre Royal: 'Long may you all in Joyous Chorus sing But [praise]
Imperial Paul and George our King', and also enclosed words of 'Rule,
Britannia'. In the same letter he advised young Mikhail 'to attend Mr
Pearson's or Mr Walker's chemical lectures.'[26] Writing back, Woronzow vividly
commented on the 'Suworow' medal. At the end of his letter – a postscript in
the diligent, still childish handwriting of fifteen year-old Ekaterina:

> I am quite glad, my dear Mr Boulton, that Papa has left me room
> to say a few words to you, to thank you for not having forgot to send us
> the famous 'Rule Britannia' which we have been singing away, & a copy
> of it has already been sent to Russia. But I am still more glad, that I
> have so good an opportunity of thanking you also, for your kindness to
> us all during our delightful stay at Soho, which we always think of with
> the greatest pleasure.[27]

James Smirnove summed up the emotions and feelings of that visit:

---

25 BAH, MS 3782/12/44/270. Woronzow to MB, August 1799.
26 BAH, MS 3782/13/107/Folder 9. MB to Woronzow, 11 September 1799.
27 BAH, MS 3782/13/107/Folder 5. Woronzow to MB, 7 September 1799.

I tell you, my dear Sir, most frankly and most candidly, that since the Count came to England, although I have the honour to see him almost every day for these 14 years past, I never saw him and his family pass their time so happily and so comfortably, as they did at Soho. If I could say so without pedantism, I would say that the Furnaces of your kindness and attention have melted him a – new. You have really set him up quite and made him stout and strong at least for half a dozen years to come...[28]

But times were changing: Russian forces had been defeated in Switzerland and the Netherlands; Paul I blamed his allies, particularly the English, and official diplomatic relations were broken off. Woronzow was dismissed from his post in disgrace. He would be restored only in May 1801 by the new Emperor Alexander I. These storms did not affect relations between the Woronzows and Soho. In November 1799 Boulton dined with Count Woronzow. Young Mikhail, following Boulton's advice, had attended Walker's lectures to prepare himself for his next visit to Soho [29] and on 25 April 1800, James Smirnove wrote:

The young Count, Mr Yakovleff, one of the gentlemen belonging to our Embassy,[30] and myself have formed a Resolution to make a little excursion to Birmingham. /.../ I do not know if you are acquainted that the young Count is to go to Russia in the month of June, to see his friends and relations. His father, our good Count, therefore wishes him once more to see Soho, and as many of its mechanical establishments, as you will allow...[31]

Despite the well established and informal relations, Mikhail Woronzow arrived with a meticulously polite letter from his father, which also outlined the educational purpose of his trip:

The object of the Excursion is to see first of all Soho and everything in it, then Birmingham and its neighbourhood. /.../ I cannot recommend them to a better Guide than my esteemed worthy friend Mr Boulton; they can profit of nobody's advise to more advantage.[32]

---

28   BAH, MS 3782/13/107.Folder 5. Smirnove to MB, 19 September 1799.
29   BAH, MS 3782/13/107/Folder 5. Smirnove to MB, 19 September 1799.
30   Lev Alexeevich Yakowlev, 1764–1839. In 1795–1796 he served in British navy and in 1798 he
      started a diplomatic career. In 1800 he made a marriage proposal to sixteen year old Ekaterina,
      to the great embarrassment of Woronzow and was nicknamed in the family 'Our Tartuffe'.
31   BAH, MS 3782/12/45/116. Smirnove to MB, 25 April 1800.
32   BAH, MS 3782/13/107/Folder 6. Woronzow to MB, 30 April 1800.

This time visitors arrived not in a 'coronetted' but in the ordinary mail coach and were prepared to stay at the New Inn. Boulton however welcomed them at Soho. The reasons for this were Boulton's hospitality, but also his wish to guarantee the young man's safety: Mikhail's arrival coincided with a food riot in Birmingham. The Riot Act was read, and Boulton commented: 'The present riotous state of Birmingham and the remembrance of the sight I saw in the year 1791 makes me feel very uncomfortable /.../ In Swinney's Newspaper of yesterday there appeared some verses which our young count cut out of my paper and sent to his father.'[33]

When Mikhail Woronzow was leaving for Russia, the parting words of his father were:

> The country to which you are going does not resemble England. Although the new reign has made our countrymen happy, although having been delivered from the most horrible slavery, they consider themselves free, they are not free in the sense of citizens of other countries, who in their turn have no idea of real liberty which is based on an unique constitution which makes the happiness of England: where people obey laws which are the same for all, and where human dignity is respected. In Russia there is ignorance, immorality as the result of this ignorance, and forms of government which spoil people, deprive them of high feelings, and encourage greed, sensuality, and a slavish, unworthy self-degradation before mighty people or favourites of the Tsar.[34]

In April 1802, Count Woronzow and his daughter went to Russia to meet the new Emperor Alexander I. They brought to St Petersburg four engraved portraits of Matthew Boulton [35] which he requested Woronzow to distribute:

1. I am not so vain or presumptuous as to offer one to the Emperor; but if his Imperial Majesty should have any collection of prints in his library I should feel myself highly honoured by having that print which is marked on the back side (a proof) placed among them merely as a Specimen of good engraving.
2. I wish to show some mark of respect to Count Samoilov.
3. Also to Mr A Schnese who sent me a silver medal of his father who was master of the Imperial Mint.[36]

---

33 BAH, MS 3782/12/45/126. MB to Smirnove, 2 May 1800. Swinney's *Birmingham and Stafford Chronicle* for 1 May 1800 is unavailable.
34 Arkhiv kniaza Vorontsova. Vol.17, pp.5–6. In French.
35 Portrait of Matthew Boulton. William Sharp after Sir William Beechey, 1801.
36 BAH, MS 3782/12/47/112. MB to Woronzow, 6 April 1802.

Count Alexander Samoilov (1744–1814) was Procurer-General and Manager of the St Petersburg bank. Matthew Boulton had dealt with him at an early stage of the Mint business. Mr A. Schnese was a son of Alexei Schnese (1743–1801), a mint master at the St Petersburg Mint. Schnese's wife, neè Schlatter, belonged to the family of mining engineers and mint-masters. Her uncle, Felix Schlatter, was head of Russian apprentices at Soho from 1797.[37]

While his friends were away, Boulton missed them, and was very pleased when they returned in December of 1802: 'Nothing could be more acceptable for me than Your Excellency's letter.... Indeed I have long looked for you with the Eyes of Argus and have some times caught a glimpse of you and your fair companions in St Petersburg...'[38] This letter he concluded with the words: 'Compliments to your dear Countess would not express my (crossed out – feelings) sensations, and yet I may be thought too free in presenting the love of an old infirm man; however I can find no other word that will so properly express my feeling which I must beg her good father will communicate...'[39] At that time Boulton was unwell and extremely anxious about the Russian Mint business, so this letter reveals his genuine affection for the Woronzows.

In their absence, changes were undertaken at Soho and visitors were not allowed any more. It caused some difficulties for Boulton, as he had to refuse some friends of young Countess: 'I could not break new Law in favour of the Countess for the most cogent reasons... without bringing upon myself a disagreeable quarrel. I therefore wrote a note to the Countess and sent her one of our prohibiting cards with an explanation and apology.'[40] This measure, however, did not last long. After the Woronzows' return to England, their relatives, friends, and protégés were welcomed as before. In June 1803, Woronzow introduced to Soho his nephew Pavel Bacounin (1776–1805) with his wife Ekaterina, neé Sablukov. In 1794 Bacounin had succeeded his aunt Princess Dashkova as Director of the Academy of Sciences, and in this role he arrived in England. Woronzow, however, was not fond of him and wrote to the Academy: 'Bacounin is my nephew and has been nearly two years with me. He is thoughtless, presumptuous and ignorant; he is the man the least proper to be the head of an Academy and will only introduce disorder and confusion.'[41] Woronzow's feelings can be seen in his letter, given to Bacounin but recommending Madame Bacounin instead:

---

37   Richard Doty in *The Soho Mint and the Industrialization of Money* (London, 1998, p.85) calls Schnese Schlatter's uncle. Their family relations were the other way round. In Russian sources there is no agreement about the date of Schnese's death: 1801 or no earlier than 1815. Boulton's letter supports the date 1801.

38   BAH, MS 3782/12/48/27. MB to Woronzow, 31 January 1803.

39   Ibid.

40   BAH, MS 2782/13/107. Folder 5. MB to Smirnove, 22 July 1802.

41   Arkhiv Kniaza Voronzova, XXII, 527. In French.

a very sensible amiable person, she is accompanied by Ms Christine Jardine, younger sister of Ms Jardine already known to Mr Boulton. They are going on a tour through England, and in their way are extremely desirous to have the honour to be introduced to Mr Boulton, whom Count Woronzow requests in a very particular manner to permit his friends to see Soho manufactory and to advise them how they are to obtain a sight of those objects which are worth the curious Traveller's notice at Birmingham. Madame Bacounin is a great friend of Countess Catherine.
Whose voice is also can be heard here:

'the Countess hopes that from the Love which Mr Boulton has so often professed to her, her friend will experience the more civility and kind attention which the Countess will be always ready to acknowledge with gratitude.'[42]

The name of the Bacounins has a special resonance for both Russian and English ears: their son Alexander was Alexander Pushkin's school friend and their daughter Catherine was the first love of the young poet and the addressee of his first poems. Madame Bacounin's brother, Nikolai Sablukov (who visited Soho in 1802), married in 1804 Juliana Angerstein, the daughter of the founder of the National Gallery, London.

In August 1803, Count Woronzow introduced to Boulton Count and Countess Zamoyski, 'very respectable friends, the Brother of the Countess is a Minister of Foreign Affairs, co-partner with my brother the Grand Chancellor of Russia, and he is a very particular friend of my brother as well as mine.'[43] Stanislaw Kostka Zamoyski (1775–1856) was the younger son of the great Polish humanist and reformer Andrzej Zamoyski. Stanislaw Kostka became known as a statesman, patriot, and patron of the arts and industry. A brother of his wife Sofia was Adam Jerzy Czartoryski, not only the Minister of Foreign Affairs, but also one of the closest friends of Alexander I. As a sign of their gratitude, the young couple sent Matthew Boulton some French tobacco along with a lump of Polish granite [44] which probably was added to his geological collection. Immediately after returning to Poland in 1804, Zamoyski founded the first Polish manufactory, producing agricultural tools and other machinery.

The introductory letters of these guests emphasise their high position and serious purpose. But in some way they also indicate that the real driving force behind them was the young Countess Ekaterina. In October 1803, introducing 'Major General Kretoff and his lady', Woronzow wrote:

42   BAH, MS 3782/12/48/169. Woronzow to MB, 9 June 1803.
43   BAH, MS 3782/12/48/245. Woronzow to MB, 6 July 1803.
44   BAH, MS 3782/12/48/267, 268. Zamoyski to MB, 19 and 21 August 1803.

Your and Miss Boulton's politeness and kindness to my daughter, Madame Bacounin, and Countess Zamoyska have created such a rivalship amongst my countryladies which has the greatest share of your affections, so that every one of those who come here wish to have the honour of being known to you in hopes of meeting with an equal success and I can only assure you that Madame Kretoff will not yield to any of those above mentioned neither in Sweetness of Temper, nor in amiable manners, nor in any things which render the fair sex virtuous and valuable. The General is an old friend of mine, and I have a great regard for him as well as for his lady.[45]

Ekaterina can also be seen behind the letter from James Smirnove introducing:

Capt. Samuel Greig, Commissioner of His Imperial Majesty the Emperor of Russia in London for the Marine Department, a very particular friend of mine, a son of the late worthy Admiral Greig, a great friend of as worthy a man our friend Count Woronzow.... Capt Greig has been in Edinburgh to marry a daughter of a very well known and much respected character Sir William Fairfax.... He will no doubt have the honour of introducing his Lady to you and to Miss Boulton.[46]

Samuel Greig was perhaps not very keen on seeing Soho, as, according to his wife, he 'had neither knowledge of, nor interest in, science of any kind.'[47] But Mary Fairfax Somerville hungered for knowledge, felt lonely and found consolation in Woronzow's house: 'The first time I went to [Italian Opera] was in London as chaperone to Countess Catharine Woronzow... who was godmother to my eldest son. I sometimes spent the evening with her, and occasionally dined at the embassy...'[48] Introducing the Greigs to Soho meant to bring Mary to the 'amiable society where entertainment was always accompanied by interesting instruction'. Mary Somerville would become a distinguished mathematician and astronomer and a member of the Royal Astronomical Society.

The Woronzows worried about Boulton's deteriorating health, and in November they came to Birmingham to see him. On the way they were caught

45   BAH, MS 3782/12/48/335. Woronzow to MB, 28 October 1803; MS 3782/12/48/357. N. Kretow to
     MB, 20 November 1803. General Nikolai Wasiliewich Kretow (1773–1839) served in the Russian
     Navy Squadron of Admiral Khanykov which, from 1795, was located in England. He participated in
     Suworow's 1799 campaign in Italy, the Napoleonic wars of 1806–1807 and 1812–1814. He was
     wounded at the battle of Borodino (1812).
46   BAH, MS 3782/12/49/223. Smirnove to MB, 3 July 1804.
47   Mary Somerville, *Personal Recollections. From Early Life to Old Age* (London, 1874), pp.75–76.
48   Ibid.

up by the overwhelming news about the victory at the Battle of Trafalgar and the death of Lord Nelson. Ekaterina hurriedly wrote from Styles's Hotel:

> Papa, Miss Jardine & myself are just arrived at Birmingham & are very anxious to hear a good account of yourself, and to send you the Extraordinary Gazette which my father received by an Office Messenger at Lichfield this morning. In case the good news it certainly has not yet spread, we think this may be welcome – one can scarcely decide which is greatest, the honour and glory you have got or the Losses you have sustained. – Perhaps some charitable soul among your party will give as a leave to tell us how you are. My father wishes to know whether you are stout enough to see people & in that case if it is no inconvenience to you, dear Sir, & that you are quite equal to seeing 3 old friends, he would beg you to allow us dine with you *en famille* tomorrow. But he hopes that you will be honest and refuse us if right and convenient.[49]

Another worrying piece of news about Boulton's health reached the Woronzows in October 1806 from Count Pavel Alexandrovich Stroganov (1774–1817). One of the Emperor's 'young friends', a Senator, and Privy Councillor, he was fulfilling a diplomatic mission to secure a Russo-British alliance against Napoleon. In Russian history, Stroganov's name has been surrounded by a romantic glow: he was in Paris in 1789, witnessed the storming of the Bastille, joined the Jacobin Club, and dreamed of political changes in Russia. After his return from England, Stroganov joined the army, and participated in the Napoleonic campaigns of 1811–1815. Matthew Boulton showed him the Mint, but was feeling unwell. This was noticed by his guest and greatly worried him. Three days later Count Woronzow wrote to reproach Boulton for scorning his health, and towards the end of the letter gave up all standard formalities, and expressed his emotions spontaneously and directly:

> In 8 or 10 days I reckon upon being in Birmingham; I shall come to Soho for 10 minutes only, merely to see and embrace you; I want nothing but to see you again, my worthy and respectable friend, for I have already seen and re-seen your admirable Machines.... I beg, nay I conjure you not to answer me – your time is too precious to loose on this. You will tell me what ever you please when we meet – in the mean time I embrace you with all my heart.[50]

---

49   BAH, MS 3782/12/50/201. Ekaterina Woronzow to MB, 7 November 1805.
50   BAH, MS 3782/12/51/169. Woronzow to MB, 28 October 1806: in French; BAH, MS 3782/13/16: English translation.

Woronzow retired in 1806, but remained in England. In 1808, Ekaterina married George Herbert, the 11th Earl of Pembroke, and became the hostess of Wilton House, Wiltshire. Matthew Boulton died the following year. Woronzow tried to keep up relations with Soho, but it seems that for him Soho had lost its magic with its old master's departure.

At the start of Soho, Russian travellers were only occasional guests as their attention was still directed towards Italy and France. They started to appear more often in the early 1790s, when, following the French Revolution, the Russian Government discouraged them from visiting France and they turned to England. The largest number of visitors appears in the early 1800s which reflects the Anglo-Russian alliance against France. Apart from the ambassadors themselves and the Russian apprentices and students who arrived to be placed at other Birmingham manufactures or in relation to the Russian Mint, about twenty-five guests – Russians, from Russia, and people recommended by the Russian Embassy – came to Soho. Among them were Count Wladimir Orlov, the youngest of the 'five celebrated brothers' who had brought Catherine II on to the Russian throne; Woronzow's sister Princess Dashkova; Alexander I's 'young friends' Prince Ivan Bariatinsky and Nikolai Novosiltsev; Prince Obolensky, General Koshelev, and the Chamberlain Nikolai Swistunov. The architect Adam Menelaws and the engineers Leon Waxel and Charles Baird also came. These names represent the élite of Russian society, and can be found on the pages of Russian political and social history of the era. But, in spite of their significance, they did not make any lasting impression on Boulton's private and business life. Only the Woronzows came to Soho as esteemed friends. Steering Russians to Soho, the Russian Ambassador enabled them to see not only modern industry, but, more importantly an example of a man with great human qualities. His last known words addressed to Boulton confirm this: 'I want nothing but to see you again, my worthy and respectable friend, for I have already seen and re-seen your admirable Machines...'

Chapter 8

WAS MATTHEW BOULTON
A STEAM ENGINEER?

Jim Andrew

There have been many references to Matthew Boulton's activities on a variety of technical matters apart from his association with James Watt. He developed production machinery for his toy trade business, made advances in producing silverware and ormolu as well as established the minting of coins and medals, yet the popular perception remains of Boulton and Watt bringing quite different and distinct abilities to their steam-engine partnership. Thirty years ago, when describing how their business was actually organised, Jennifer Tann mentioned this myth as "the portrayal of Watt as a hopeless businessman, partnered by Boulton the sharp entrepreneur who was, more or less, technically inept".[1] I think that there is much to be gained from presenting Matthew Boulton as an example to show that an individual does not have to be either "technically" or "financially" competent to have a successful business, but it would be, of course, useful to have a suitable blend of each ability. Here we will look at examples of Boulton's technical ability in relation to the steam-engine business and then seek to offer some reasons for this enduring myth.

In 1854 J.P. Muirhead reproduced many of the letters between the partners which show that, for example in 1775 and 1776, while Watt was in London and Scotland, Boulton wrote in detail of the development testing in Birmingham of the first Watt steam engine, while giving both technical details and firsthand accounts of progress.[2] Later Boulton and Watt were often apart as one was in Birmingham while the other travelled the country seeing customers and reporting on progress and modifications to engines, which had been installed. Their letters included technical and business matters and

---

1   J. Tann, 'Boulton and Watt's Organisation of Steam Engine Production before the opening of Soho Foundry', *Transactions of the Newcomen Society* 49, 1977–78, Note 1, p.51.

2   J.P. Muirhead, *The Origin and progress of The Mechanical Inventions of James Watt,* 3 Vols, (London, 1854).

show Watt as a competent if cautious businessman and Boulton as happy dealing with technical matters. There is no shortage of books published since Muirhead which show similar details of Boulton's technical work including *James Watt and the Steam Engine* by Dickinson and Jenkins [3] and, more recently, Richard Hills' fine three volume work on Watt.[4]

Someone dealing competently with a piece of technology like developing an engine could act in one of two ways. They could either understand the theory and practice of what is to be done and instruct technical staff to carry out the work, or they could both understand the theory and carry out the work themselves – the hands-on approach. Boulton was a busy man with many calls on his time in several different businesses and we might expect him to direct activity, but like many good engineers he was also quite capable of getting his hands dirty.

It seems that Boulton was concerned about the shortcomings of the water power available at his Soho Manufactory from well before he heard of Watt and of his potential improvements to the steam engine.[5] At that time many were aware that Newcomen and even Savery steam pumps could be used to return water to water wheels where water supply was limited. These engines and this approach, however, were very inefficient and a poor proposition where coal was expensive, as it was in Birmingham before the arrival of the first canals.[6] Hearing of Watt's ideas, Boulton was interested both in the improved efficiency and in the prospect of a direct rotary steam engine, the "steam wheel", which resembled a ring doughnut, two metres in diameter, rotated by a liquid piston acting under steam pressure.[7]

John Roebuck, who was funding the development of Watt's ideas, needed efficient pumps for his mines in Scotland. He wanted Watt to concentrate on his beam pumping engine and had little interest in the "steam wheel". There is some evidence that Roebuck agreed to Boulton working with William Small, in Birmingham, on developing Watt's rotary design, while Watt concentrated on the beam engine in Scotland. Almost all the letters to Watt about the "steam wheel" were written by Small and tend to show Boulton and Small instructing technical staff rather than doing the work themselves although they made various recommendations about the design.[8]

---

3   H.W. Dickinson and R. Jenkins, *James Watt and the Steam Engine* (Oxford, 1927 reprinted Ashborne, 1981).

4   R.L. Hills, *James Watt*, 3 Vols (Ashbourne, 2002–2006).

5   Ibid, Vol.1, p.417.

6   R.L. Hills, *Power from Steam* (Cambridge, 1989 reprinted 1997), pp.31–33 & 37.

7   Hills, *op. cit.*, Vol.1, pp.424–436.

8   Muirhead, *op. cit.*, Vol.2, pp.1–75.

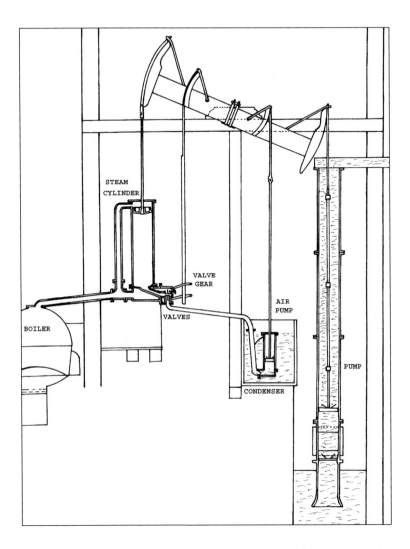

Fig. 8.1. A Boulton and Watt pumping engine designed in 1777. Diagram by the author.

Although Boulton and Small did not complete any test runs with the rotary engine before Watt moved to Birmingham, they had ordered parts, supervised assembly, tested various aspects of the design and recommended modifications. Their work certainly bore fruit because a steam wheel was run within months of Watt's arrival in Birmingham, but little appears in letters because Watt, Boulton and Small were together at this time. Sufficient tests were carried out for favourable reports to be made to the Parliamentary Committee looking at extending Watt's patent in 1775[9] but

9   Hills, *op. cit.*, Vol.1, p.434.

these tests probably showed the limitations of this design and the need to concentrate on the improved beam engine. Watt had brought his incomplete and poorly performing experimental beam engine from Scotland to Birmingham in 1774.

1775 and 1776 were fruitful years. Watt was in London for over three months in 1775, at Parliament dealing with the Bill to extend his patent. He was then in Scotland for another two months that year, winding up his affairs, before returning for well over a month in 1776 to marry his second wife and then bring her and his children down to Birmingham. These years were also a time of extensive development work and testing on Watt's experimental engine and of starting the commercial exploitation of the new engine design.

Boulton's letters to Watt during these two years reveal of his involvement in the technology of these engines: for example, in April 1775, Boulton wrote of the arrival of a really accurately bored, cast-iron cylinder from Wilkinson and of his directing staff in setting it up in the engine.[10] In May 1775 Boulton wrote of his testing parts of the engine, trying various components for excessive friction and directing their mechanics to take action to improve things.[11] In June that year he sent Watt details of temperatures and pressures found while working the engine and asking for Watt's suggestions for further work.[12] He also started recording the amount of coal burnt on test runs. More technical details were sent while Watt was in Scotland in both years, and Boulton wrote in the first person of further tests on coal consumption.[13]

With Watt's return they began travelling to see engines in progress, and many letters were sent between them containing ideas to improve specific engines or for future developments. When visiting engines, prompt action was often required to solve problems, and Hills records Boulton assisting by packing grease into the piston of the Chacewater engine in September 1778.[14] In later correspondence, Boulton continued to make suggestions about improvements to the engines' design and to report on problems found with specific engines, which customers had installed. There does seem, however, to be less of his hands-on approach than between 1775 and 1778. As the beam engine became a working proposition, Boulton's mind returned to the need for factory power units and he pressed Watt to direct his attention to rotative engines based on the beam engine design.

Some work had continued on developing the steam wheel while establishing the business based on Watt's beam engine design. As late as 1779

10   Muirhead, *op. cit.*, Vol.2, p.84, Boulton to Watt, 24 April 1775.
11   Ibid, p.86–89, Boulton to Watt in two letters in May 1775.
12   Ibid, p.90, Boulton to Watt June 1775.
13   Ibid, p.91, Boulton to Watt a second letter in June 1775.
14   Hills, *op. cit.*, Vol.2, p.106.

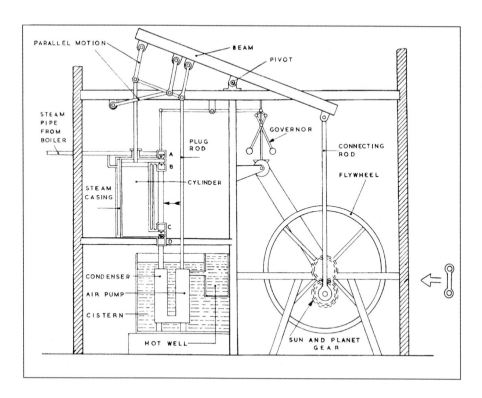

Fig. 8.2. A rotative engine showing Boulton's link, which was fitted behind the sun and planet gears (note that the valve gear is not shown). Diagram by the author.

patterns for castings of components for a steam wheel were being sent to Wilkinson [15] but there was little real progress and, despite mentions in Watt's later patents, the rotary engine seemed to have slipped into limbo. Indeed the idea of such engines, steam or even internal combustion, remained something of a pipe-dream for the best part of another two centuries. Meanwhile several engineers had tried various methods of obtaining rotary, or rotative motion as it became known, from Newcomen engines and possibly even pirated Watt beam engines.[16] These crude devices seem to have been satisfactory for winding coal but were too irregular to work machinery. Meanwhile Boulton continued to press Watt for factory power units with an emphasis on their commercial possibilities.[17]

In October 1779, Watt wrote to Boulton that he would turn to producing designs for "circular motion" when he had time.[18] Watt was well aware that

---

15   Dickinson and Jenkins, *op. cit.*, p.147.

16   L.T.C. Rolt and J.S. Allen, *The Steam Engine of Thomas Newcomen* (Hartington, 1977), pp.120–123.

17   Dickinson and Jenkins, *op. cit.*, p.159.

18   Hills, *op. cit.*, Vol.3, p.54.

designs were needed that would not only turn reciprocating motion into circular motion but a design with the smooth controlled operation needed to drive machinery, as was already available from waterwheels. As early as 1767, Watt had thought that a double-acting engine, with the piston forced up as well as down, would give smoother movement, but the simpler single-acting motion had been satisfactory for pumping engines and the chains and arch-head design was certainly easier than trying to have straight-line motion which pushed up as well as pulling down. Flywheels were being tried to deliver smoother motion, by engineers working on rotative Newcomen engines, and Watt had this in mind when he commented that Murdock's suggestion of the sun and planet gear had the advantage of doubling the speed and hence quadrupling the smoothing effect of a flywheel on the engine shaft.[19]

Many discussions must have taken place between the partners about the various devices needed for a satisfactory design of rotative engine and only a few of these discussions were conducted by letter, so we have relatively little evidence for either man's contribution to the engine's development, but in January 1782, Boulton wrote to suggest a much simpler arrangement for the sun and planet gear than the one which Watt was intending to patent.[20] He added Boulton's idea, for the simple link shown in Fig. 8.2 to the patent, and this became the standard way of linking the sun and planet gears together on the partners' rotative engines. Accommodating the double acting idea led to the development of the parallel motion, probably Watt's most visually pleasing invention.

The examples provide a good indication that Boulton was contributing significantly to the technical development and exploitation of Watt's ideas for steam engines but this suggestion has only drawn on some letters reproduced in two or three books. Other books and the many letters in the Archives of Soho may well give many more instances of Boulton showing understanding of steam and making contributions to the development of the engines. Some of this investigation would have to be on the assumption that, in the past, the perception of Boulton as technically inept, together with some researchers' limited knowledge of eighteenth-century steam technology, could easily have led to relevant evidence being overlooked.

We can again ask "Why is there a popular perception of Boulton as a businessman with no technical ability?" We can start with something which bedevils anyone working on the history of famous people who were multi-taskers or polymaths. One obtains the impression that the authors of

---

19   Dickinson and Jenkins, *op. cit.*, p.56.
20   Hills, *op. cit.*, Vol.3, p.24.

popular books on innovation want to claim that famous people are famous for just one great contribution. There are many examples such as: Darwin and evolution, Stephenson and railways, Edison and the light bulb and Parsons and steam turbines. The reader can probably think of many more! People seem to become confused when faced with a same person working on another innovation, so Watt was the great steam engineer, but his contribution to the copy press is largely forgotten and Boulton was a splendid businessman, who did not know anything about steam engineering. Many authors have fostered this belief by simplifying the activities of their subject and, for example, some biographies of Watt do not mention the copy press despite its contribution to business systems and the extensive records which survive from the partnership.[21]

Another deeply entrenched idea that has also worked against Boulton's steam engineering ability is the perception that people are either practical or intellectual, businessmen or technologists and thinkers or doers. These distinctions may apply to some people, but there are others whose breadth of ability and aptitude is remarkable and the possibility of their contributing insights in diverse fields should not be underestimated. There is no reason why Boulton the businessman should not have also contributed to steam engineering.

When we look back to some of the great names of the Industrial Revolution, we tend to be influenced by the heroic view of interpreting history which was so beloved by the Victorians. They loved a good story with a simple moral about how to get on in the world or make a contribution.[22] They wished to romanticise "the eureka moment" rather than draw attention to the slow and steady progress towards a great discovery. Thus the role of team work and the process of cooperation, discussion, consensus and evolution of successful ideas were largely ignored compared to the ways in which great men produced individual achievements.

There have been many more books about James Watt than about Matthew Boulton and their authors, influenced by these notions, have felt the need to emphasise Watt's technical genius by playing down his business skills. They have also needed to inject business acumen into the exploitation of the steam engine and have consequently emphasised the contribution of Boulton's

---

21 Boulton funded the setting up of a separate company to produce copy presses and the materials they used, the first commercial document copying process. J.H. Andrew, "The Copying of Engineering Drawings and Documents", *Transactions of the Newcomen Society* 53, 1981–82, pp.1–15. Hills, *op. cit.*, Vol.2, p.190–211.

22 Stories like James Watt watching a lifting kettle lid, irrelevant to his contribution to steam power, or James Brindley as the almost illiterate but self educated man, which is hard to believe when one looks at his achievements, are just two contributions to the confusion about technical developments.

business skills and played down his involvement in technological improvement. It is natural enough for this to happen, sadly the author now realises that he has done this himself, and over many years and many publications that perception takes on a life of its own.[23]

The perception of Boulton as a non-technical man could even be confirmed if his correspondence was examined by someone with knowledge and experience of using steam in more modern engines. It should be explained that in over thirty years since the author became closely associated with early steam engines he has had many conversations with engineers whose knowledge of steam derived from working on much later designs of engines using high pressure steam, modern instrumentation and the established laws of thermodynamics. Life was very different for early steam engineers but they did have an intuitive understanding of some of the things that were going on inside their engines and of what those engines could achieve. Let us look at two examples which have caught out many a modern steam engineer and brought home to the author that they didn't necessarily "know it all".

Watt's engines evolved over several years and most of those designed before the middle of 1778 had no valves between the water in the boiler and the piston in its cylinder. The only way to reduce the power from the engine – to "take your foot off the throttle" we might say – was to reduce the vacuum in the condenser, which was not easy, or reduce the boiler steam pressure by reducing the boiler temperature. Damping down the fire or firing less coal would achieve this and in extreme cases this could produce some interesting effects. John Farey in Rees' *Cyclopaedia* writes of boiler temperatures as low as 185°F or 85°C and this means the boiler was producing steam at below atmospheric pressure.[24] Thus if the boiler failed we would not have an explosion rather the boiler would implode – the reader may have seen a can filled with steam collapse when that steam cools and condenses. This boiler pressure was safe but very confusing for those brought up on the dangers of boiler explosions.

Secondly one of the terms used about pumping engines throughout the time when Watt was designing steam engines was the "load on the piston" which was given in pounds per square inch and seems to refer to the steam pressure applied to the engine. In fact, it is a design characteristic of the engine and pump, which just happens to have the same designation as the steam pressure found in engines and a not dissimilar value from that used at

---

23   Fortunately the author's most specific statement about Watt the engineer and Boulton the business man was in the commentary on a video presentation for display in museums and which was only used for a short time.

24   *Rees' Cyclopaedia* (London, 1816; reprinted Newton Abbot, 1972), p.98 of the reprint.

the time. Paradoxically a low "load on the piston" indicates that a Watt engine was being designed for greater efficiency, something also achievable by using an increased steam pressure. It is easy to see how this could cause confusion.

It takes a long time to understand the eighteenth-century approach to testing, recording and calculating the performance of steam engines. The problem in looking at Boulton's technical reputation is that the details of pressures, temperatures and other data about the engines which he was reporting in his letters to Watt can easily look, to later generations of engineers, as a naïve attempt to be helpful rather than actually giving the information which Watt needed to assess the engine's performance. A parallel would be giving the size and colour of a book, instead of its title and author, to someone seeking that book in a library. In fact Boulton's letters did contain the information which Watt would use, given his understanding of the engines, to judge the benefits of the adjustments and modifications made by Boulton or to carry out calculations on the engine's performance. We can imagine other situations where failure to understand the operation of early Watt engines made Boulton's suggested improvements also appear naïve or based on naïve assumptions about what was happening in the engine. It would not take too many comments on Boulton's apparent failings for authors to dismiss his contribution as that of a technically inept businessman.

The author is quite sure that Boulton could have become established as a competent steam engineer just as he showed other technical abilities in his partnerships in the toy trade, silverware and ormolu manufacturing and minting. Just as Watt's scientific genius overshadowed his business ability, it was Boulton's business skill which overshadowed appreciation of his ability as a steam engineer.

Chapter 9

POWER AT THE SOHO
MANUFACTORY AND MINT

George Demidowicz

I was first attracted to the study the Soho Manufactory about twenty years ago as part of a commission initiated by Stephen Price, then Keeper of Local History at Birmingham Museum, to research water mills and water power in Birmingham.[1] I was intrigued to find that in the nineteenth century a water wheel was still in operation at a place legendary for the production of steam engines under the partnership of Boulton and Watt. It did not take long to discover that the firm of Boulton and Watt was not synonymous with the Soho Manufactory and that the engine works was a latecomer to this illustrious and multi-faceted industrial establishment. Although a number of steam engines were installed at the Manufactory and its offspring, the Soho Mint, even more surprising was the fact that a water wheel probably operated well into the 1840s. The complex was gradually demolished during the 1850s, the classically inspired 'principal building,' featuring in most of the best-known views, being the last to come down in 1863.[2]

This chapter analyses the power systems at the Soho Manufactory and Soho Mint and chronicles their development over a period of roughly a century from the early 1760s to their demise.[3] These two industrial establishments were the physical expression of Matthew Boulton's far ranging scientific, industrial and commercial endeavours. The buildings were part of his landed estate at Handsworth, his personal property to which each of the firms paid a rent for their part of the works (Fig. 9.1). Apart from limitations of space, there is good reason, therefore, to exclude the Soho Foundry from this analysis, since it was not established by Matthew Boulton, but by the

---

1   The information was used to enhance the displays at Sarehole Mill.

2   *Building News,* 2 January 1863.

3   The chapter is based on documentary research, field work and archaeological excavations. A book is forthcoming on the origins, development and decline of the Soho Manufactory, Soho Mint and Soho Foundry. This work should be consulted for details of sources.

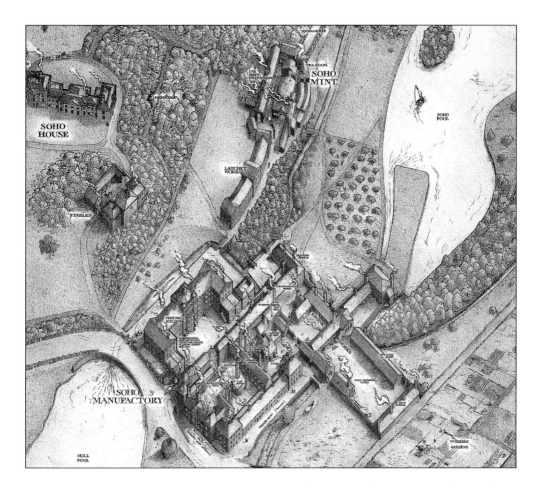

Fig. 9.1. Axonometric of Soho Manufactory and Soho Mint, based on a drawing by George Demidowicz. Copyright Bremner and Orr.

second generation of Boulton and Watt, and in particular James Watt Junior. It should be noted in passing, however, that the Foundry was the first purpose-built steam engine manufactory in the world. Matthew Boulton delivered an eloquent speech at its opening in 1796, but had little involvement in the development of this new enterprise.[4]

The Water Mill

The *Victoria County History* for Birmingham rightly includes the Soho Manufactory in its chapter on water mills.[5] Reference is made to a water wheel

4   *Aris's Birmingham Gazette*, 1 February 1796.

5   *VCH Warwick*, vii (London, 1964), pp.258–9.

in use in 1818, but it suggests that it fell out of use soon after. The life of the Soho water wheel should in fact be extended for perhaps another thirty years. The VCH is however, accurate in its account of the origins of the water mill at Soho.[6] Matthew Boulton needed water power for his toy-making business based at Snow Hill in Birmingham. This was to be used for rolling metal but mainly for polishing finished goods to which water power was not usually applied. In the late 1750s he held a sub-tenancy at Sarehole Mill, but this was insecure and when in 1761 the opportunity arose to take over full control of a newly built mill at Soho, he grasped it immediately. Only four years before, in 1757, Edward Ruston and John Eaves had constructed the mill on Handsworth Heath, but they were willing to assign their lease to Matthew Boulton, perhaps enticed by £1000 that he offered. Boulton quickly knocked down the infant mill in the summer of 1761 and with the help of John Wyatt, the inventor, working on the machinery, a new mill was constructed within a year. The water wheel turned for the first time on 28 August 1761.[7]

The construction of the mill took place within a much bigger building site, which included a warehouse, workshops and a row of workers' houses. The steep bank on which the mill was located for its head of water (here called the 'great bank' for convenience) was to form a prominent topographical feature of the Soho Manufactory complex, even at it maximum extent, dividing it into two main levels. For a few years the Dutch gable of the mill could be seen rising from the 'great bank' on the approach across the heath from the present Soho Road. The imposing classical 'principal building' designed by William Wyatt to house the new silver and plated works, was constructed on the upper level between 1765 and 1767 and obscured the mill from view. All this required a radical reconstruction of the head race to the mill, the first section of which coincided with the new canal fronting the terrace of the 'principal building,' the water then entering a culvert which passed under the new building itself.

The earliest drawings showing the mill were probably produced by Edward Rooker in 1768, the year after the completion of the 'principal building' (Figs. 9.2 and 9.3). An external water wheel can just be discerned on the shadowed long elevation in the view from the front (Fig. 9.2). We know from later evidence that this was about 17ft in diameter. James Watt, when visiting Soho for the first time in 1767, observed that it 'was employed in Laminating metal for buttons, plated goods &c and to turn laps for grinding & polishing steel work.'[8] It is likely that 'laminating' or rolling of metal took

---

6   This was based on S. Shaw, *The History and Antiquities of the County of Stafford*, ii pt.1 (London, 1801), pp.117–19; H.W. Dickinson, *Matthew Boulton*, (Cambridge, 1937), pp.41–44.

7   University of Birmingham Special Collections, Wyatt Papers/20, John Wyatt to [a friend], 29 August 1762.

8   Dickinson, *op. cit.*, p.202; Wyatt Papers, ibid.

Plate 1. Soho House, Handsworth, Birmingham, the home of Matthew Boulton, 1766–1809. The house was progressively expanded and developed during Boulton's lifetime and formed part of a 'polite landscape' close to the Soho Manufactory. The house is smaller in size than it was in Boulton's time and the extensive grounds and manufactory no longer survive. In 1995 it was opened as a museum by Birmingham City Council. Photograph by Mohsen Keiany.

*Plate 2. Matthew Boulton by J.S.C. Schaak, 1770.
Birmingham Museums and Art Gallery.*

Plate 3. Matthew Boulton by C.F. von Breda, 1792.
Birmingham Museums and Art Gallery.

*Plate 4. Matthew Boulton by Sir William Beechey, 1798.
Birmingham Museums and Art Gallery.*

Plate 5. Matthew Boulton by L.F. Abbott, 1797–1801.
Birmingham Museums and Art Gallery.

Plate 6. Boulton and Fothergill: Candle vases, ormolu and green enamel. Height 7.8 inches. Private Collection.

Left: Plate 7. Tortoiseshell box, probably by Boulton and Fothergill or Boulton and Scale, jasper cameo of 'Sportive Venus', impressed 'Wedgwood' on reverse. Height 1 inch, width 2.9 inches. Wedgwood Museum. Right: Plate 8. Jasper cameo 'Hope', impressed 'Wedgwood and Bentley' on reverse. Height 3 inches. Wedgwood Museum.

Plate 9. Boulton and Fothergill: candle vases, ormolu and white marble.
Height 11.4 inches. Private Collection.

Plate 10. Boulton and Fothergill: Pattern Book 1, p.80, drawing for ormolu frames. Archives and Heritage, Central Library, Birmingham.

Plate 11. Jasper cameo 'Socrates', impressed 'Wedgwood' on reverse, set in ormolu frame possibly by Boulton and Fothergill or Boulton and Scale. Height 2.6 inches. Private Collection.

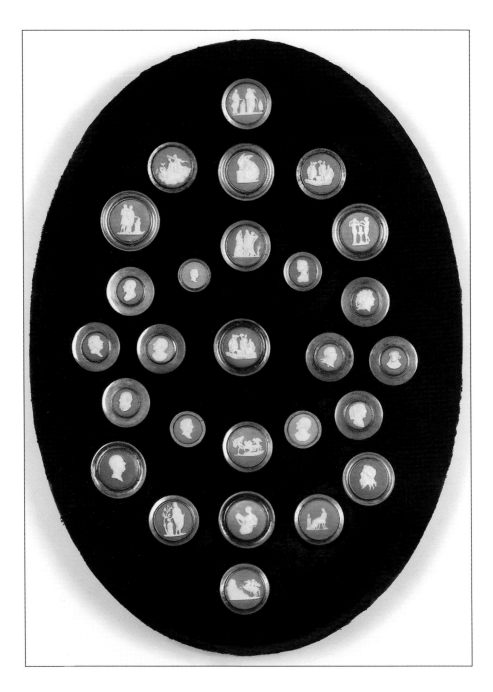

Plate 12. Jasper cameo buttons by Wedgwood set in brass, maker unknown.
Wedgwood Museum.

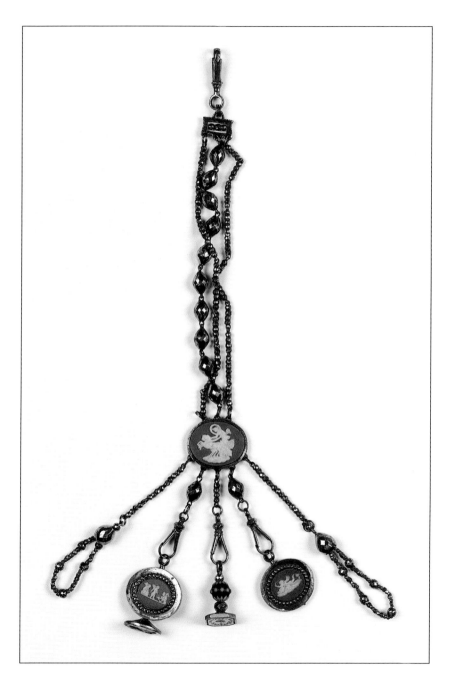

Plate 13. Jasper double-sided cameos by Wedgwood, including Aurora, set in cut steel chatelaine. Height 9.9 inches. Wedgwood Museum.

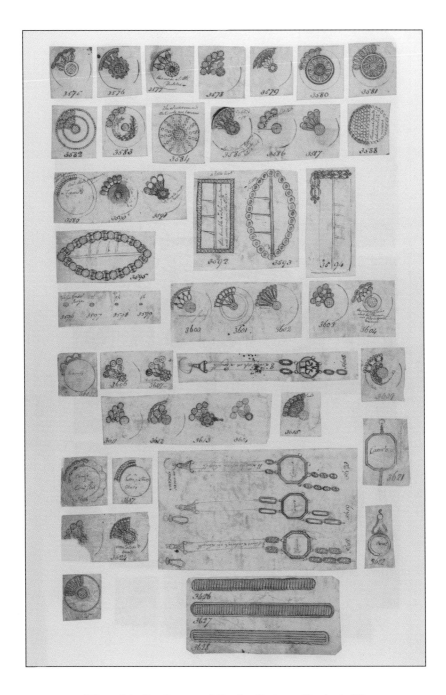

Plate 14. Boulton and Scale: Pattern Book, p.62.
Archives and Heritage, Central Library, Birmingham.

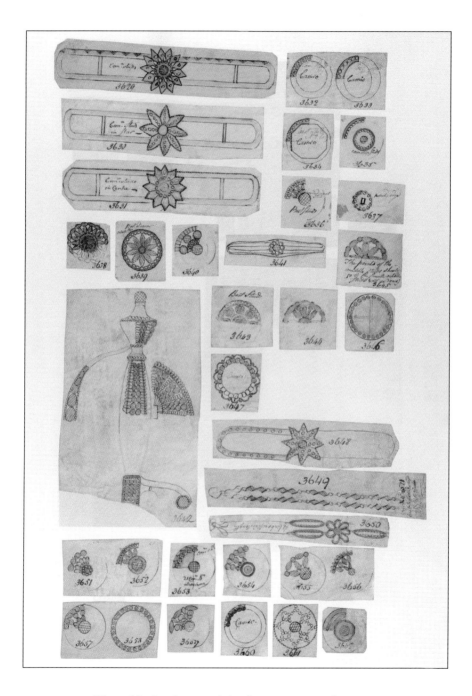

Plate 15. Boulton and Scale: Pattern Book, p.63.
Archives and Heritage, Central Library, Birmingham.

Plate 16. Black basalt intaglios Venus and Cupid and Atlas, impressed 'Wedgwood and Bentley' and '68' and '10' respectively on reverse, set as seals in gilt brass frames, probably by Boden and Smith. Overall depth 1.1 inches. Wedgwood Museum.

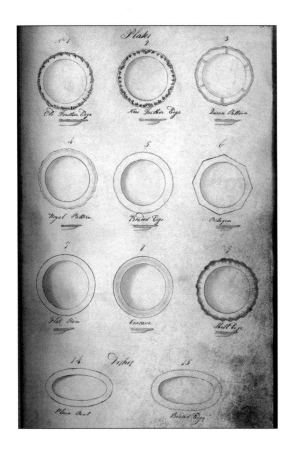

Plate 17. A page from Wedgwood's 'Shape Drawing Book' (1802) showing the principal plate shapes in production in the eighteenth century, including the Royal and Queen's pattern plates and the 'feather' edge. Wedgwood Museum.

Plate 18. The Brasshouse, Broad Street, Birmingham. Currently, the Brasshouse is a restaurant and bar. Formerly, it was the frontage of the Brass House, built in 1781, which manufactured the metal alloy from copper and zinc to avoid the need to transport raw brass from elsewhere. Boulton was one of several businessmen who were part of a consortium to establish the Brass House. The foundry itself no longer survives, but the Brasshouse is one of the few existing buildings in the centre of Birmingham from Boulton's time, which has a direct connection with him. It is described by Andy Foster as the 'finest surviving secular building'[1] of the eighteenth-century town. Photograph by Mohsen Keiany.

[1] Andy Foster, *Birmingham*, Pevsner Architectural Guides (New Haven and London: Yale University Press, 2005), p.154. See also Doreen Hopwood, 'The Brass Industry and Brass Workers in Birmingham', section 6 of http://www.search.revolutionaryplayers.org.uk/engine/resource/exhibition/standard/default. asp?resource=2022.

Plate 19. Statue in Broad Street, Birmingham of, from left to right: William Murdock (1754–1839), Matthew Boulton, (1729–1809) and James Watt (1736–1819), by James Bloye (1956). The three colleagues are portrayed in a 'conversation piece', examining mechanical drawings. The statue represents the collective nature of scientific and technical development in late eighteenth-century industrial Britain, but it also indicates the different social status of the three men. Boulton, the captain of industry, is directing the scene through his assertive gestures and confident gaze. He wears a wig and is the most elaborately dressed of the trio.

The bareheaded inventor, Watt, points to the plans whilst Murdock, the artisan engineer, also bareheaded, bows his head and listens. Photograph by Simon Russell.

Plate 20. Commemorative copper or bronze medallion of Matthew Boulton produced after his death in 1809. The obverse shows a bust of Boulton with two cherubs, one holding a lighted torch and the other holding a branch of laurel leaves above a representation of the Soho Manufactory. Boulton's scientific interests are indicated by the initials F.R.S., Fellow of the Royal Society, after his name. The reverse contains several lines in praise of Boulton. The Birmingham Assay Office.

Figs. 9.2. and 9.3. Views of the Soho Manufactory from the front and the rear c.1768. The water mill (circled) has a Dutch gable. Archives and Heritage, Central Library, Birmingham.

on the ground floor, the rolls needing a solid foundation, whilst polishing was housed on the first floor. The laps or polishers were driven by leather belts attached to drums in a room on the opposite side of the wheel to the metal rolls. It must be stressed, however, that most of the industrial processes that took place in the Manufactory were accomplished by hand or by hand-operated machines such as stamps and presses.

The power supplied by water mills was prone to variation caused principally by extremes of weather. Drought could bring the water wheel to a stop and floods could destroy not only the wheel and its associated structures, but also the mill leats and dam. Boulton suffered shortages of water in the summer of 1763, 1764 and 1765 and at times horses were used to drive a gin, connected directly to the wheel. Boulton could not afford these interruptions to production in his hugely expanded manufactory which needed a high and sustained level of fulfilled orders to provide a return on the huge investment in buildings and machinery. It is worth speculating whether Boulton would have become involved in steam engine production had his mill been assured of a more copious and reliable flow of water. Immediately below the Manufactory he could see his spent mill water filling Great Hockley Pool, itself used to supplement the supply to Aston Furnace farther downstream. His solution to the wastage was to intercept the outflow and return the water to the mill with the aid of a steam engine attached to a pump. Matthew Boulton's far-reaching antennae detected that a Scotsman, James Watt, was working on much improved steam engine using an independent condenser. Boulton's genius was to perceive both a solution to an immediate problem, but also to recognise the commercial opportunities of a brand new invention. Newcomen engines were used mainly to pump water out of coal and tin mines, but they were inefficient and Boulton could see himself selling Watt's engines to a world eager to reduce its coal bill.

The Watt Pumping Engine

The extrovert, Boulton, finally met the introvert, Watt, at Soho in the late summer of 1768, unlikely partners on the face of it, but the event should be seen as one of the great conjunctures of industrial history.[9] It was not until 1773, however, that Watt's first full-sized engine was shipped from Kinneil in Scotland to Soho. It was not assembled until the following year when Watt himself arrived on 31 May 1774 to settle permanently at Soho.[10] Boulton was anxious that the engine quickly paid its way and it was set up on the 'great bank' and an engine house constructed in the summer and autumn of 1774. Significant expenditure on waterworks was needed as a new culvert was constructed from the mill tail race to the base of the engine house. The engine with a cylinder 18in diameter and a stroke of 5ft lifted water at fourteen to fifteen strokes a minute from the culvert to the top of the 'great bank', a height of 24ft. From here a short section of new channel was constructed to connect with the canal on the Manufactory frontage and the circuit was completed to recycle Soho Mill's water (Fig. 9.4). In short the first working James Watt engine in the world had come to the aid of a water mill. Although tail race water was intercepted by the new engine, much water would still have by-passed the system if it were not contained before entering Hockley Pool. Accordingly a new upper reservoir was built on land that Boulton jointly purchased through the firm of Boulton and Fothergill, the main partnership at the Manufactory. The new dam followed the contour at the tail end of the now lower Hockley Pool.

In 1777 the original 18in cylinder was replaced by a 33in cylinder working on the expansive principle. It was originally called 'Beelzebub' from its jerky and violent action. A fire erupted in the engine house in July 1778, but the engine survived the flames. The considerable reconstruction that followed allowed a better fit and the larger engine appears to have worked more satisfactorily, eventually known more affectionately as 'Old Bess'. She certainly earned her keep as she remained in service, tied inexorably with the

9   Other ingredients were needed to complete the conjuncture such as the withdrawal of John Roebuck's, Watt's principal financial backer. This was caused by his losses in the trade depression of 1772–3.

10   See H.W. Dickinson and R. Jenkins, *James Watt and the Steam Engine*, (London, 1927), pp.108–111 on the early days of the engine at Soho and the experiments that were conducted on it to make it work. Richard Hills has published a comprehensive three volume biography of James Watt published by Landmark (2002–2006).

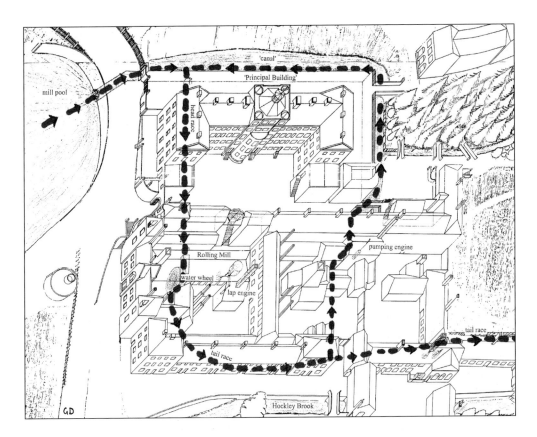

Fig. 9.4. Axonometric of Soho Manufactory showing water circulation system and position of steam engines. Drawing by the author.

working of the water wheel, until the late 1840s. Today Old Bess can be seen on display in the Science Museum at South Kensington.[11]

Rebuilding the mill, 1785

Despite the successful application of rotary motion to the Boulton and Watt engine in the early 1780s, the decision was made in 1785 to rebuild the mill using water power alone. The worn out structure and machinery were demolished and the new building was constructed at right angles to the old site on a footprint over two and a half times greater than the old mill. Although

---

11 The engine was sold as part of the Soho Mint sale on 29 April 1850, Birmingham Archives and Heritage (BAH), MS 3147/10/74. It passed eventually to Samuel Walker, a metal roller who set it up on an island in his mill pool mill at Heath Mill, Deritend (mistakenly given as Derrington Pool in the sources). Mr Walker later sold it to Messrs Branson and Gwythens's Builders of Birmingham, who subsequently presented it to the Commissioners of Patents for the Patent Museum, situated in part of the original Science Museum, the 'Brompton Boiler.' (Dickinson and Jenkins, *op. cit.*, p.123.

metal rolling was to figure more prominently, 'the greater part [of the power] was employed to turn the grinding and polishing Laps with other Machinery belonging to the Steel and Plated Manufactories.'[12] The construction of Boulton's new power house was aided by a young John Rennie, who soon after established a reputation as an engineer in his own right.

The new water wheel was installed in roughly the same position as earlier but was made 3ft wider in diameter (20ft) and placed internally within the centre of the building. It powered a rolling mill on the north-west side and two pairs of drums on the south-east side, connected via leather belts to the laps on the floor above. As the mill neared completion during the summer of 1786, Boulton's mind had already turned to the production of coinage and he obtained a contract to supply copper blanks to the East India Company. Boulton was determined to secure the prestigious contract for the national coinage but with a difference that reflected his panache and innovative drive. He would be the first to make coins with machinery powered by steam engines. As a consequence the coins would be made more rapidly, be more consistent in quality and size and, and with Soho good taste and craftsmanship, beautifully designed. This innovation, however, would not be feasible without significantly increasing the capacity of his rolling mill and the quality of production of copper sheet.

Steam Power at the Soho Mill, 1788
Early in 1788 Boulton began constructing a mint on a separate site about 120 yards (110m) away from the main Manufactory complex. At the same time he planned another rebuilding of his mill. No longer would it primarily serve his button and plated ware business, but from now on be applied mainly to the task of rolling out into thin sheets the raw material received from the Parys mines in Anglesey, copper 'cake'. In the same room the finely rolled sheets would then be cut into strips for the next stage in coining-cutting out blanks. The 20ft diameter water wheel was not capable of running the powerful train of rolls required and, at the same time, the polishing laps at the other end of the mill. There was much discussion on how to solve the problem with John Rennie providing drawings and estimates. By July 1788 it had been decided that the water wheel would be dedicated to powering the rolls alone, whilst a steam engine was to be erected at the end of the lapping mill to drive the polishing wheels. In the summer and autumn of 1788 the lap engine house was constructed, increasing the size of the mill by approximately 40%, more than would be

---

12   BAH, MS 3782/13/49/124, Memoir of John Rennie 1823. It is not well known that Boulton leased Holford Mill on the Tame from the mid 1760s to 1781 to provide additional rolling mill capacity.

expected in an already large building. The reason for this was that the additional power provided by the new steam engine was also transmitted to an eight place cutting-out press arranged in a circle and positioned on the first floor adjacent to the rocking beam of the engine. Despite the extra size of the engine house, space was at a premium and around 1790–91 the boiler was removed and placed in an adjacent lean-to building.

The engine itself was double-acting (i.e. capable of power in both the up-and-down stroke) with an 18-inch cylinder manufactured by the Wilkinson brothers at Bersham, Shropshire. It was the only rotary steam engine to be erected in the mill at Soho, following many experiments carried out in 1782–3 with other engines applied to tilt hammers and corn grinding machinery; it was the first to use a centrifugal governor, already familiar in water mills, to regulate the speed. The engine was to remain at work until the late 1840s and also eventually found its way to the Science Museum, South Kensington, where it forms an important part of the display of early rotative engines. Strictly speaking, it should be called the 'Lap and Cutting-out Engine', although the cutting-out presses were removed in 1824 and sent to the new Bombay mint, the reason for which is explained below.

The Soho Mint

Despite Boulton's intense effort in lobbying for the national coinage contract, he was initially unsuccessful. He had, however, committed himself to building a mint, consisting of a coining room and an engine house, and which was hidden, for secrecy, amongst his menagerie and other garden buildings. Early ideas for placing the coining presses in parallel rows were abandoned and by November 1788 a circular arrangement had been adopted, which was also used for the cutting-out presses in the Lap Engine house (see above). Many of the engineers at Soho were involved in developing the machinery, including James Watt, John Southern and James Lawson and a patent was applied for in 1790 for which the drawings were made of the actual Soho machinery installed.[13] The presses were not directly steam powered, but the steam engine with its 16in cylinder, the third rotary engine to be installed at Soho, drove via a 'sun-and-planet crank' a horizontal and then a vertical shaft. The latter turned a horizontal wheel with curved cams that engaged with pins on each of the fly arms of the eight coining presses. Each of the fly arms in turn were connected to a vacuum pump and the revolving of the cam wheel first forced the piston up the cylinders, inducing a vacuum, and then a sudden release, imparting energy to the fly which revolved the screw of the press downwards.

---

13   Dickinson, *op. cit.*, fig. 5, 141, Patent 8 July 1790, no 1757.

Boulton had developed the first stream-powered mint in the world, constructed at considerable expense, but was forced to seek private coining contracts in the early 1790s. It was to be another decade before Soho could impress the national coinage.

The Engine Works

It must be stressed that when Boulton and Watt began selling their patented steam engine in 1776, on offer was an idea or an advantage (gained by using less coal) rather than a piece of hardware. The Soho Manufactory was not immediately extended as an engine works, for the decision was made to act as agents for Watt's invention rather than manufacturing and supplying a complete engine. This had to wait another twenty years until the foundation of the Soho Foundry. Purchasers of Boulton and Watt engine licenses had to find other manufacturers to produce the parts required, the most notable being the Wilkinson brothers in Shropshire, who supplied the engine cylinders.

The engine works at Soho was initially therefore a modest establishment concentrating on making only specialist parts such as valves. By late 1782 there were only two purpose-built workshops (a forge and a fitting shop) arranged at right angles to one another and with no power. It was here, however, that experiments in applying rotary motion to a number of steam engines took place. The distinctive Boulton and Watt 'sun-and planet crank' observed by John Scale, manager of the button works, newly working on 11 November 1782, was probably attached to a double 15in cylinder arrangement.[14] The engines were most likely positioned at the junction of the two workshops and an engine house was constructed for a new 18-inch engine in late 1782, connecting all together. Early in 1783 the 18-inch engine was attached to corn milling machinery, and these experiments led directly to the establishment in 1785–6 of the largest commercial steam-powered corn mill at that time near Blackfriars Bridge, London. After the extensive trials were completed, a 15in cylinder engine, perhaps part of the experimental double cylinder, was eventually installed to run lathes and drills in the two workshops and the engine works became powered for the first time. By 1790 the forge had moved to a new workshop on the south-east side of the engine house, so that three shops now projected from it.

The New Engine Yard 1801–1804

Following the construction of the Soho Foundry in 1795–6 it was decided to extend considerably the engine works at the Manufactory in order to

---

14   BAH, MS 3782/12/72/46, letter John Scale to Matthew Boulton.

produce more engines, particularly smaller sizes for which demand was quickly rising. By this time both Matthew Boulton and James Watt had withdrawn from active involvement in the engine business and their sons, Matthew Robinson Boulton and James Watt Jr, were effectively running the new firm of Boulton, Watt and Company. As the Manufactory formed part of Matthew Boulton's private estate, Matthew Robinson took charge of the design and construction of the new engine yard at the Manufactory. This was extended across the Hockley Brook, which was culverted, and for the first time part of the Manufactory found itself in Birmingham parish. The engine house was stripped of its 15in cylinder engine and its machinery, which included in a complicated array of two lathes in the same room, and more lathes and two drills in the adjoining shops.

Of most significance was the contribution of William Murdock to the design of the new engines. He had returned from Cornwall in 1797, where he had erected many engines in the tin mines, and solved the problems of vibration that bedevilled the Boring Mill at the Foundry. Part of the solution was to use small engines running lathes and boring machines independently preventing any single engine becoming overloaded with too many functions. William Murdock had invented two types of beamless engine, a bell-crank engine and a table top engine, the latter made more famous by Henry Maudslay who patented a similar design in 1807.[15] Two table-top engines were installed in 1803–4, the first of 1hp running the piston rod lathe, which was moved out of the engine house and the other of 3hp connected to a lathe that remained in the room. The bell-crank engine boasting 6hp was distinctive, aside from the pair of bell cranks transmitting motion to the crankshaft, for the cylinder sat directly on a solid rectangular cast iron block acting as a cistern. It powered machinery in a new workshop in the 'Birmingham' yard so that the reconfigured engine house now stood at the centre of a cross of workshops. Well over a hundred bell-crank engines were to be sold before 1814, many to the West Indies sugar plantations.

The New Mint 1798–9
Private coinage business was insufficient to keep the mint in operation and Boulton decided to enter a partnership with the Smith brothers, James and Benjamin, to make a patent flexible buckle called a 'latchet', which could be transferred from shoe to shoe. The Latchet Company took over the underused mint workshops, themselves extended in 1791, but a new works were erected on a site between the Mint and the Manufactory, known as the Crescent building. It was only partially constructed as originally conceived – the south

---

15   H.W. Dickinson, *A Short History of the Steam Engine* (Cambridge, 1938), pp.109–110.

Fig. 9.5. Eginton view of Manufactory c.1800 showing 'Latchet' or Crescent building (partly obscured by tree trunk) in S. Shaw, Staffordshire, Vol.II, Plate 17.

crescent wing in 1794 and the central three-storey bay in 1798. The north wing had to wait until 1824–6, although most drawings of the Manufactory frontage show the scheme as if completed (Fig. 9.5). The Crescent building was not to have any powered machinery for thirty years (see below).

Despite having been diverted to making patent buckles, the indefatigable Boulton did not give up petitioning for the national coinage and was finally rewarded for his persistence with a contract signed on 9 June 1797 for 500 tons, the vast majority of which were penny pieces. The intermittent use of the presses in the years previously had demonstrated that the 1790 patent machinery was not up to the task. The massive and high frequency recoil in eight screw presses in close proximity to one another was capable of shaking to pieces both the circular frame that contained them and the working gears. John Southern, head of the engine works drawing office and an accomplished engineer, suggested an entirely different arrangement and in January 1798 Matthew Boulton agreed his plan 'for working of Coining Presses by means of a partial vacuum.'[16] The steam engine would no longer drive any mechanical shafts, cogs and cam wheels for its duty henceforth was induce a partial vacuum in a long tube running parallel to presses now arranged in a line. There was a piston and cylinder for each press, attached to the top of the vacuum tube. The piston was connected by vertical and then horizontal levers to a hollow elongated 'trumpet' attached to the top of the

16   BAH, MS 3782/13/120 folder 3, copy letter 17 January 1798, Matthew Boulton to John Southern.

screw and weighted fly of the press. Using the expansion of air let into a partial vacuum below and atmospheric pressure above, the sudden motion of the piston downwards imparted motion to the screw. A heavy balanced beam above, connected to the screw at one end and another small cylinder and piston on the other, helped return the screw to the upper position and reduce the violence of the recoil.

Not only was the machinery radically altered, but the existing mint coining room and engine house were abandoned. In the latter part of 1798 and during 1799 a new coining room was constructed below and adjacent to them on the site of former menagerie pens, following the contour of the hill slope on which they were located. As a consequence the eight presses were arranged in a slight curve. A new 23in beam engine was erected in an existing workshop replacing the ten-year-old 16in steam engine. The vacuum pipe was not directly linked to this engine, but via another tilting beam attached to the beam of the steam engine, both moving in unison. The rotary capabilities of the engine were, therefore, not the principal requirement and it is not clear if indeed they were exploited at all. During the experiments with the new machinery and the reconstruction period, Boulton's patience was tested to the limit. For much of the time he was in London renegotiating a larger contract with more denominations. It was to until 1 May 1799 that the eight presses in the new coining room worked together for the first time on the production of the nation's pennies. Boulton's ambition of producing a high quality coinage of the realm had at long last been fulfilled. By the end of 1799 his new presses had delivered 1818 tons of coinage, an unprecedented rate of production.

Power in 1805

By 1805 the Manufactory had more or less reached its maximum extent as illustrated in Fig. 9.1. The steam engines at work were as follows:

- ROTARY ENGINES
  The lap and cutting out engine in the mill (c.10hp, 18in cylinder)
  Small table top engine (1hp) in the engine works
  Small table top engine (3hp) in the engine works
  Small bell-crank engine (6hp) in the engine works

- PUMPING ENGINE
  'Old Bess' lifting water from the tail race to the canal and head race (30hp, 33in cylinder).

The Mint operated with one engine (c.20hp, 23in cylinder) using its beam to pump a vacuum. A redundant 16-inch engine remained in the old engine house to pump water onto the Soho House gardens. Little change took place to the power units during the remaining history of the Manufactory, a period of over 50 years. The lack of modernisation during a time in which steam engines considerably improved their output and efficiency was one of the factors in the decline of the works and their ultimate demise.

The Engine works
In 1815 the 6hp bell-crank engine in the engine works was replaced by a 14hp beam engine, a popular Boulton and Watt model. It was an elegant looking machine with an integral cast iron frame consisting of six Doric columns standing on a tall classical plinth and surmounted by a classical entablature. At Soho, art and industry happily cohabited. After 1820 the engine works concentrated on the production of marine engines, which became an important part of the Boulton and Watt business. In 1831–2 the original Murdock 1hp and 3hp table top engines were replaced by two 3hp units running lathes and drills as previously. These three engines were removed to the Soho Foundry when Manufactory engine works were demolished in about 1853. James Watt Jr. had died in 1848 and with him the firm of Boulton and Watt. The new firm that took over, James Watt and Co, had no Boulton or Watt family connection and one of its first decisions was to abandon the Manufactory site and consolidate production at the Foundry in Smethwick.

The Plated and Button works
The button business, later known as the steel trade, had been the principal user of the laps in the mill, but demand for these had declined from the beginning of the nineteenth century when up to 32 laps and a brushing machine were available for use. From about 1794 to 1807 the Latchet Company (dissolved c.1808–9) took over part of the lapping mill for a glass grinding shop, which it shared with the Boulton Plate Company. In 1834 the latter was sold by Matthew Robinson Boulton, adopted the name the Soho Plate Company, and immediately undertook a major overhaul of the lap engine. The plated company vacated Soho in 1850, and in 1852 its premises were taken over by James Toy and Son, manufacturers of metal bedsteads, gas chandeliers and general brass founders. They installed the last steam engine at Soho, housed in a large lean-to in the yard at the rear of the 'principal building.' This was a horizontal Boulton and Watt engine originally intended for the London, Croydon and Epsom Railway, a bold but ultimately

unsuccessful venture.[17] James Toy and Son traded for only about ten years, moving to new premises in Spring Hill in 1862. Within the year there were no buildings left standing at Soho.

The Rolling Mill

The rolling mill continued to be used principally by the Mint business with the plated company as a customer for rolled metal sheet. During the late 1820s, 1830s and 1840s extensive repairs were carried out to water wheel, the rolling mill and the pumping engine and it is clear that water and steam power were still interdependent.

In 1850 the Mint plant and equipment were sold by Matthew Piers Watt Boulton, grandson of Matthew Boulton, and the main demand on the rolling mill was extinguished. His father, Matthew Robinson, had died in 1842 and it was clear that this third generation Boulton did not share the family enthusiasm for running a mechanised coining business. The pumping engine was disposed off with all the other machinery and, although the water wheel was also offered for sale, it may not have found a buyer.[18]

In January 1853, Frederick Jenks, a *papier-mâché* maker, took a lease of the rolling mill with the lap engine, now the only source of power. The water wheel had probably already been removed, for early in 1853 the mill pool was permanently drained. The lap engine worked for approximately another five years, contributing to a total operating life of seventy years from its original installation in 1788. It is fortunate that in about 1858 this venerable workhorse was rescued and removed to the Science Museum in London.[19] Its historical importance in the development of steam engines in general and as the earliest surviving Boulton and Watt rotary engine had fortunately been recognised.

The Mint after 1805

Unlike the Manufactory, where the power systems essentially fossilised after 1805, the Mint underwent a major reorganisation between 1824 and 1826 under the direction of Matthew Robinson Boulton. This not only involved a change of engine but also a radical reconstruction of the buildings and a concomitant rearrangement of the power transmission systems. Doty has claimed that the new Mint was erected in the hope of an eventual sale to Gran

---

17   BAH, B&W Catalogue of Old Engines by Henry Hazelton 272–3; MS 3147/5/674; MS 3147/3/135 f.528, letter J.W. & Co to Alfred Toye, 16 September 1852; MS 3147/4/12, 25 September 1858; the 'atmospheric' railway was to be powered by a vacuum tube laid along the track pumped by a series of steam engines.

18   See note 11 above.

19   S. Smiles, *Lives of the Engineers Boulton and Watt* (London 1902), pp.298–99.

Columbia in South America.[20] The nature and extent of the work, however, strongly suggests that the new Soho facility was not a temporary holding place before export. Matthew Robinson wished to improve the Soho Mint for his own needs of production, a reorganisation which he himself stated that he had 'long contemplated.'[21]

The 'production line' for making coins at Soho had not been ideal, despite its revolutionary technology, with the rolling of copper sheet carried out at some distance in the Manufactory mill along with cutting out of blanks. Matthew Robinson decided to move the cutting out presses nearer to Mint by installing a new set of six machines in the traditional circular arrangement in the former Latchet works. A drive shaft was installed below ground to connect the cutting out presses to a new steam engine in the main Mint complex. The length of the drive shaft tunnel was about 200ft (61m). The new cutting out room was high and spacious, occupying the trapezoidal three-storey bay of the Crescent building, from which the floors had been removed. The Crescent was finally completed as originally intended with a second storey added to a makeshift north wing, so that the new cutting out room found itself in the centre of a symmetrical building (Fig. 9.1). With the power shaft passing under the south wing, the opportunity was taken to install other mint machinery on the ground floor. Power was transmitted from the underground drive shaft via pulleys and leather belts.

At the Mint itself, the machinery that had produced the national coinage in 1799–1800 was sold and transported to Bombay in 1824. A new 10hp engine with a 19¾in cylinder, the third to be used at the Mint, was installed in an existing room on the north-east side of the 1798 engine. It needed to be closer to a narrow yard that penetrated deep into the Mint complex, the course chosen for part of the drive shaft tunnel. The eight-press coining room was demolished and replaced with a new four-press facility relocated on the site of the original 1788 coining room. The structure was radically rebuilt and widened to accommodate the very different machinery. A shorter and now straight vacuum pipe was installed between the presses and the external wall to the narrow yard. The new engine no longer required a second pivoting beam to do its work, but transferred its power to the two cylinders evacuating the vacuum pipe by rotary motion via a main axle, cranks and levers. The same axle turned a 5ft-diameter pulley connected by 56 feet of leather strap to a 3ft pulley fixed to the underground drive shaft below the yard. This extensive work was completed by mid 1826, but it appears that the presses were not fitted up to impress coinage until 1830 and initially only coin blanks were produced.

20   R. Doty, *The Soho Mint and the Industrialization of Money* (London 1998), pp.65–66.
21   BAH, MS 3782/3/138, letter MRB to J. Moseley, 23 January 1826.

This major rebuilding and re-equipping project is well documented, although no plans survive and the course of the underground drive shaft tunnel can only be surmised. Was the reorganisation in fact implemented as so meticulously planned? In 1996 the Channel 4 'Time Team' programme, after some persuasion, agreed to their first industrial archaeological dig – to rediscover the Soho Mint in the back gardens of Handsworth. As a result of these excavations the working hypothesis on the layout of the power transmission system was confirmed. Parts of the drive shaft tunnel were uncovered: firstly, in the former narrow Mint yard at the junction with the steam engine where the 3ft pulley that turned the long cast iron shaft was firmly fixed to bearings on massive sandstone blocks (Fig. 9.6) and secondly, where the tunnel entered the southern bay of the old Latchet building. A small fragment of the cutting out room was also found under the slabs of a garden patio. As excavations progressed, it became clear that much of the main Mint complex had been destroyed by excavations for building sand in the early twentieth century.

Fig. 9.6. Soho Mint drive shaft tunnel c. 1824-6 excavated 1996. The stone blocks in the middle distance supported the pulley connected to the steam engine. Author's photograph.

In the early 1850s, following the sale of the Soho Mint plant and machinery, the buildings themselves had been gradually brought down to the ground. This demolition accompanied that of the engine works and culminated in the tragic loss of the 'principal building' in early 1863, the last building on the site. An industrial complex of national significance, founded only a century earlier by Matthew Boulton, had been finally eradicated. It is fortunate, however, that the below-ground remains of industrial buildings and their power systems have been proved to be deep and robust and more await rediscovery in the future, as parts of the site come up for redevelopment.

Acknowledgements
I would like to thank Toni Demidowicz for reading the manuscript and Fiona Tait for help with updating references.

Chapter 10

'I ALMOST WISH TO BE A POTTER': MATTHEW BOULTON'S RELATIONSHIP WITH JOSIAH WEDGWOOD

Nicholas Goodison

The purpose of this chapter is to record the ways in which Matthew Boulton, metal manufacturer extraordinary, sought to capitalise on Josiah Wedgwood's expertise in the production of vases, cameos and intaglios, and acted as a merchant for the export of Wedgwood's 'useful' wares.

Friends and businessmen

Born only two years apart, Boulton and Wedgwood became two of the most notable businessmen of their age. They both built large manufactories on new sites, and took big financial risks in doing so. They married wives whose fortunes eased their stretched finances. Both sought to profit in the late 1760s from the new fashion for the 'antique taste' and the craze for vases that accompanied it. They set about selling their fashionable wares to the nobility and gentry in similar ways. Their manufactories were renowned destinations for tourists. They used the same range of contacts, including factors, agents and ambassadors, to generate exports. From time to time they supplied each other with goods. They cooperated over investment in canals, in Cornish mines and the Cornish Metal Company, in scientific experiments (they were both members of the Lunar Society), and over such political projects as trade with Ireland and elsewhere and the abolition of the slave trade. Both became Fellows of the Royal Society. They were close friends.

It is not clear how they first met. The earliest archival evidence of contact between them is a letter from Wedgwood in the autumn of 1766 acknowledging a 'draft on the Navigation account' which Boulton had sent him.[1] This refers to the financing of the Trent and Mersey Canal (also called the Grand Trunk), which Wedgwood had tirelessly promoted from 1764 and which Parliament had approved in April 1766. Wedgwood was the Treasurer. Boulton was one of the many subscribers. Wedgwood's interest in building the canal was acutely personal. The proposed route lay through the land that he acquired for his new Etruria factory, which would stand on the bank of the canal.[2]

Wedgwood first visited Boulton's factory and home at Soho in May 1767.[3] He wrote to his partner Thomas Bentley that Boulton was 'the most complete manufacturer in England in metal' and that he was 'very ingenious, philosophical and agreeable.' He was impressed by Boulton's willingness to offer him 'every improvement' that he might need in developing his business.[4] After his first visit to Soho, Wedgwood sent some vases to Boulton. They were a token of friendship that Boulton eagerly accepted: '... my wife returns you a thousand thanks. She admires your vases very much & indeed so do I, even so much that I almost wish to be a potter...'[5] In March 1768 Wedgwood stayed at Soho. He wrote afterwards to

---

MBP signifies the Matthew Boulton Papers in the Archives and Heritage section of Birmingham Central Library, WMA the Wedgwood Museum Archives, MB Matthew Boulton, JW Josiah Wedgwood, TB Thomas Bentley, B and F Boulton and Fothergill, and B and S Boulton and Scales.

1 MBP, 3782/12/81/32, JW to MB, 11 October 1766.
2 See Robin Reilly, *Josiah Wedgwood* (London, 1992), pp.56–8 and pp.66ff. The Bill authorising the canal was passed by Parliament on 21 April 1766. By the summer of the following year Boulton preferred to concentrate on his investment in 'the Birmingham navigation', which was as close to his own interests as the Grand Trunk was to Wedgwood's. He was happy to sell his Grand Trunk shares if Wedgwood became aware of a buyer at par, having only subscribed to show his 'approbation of so great and good a scheme' (MBP, 3782/12/1 MB to JW, 10 July 1767). Canals were the key to better transport both for raw materials and for finished goods, along with the simultaneous development of better roads through Turnpike Trusts. The reductions of raw material costs that canal transport brought about were in many cases dramatic, and exports through ports such as Liverpool and Hull were greatly increased. For Wedgwood's promotion of the Grand Trunk, see Robert Schofield *The Lunar Society of Birmingham* (1963), pp.39–42, Robin Reilly, *Josiah Wedgwood op. cit.*, pp.49–57.
3 'Register Book' (Tew Park MSS), 14 May 1767: 'Mr Wedgwood, Potter to her Majesty at Baselom [i.e. Burslem]'. The Register Book was a record of visitors to the Soho Manufactory.
4 WMA 18147–25, JW to TB, 23 May 1767. He says the same of the leading Birmingham manufacturer John Taylor but thinks that Boulton is far the more spirited of the two. Boulton would have liked to hear it.
5 MBP, 3782/12/1, p.4 onwards, MB to JW, 10 July 1767. Three and a half years later Wedgwood wrote to Bentley (WMA 18336–25, the letter is undated but was written in January 1771) expressing a sense of 'disgrace at Mr Bolton's from some of my first vases which I made him a present of' because they did not stand up as worthy specimens against the vases made at Soho, and he feared the 'odious comparisons they must give rise to.' The vases were 'two middle-size Chetwynd vases and 2 Orfords creamcolour, engine lathed and gilt, such as you have now stowed in the garret out of the way, and such a situation Mrs Boulton has promised me for hers when we send them better.' He offered to replace them with painted Etruscan vases. Four were needed for the chimneypiece and he asked Bentley to send them from London as soon as possible.

thank Boulton and his 'good lady for the genteel treatment and hospitality I ever meet with at Soho'.[6] Later letters continue in this strain. They show that the two men enjoyed each other's company, rivalled each other with their hospitality,[7] and expressed mutual concerns at each other's health. The tone of their correspondence for the next twenty years was one of constant admiration and friendship.

Not surprisingly they sometimes bought things from each other for their personal use. In the early years of their friendship Boulton and his wife Anne bought quantities of china-ware,[8] including a pair of 'each of all the eliggant Etruscan ones [i.e. vases] for my cabinet, I being impatient as a child for them.'[9] He placed some Etruscan vases on his chimneypiece, which prompted Wedgwood to comment that he was 'proud of the honour you do them.'[10] Later, it is highly likely, but not proven by any archival reference, that he bought other black basalt wares including a library bust of Venus, an oval plaque of a portrait of Louis XIV, and an oval jasperware plaque of a piping faun, modelled by John Flaxman in 1776.[11] Later still he bought ceramic pans and other equipment for his collection of fossils.[12]

There is no evidence that Wedgwood bought any of Boulton's vases, but he was impressed by Boulton's range of products. He wrote to his partner Thomas Bentley after a visit to Soho in 1772 of Boulton's 'superb gallery in which there is a great many good things of his manufacture beside the vases', and he bought four plated candlesticks to give to Bentley.[13] He bought a set of buttons for himself.[14] The archives record other purchases from time to time. He ordered urn-shaped knife cases in 1780,[15] having admired examples

---

6   MBP, 3782/1/81/35, JW to MB, 19 March 1768. Two months later Wedgwood had his right leg amputated. It seems inconceivable that Boulton did not write to express his sympathy and good wishes, but no letters appear to survive.

7   MBP, 3782/12/81/37, JW to MB, 19 February 1771, in which Wedgwood hopes that Boulton will come to Etruria with his wife and 'the infantry', i.e. Boulton's two children. 'We shall have room enough if we can once get into our new habitation.'

8   MBP, 3782/12/81/34, JW to MB, 24 August 1767; MBP, 3782/12/81/36, JW to MB, 24 March 1768.

9   MBP, 3782/12/2, p.4, MB to JW, 28 December 1768.

10   MBP, 3782/12/81/37, JW to MB, 19 February 1771.

11   Christie's sale of objects at Tew Park, 27–29 May 1987, Lots 658, 659 and 660. The bust of Venus was based on the Medici Venus.

12   MBP, 3782/12/81/39, Invoice dated 29 May 1781; MBP, 3782/12/81/40, JW (Peter Swift) to MB, 26 May 1782; MBP, 3782/12/8/41, JW (William Cox) to MB, 27 May 1782.

13   WMA 18380–25, JW to TB, 13 July 1772.

14   WMA, 18383–25, JW to TB, 29 July 1772. They were delivered with the candlesticks he had bought for Bentley, and Wedgwood asked his partner to forward them 'immediately or I shall be ruined in losing the opportunity of shewing away with them this summer.' Boulton and Scale sent a further invoice for 30 'fine steel coat buttons' in 1786 (WMA 4736–4, 24 January 1786).

15   MBP, 3782/1/11, p.611, B&F to JW, 18 July 1780 and p.629, 28 August 1780.

that he had seen when he visited Soho four years earlier,[16] and he bought some silverware in 1782.[17]

The two men's incipient friendship suffered a bit of a hiccough when Boulton aired that thought in his thank-you letter in July 1767 that he might become a potter himself. The remark troubled Wedgwood, even though Boulton said of his potting ambitions in the same letter:

> I shall not begin before all our navigations are compleat as then we may be able to draw your clay etc. here upon easy terms but as that will require some few years I shall be content in the interim if you will permitt me to contribute now and then a little mite towards the large fund of improvements you seem to be possessed of.[18]

This was not exactly a renunciation of a potting ambition. It must have added to Wedgwood's fears, indicating that Boulton was a potential competitor once the new canals had brought down the cost of transport of raw materials and finished goods. And it was typical of Boulton to want a share of the action in a new venture, even though his own much enlarged business at Soho needed all the capital he could find.[19] Wedgwood did not take up Boulton's offer of a mite. He remained friendly, but wary of a man whose energies and ambitions could turn him into a competitor.

Vases

Boulton's early interest in ceramics centred on vases. By the end of 1767 he was fired with cashing in on the craze for ornamental vases. Why should the French metalworkers have it all their own way? He told Wedgwood early in 1768 that he would be surprised to learn the extent of the trade that had:

---

16 WMA 18707–25, JW to TB, 25 October 1776. Wedgwood included a drawing of the vase (which held the knives and forks) on its pedestal (which had drawers for the spoons) in his letter. The vase he saw was of 'black japanned iron'. He thought that Wedgwood and Bentley might produce the vases and the knife and fork handles, and the drawers could be embellished with cameos. See Nicholas Goodison, *Matthew Boulton: Ormolu* (London, 2002), pp.261–5.

17 MBP, 3782/1/11, p.987, B&F to JW, 22 June 1782. B&F also sent some pictures, which 'our Mr Boulton desires your acceptance of.' These were presumably examples of Boulton and Fothergill's 'mechanical' pictures. See Eric Robinson and Keith R.Thompson 'Matthew Boulton's Mechanical Paintings', *Burlington Magazine*, August 1970.

18 See note 5. Wedgwood's 'large improvements' were the building of the Etruria works, the first phase of which was completed in 1769.

19 The extension of the Soho Manufactory was built in 1765. The expense of this large expansion placed a heavy financial burden on the Boulton and Fothergill partnership throughout its duration.

lately been made out of vases at Paris. The artists have even come over to London, picked up all the old whimsical ugly things they could meet with, carried them to Paris, where they have mounted and ornamented them with metal, and sold them to the virtuosi of every nation, and particularly to *Millords d'Anglise*, for the greatest raritys.[20]

By November 1768 Boulton was buying ceramic vases in London. Wedgwood met him there and joined in the hunt. He wrote to Bentley:

Mr Boulton is picking up vases, and going to make them in bronze. You know how old China bowles, jarrs etc. are mounted in metal. He proposes an alliance betwixt the pottery and metal branches, viz. that we shall make such things as will be suitable for mounting, and not have a pott look, and he will finish them with the mounts. What do you think of it? Perhaps you would rather he would let them alone. Very true, but he will be doing, so that the question is whether we shall refuse having anything to do with him, and thereby affront him and set him of doing them himself, or employing his friend Garbett.[21]

We do not know Bentley's reply. But a month later Boulton wrote to Wedgwood just as the first vases were emerging from the Soho workshops at the end of 1768:

When I have the pleasure to shew you some of my vases I flatter myself you will prefer English workmanship to French in that article but I perceive it will be some time before I am ready to execute any quantity.[22]

Whatever Wedgwood and Bentley decided about the principle of supplying Boulton with vase bodies, they received some orders from him before the end of the year for some green china 'vessells' that he could mount as vases. Some of the smaller ones could 'be of the black Etruscan clay, some green, some blew or any other simple coulor you think proper'.[23] Wedgwood thought that he must either comply with Boulton's order or 'affront him, and set him a-trying to get them elsewhere, and they are so simple, the drawings he has sent me, that he may get them done'.[24] Another order for small china vases followed in January 1769 when Boulton made it clear that he was producing mounts in quantity

---

20   WMA 18193–25, JW to TB, 15 March 1768.
21   WMA 18215–25, JW to TB, 21 November 1768.
22   MBP, 3782/12/2, p.4, MB to JW, 20 December 1768.
23   MBP, 3782/12/2, p.4, MB to JW, 28 December 1768.
24   WMA 18222–25, JW to TB, 3 January 1769 (marked 1768 on the MSS).

from standard patterns. The vases would have to fit the mounts. Boulton added: 'I find the mounting of vases is a large field for fancy in which I shall indulge as I perceive it possible to convert a very ugly vessel into a beautifull vase.'[25]

Early in 1769 Wedgwood thought that Boulton was no longer a threat as a potential potter. 'Never trouble yourself about Boulton's vases,' he said to Bentley in February, 'he is making enameld ones for himself.'[26] The bodies of several of Boulton's early candle vases were indeed made of enamelled copper (Plate 6). But later in the year Wedgwood's worries came back. He was told that Boulton and Fothergill were:

> affronted at my not complying with their orders for vases to be mounted, and likewise for a pair of each sort, colour etc. which Mr Boulton desired I would send him as I got them up. This they mentioned to Mr Cox [one of Wedgwood's employees], and told him, that though I had refused them they had been offered vases for mounting by several potters, but were now determined to make the black vases (earthenware vases, they took care to tell him) themselves, and were building works for that purpose! If this be true, I expect every day to hear of their offering some of our principal hands two or three hundreds a year to manage the works for them.
>
> Mr Cox thinks farther from what he heard them say, and the hints they gave, that they are to be concerned with Cox of Shoe Lane,[27] they talked to him in the stile and manner of rivals to us, big in their own conceits, with some mighty blow their uplifted hands were prepared to let fall upon us. So stand firm my friend, and let us support this threatened attack like veterans prepared for every shock, or change of fortune that can befall us. If we must fall, if Etruria cannot stand its ground, but must give way to Soho, and fall before her, let us not sell the victorie too cheap, but maintain our ground like men, and indeavour, even in our defeat, to share the laurels with our conquerors. It doubles my courage to have the first manufacturer in England to encounter with. The match likes me well. I like the man, I like his spirit. He will not be a mere snivelling copyist like the antagonists I have hitherto had, but will venture to step out of the lines upon occasion, and afford us some diversion in the combat.[28]

---

25 MBP, 3782/ 12/2, p.7, MB to JW, 4 January 1769.

26 WMA 18228–25, JW to TB, 11 February 1769.

27 Robert Charleston (ed.), *English Porcelain* (1965), article by J.V.G. Mallet, 'Chelsea', pp.37–8, in which the author suggests that Cox, a jeweller in Shoe Lane, was probably attracted to the purchase of the Chelsea factory by hopes of a link with Boulton for the production of ormolu-mounted porcelain. But apart from Wedgwood's letters there is no evidence for this. Cox re-sold the factory to William Duesbury in February 1770.

28 WMA 18261–25, JW to TB, 27 September 1769.

This chivalrous expression of rivalry summed up the tension between the two men at this time. Both were determined businessmen. But they were also friends, and they admired each other. Battle they must, if the demands of the business dictated battle. But there would be no acrimony. Wedgwood refused to be fearful and commented a few days later:

> I have no fear at all even from the combination of Chelsea and Soho. If that should ever happen, we have got and shall keep the lead so long as our lives and healths are continued to us. I am persuaded they are thoroughly in earnest at Soho. Mr Fothergill told Mr Cox that the vase trade would be inexhaustible. It would be impossible to supply the demand for good things in that way. This is a right, just and true idea, and was not of Mr Fothergill's own manufacture I am pretty certain. The field is vast indeed! It seems to grow wider and every way more extensive the farther you advance into it. The harvest truly is great, and the labourers (thanks be praised – there's my outward man for you, he will be stealing a march now and then upon me) but few.[29]

In the event, there is no evidence that Boulton and Fothergill seriously intended to produce their own china or earthenware vases or to buy vases from the Chelsea factory. Whatever they threatened in the autumn of 1769, they seem to have decided at an early stage to use materials other than china for their vase bodies, and no china bodies with Boulton mounts have yet come to light. They concentrated on enamelled and gilt copper, and especially on blue john and white marble which they bought from stone merchants in Derbyshire. They were not trying merely to ornament the vases, but to turn them into usable candle vases and perfume burners. The body of the vase had to be pierced to fix the gilt metal mounts, and to be strong enough to bear their weight and to stand up to regular handling. China was not a suitable material. It was also expensive to buy from potters such as Wedgwood, who was not a producer of 'old whimsical ugly things'.

Boulton was still asking Wedgwood to make ceramic parts for ormolu tea vases in 1770, but these were exceptional.[30] He was also still hinting that Soho and Etruria could be working more closely together to exploit the fashionable market. Wedgwood replied with the greatest tact: 'You flatter me very agreeably with your desire to unite the powers of Corinth

29   WMA 18264–25, JW to TB, 1 October 1769.
30   WMA 18334–5–25, JW to TB, 24 December 1770, MBP, 3782/12/81/37, JW to MB, 19 February 1771.

[their nickname for Soho] and Etruria. I assure you, my dear friend, I wish it exceedingly...'[31]

The wish wasn't convincing. He thought his own competitive position was good enough.[32] 'Vases –,' he wrote to Bentley in 1770, 'Vases are the articles for us to get money by, if we can but sell them, and surely the world is wide enough to take 5 or 6,000 per annum... off our hands...'[33] He rightly saw that Boulton could add very little to his business in ceramic vases.

As the years passed and Boulton's vase business foundered, Wedgwood's fears of Boulton as a possible competitor petered out. By 1786 he knew that his friend's major preoccupation was with the engine trade. He added a postscript to a letter in that year that he had turned down an offer of making his fortune through a proposed partnership 'for making steam engines of a new improved construction, and by patent.'[34] It probably gave Boulton a good chuckle.

Cameos and Intaglios

Wedgwood wrote to his partner in September 1769 that 'gems are the fountain head of fine and beautiful composition, and we cannot you know employ ourselves too near the fountain head of taste.'[35] His remarks were in the context of the rising production of black basalt, or Etruscan, ware. By 1771 production was in full swing, and in 1773 Wedgwood and Bentley produced their first catalogue of cameos, intaglios and other ornaments, which were offered for sale in their London showroom in Great Newport Street. The introduction to the catalogue emphasised how cameos and intaglios could be used to enrich objects such as rings and bracelets, and even furniture.[36]

To begin with, Wedgwood made cameos in black basalt and white biscuit. Boulton and Fothergill took to using cameos for decorating some of their boxes. They made snuff boxes, often made of tortoiseshell, from at least 1767. In 1772 they were advertising gilt, silver, plated, shagreen, tortoiseshell, and

---

31   MBP, 3782/12/81/37, JW to MB, 19 February 1771. Boulton had suggested again that he and Wedgwood should be uniting their powers to exploit the market. Back in 1768 Wedgwood had been optimistic about cooperation on ceramic vases, having been impressed by Boulton's ability to decorate creamware with enamel and gold. But nothing seems to have come of this plan either – WMA 18193–25, JW to TB, 15 March 1768.

32   WMA 18325–25, JW to TB, 13 October 1770. In this letter Wedgwood reports on a discussion with the architect James Stuart about the wisdom or otherwise of having Boulton and Fothergill's showroom in London as a neighbour. He reckoned that 'Etruria stood a pretty good chance with any competitor.' In the event Boulton did not pursue the idea of a London showroom.

33   WMA 18320–25, JW to TB, 24 August 1770.

34   MBP, 3782/12/81/65, JW to MB, 14 June 1786.

35   WMA 18263–25, JW to TB, 30 September 1769.

36   Wedgwood and Bentley, *A Catalogue of Cameos, Intaglios, Medals and Bas-Reliefs; with a general account of Vases and other Ornaments, after the antique, made by Wedgwood and Bentley; and sold in their rooms at Great Newport Street, London* (London, 1773). Later editions were published in 1774, 1777, 1779 and 1787.

inlaid snuff boxes.[37] Wedgwood was eager to develop the use of his cameos in this way. He received an order from Soho in June 1773 for a small assortment of cameos 'suitable for setting in boxes, lockets, bracelets etc. etc, as Mr B. thinks he may have many opportunitys of disposing of some this year'.[38]

Wedgwood wrote to his partner, after a visit to Soho, in late 1773:

> Cameos. They sell very well in tortoiseshell boxes, which is the only way they have tryed them in at present. I have mention'd several more to them. In pedestals cases, candlesticks, etc. Cameo buttons Mr Fothergill believes would sell abroad for the sleeves, cloaks, and ladies dresses, and provided they could be made cheap enough would sell in large quantitys. I am persuaded we can make them very cheap in a way to answer their purpose. They set them all under chrystals and would therefore be content with them of a white bisket, without polish or colored grounds, as they would do the latter themselves in water colors. They have done some cameos for boxes in that way, and they look much better than our burnt in grounds, and being covered with a glass are sufficiently durable. In this way we can make cameos cheap enough for anything... I mentioned black polished buttons to Mr Boulton. He said black glass ones had been made and he supposed ours would not be better than those but is willing to try them. They sell a good many seals [intaglios], polish a few, and mean to polish all, and to sell a great many. They have bought most of what they have had from Boden and Smith,[39] but I am to send a sortment from hence.[40]

He mentioned in the same letter that John Fothergill had suggested that Wedgwood and Bentley might sell some of Soho's articles in their show room in London. Boulton and Fothergill would reciprocate and offer Wedgwood products in the Soho show room. Wedgwood's instinct was to sell only goods 'in which our manufacture had a place' and agreed to write about it. Bentley, who was in charge of the London show room, was not keen on 'becoming jewelers', but Wedgwood did not see any difficulties in selling finished goods such as set seals or bracelets.[41]

The archives show that in 1774–5 Boulton and Fothergill supplied dozens of tortoiseshell boxes for sale in Wedgwood and Bentley's show room in London,

---

37 See Goodison, *Matthew Boulton: Ormolu*, pp.20–1.
38 WMA 18469–25, JW to TB, 7 June 1773.
39 Boden and Smith were one of two or three stockists for Wedgwood and Bentley in Birmingham. See WMA 18501–25, JW to TB, 21 November 1773, WMA 18504–25, 2 December 1773. They also mounted Wedgwood's seals in gold and other metals.
40 WMA 18500–25, JW to TB, 22 November 1773.
41 WMA 18501–25, JW to TB, 21 November 1773.

many of them ready for fitting with cameos and some already fitted with cameos, some mounted in silver, some in gold (presumably gilt copper), and some without any mention of mounts.[42] Plate 7 shows a tortoiseshell box, with a jasper cameo of 'Sportive Love', impressed with 'Wedgwood' on the reverse and set in fine gilt mounts. It dates from ten or so years later, but is likely to be similar to the boxes supplied to Wedgwood in the 1770s.[43] The invoices in the 1770s also include enamelled gilt snuff boxes with cameos, which Boulton and Fothergill hoped would sell immediately – 'they being new induced us to take the liberty of sending them, supposing they would be likely to please you'[44] – gold bracelets with cameos,[45] and women's steel and gilt chains with cameos.[46]

These products all suggest that Wedgwood was either supplying cameos to be mounted and returned or that Boulton and Fothergill were buying the cameos and then selling them back once they were mounted. The archives suggest the latter. Boulton and Fothergill bought plenty of cameos, and their invoices for the finished goods, which allowed for discounts of 15%, suggest that they charged Wedgwood and Bentley for the whole cost and not just the boxes or mounts.

Wedgwood wasn't entirely happy selling plain cameos to Boulton, because the price would be too low:

> I do not know how to manage with Mr Boulton about grounding cameos in water colours for he is one of those high spirits who likes to do things in his own way, and if cross'd in that, will perhaps do nothing at all or worse. I will attempt to confine the water colouring to cameo buttons but if he will order plain white cameos it will be dangerous to refuse him...

He went to Soho and continued the letter to Bentley the next day, having found that Boulton was:

> much set upon having white cameos to do what he likes with, he still insists that when covered with glasses, oyl, or water colours are as good as

---

42   Invoices, B&F to Wedgwood and Bentley, London, WMA 4746–28, 2 April 1774: WMA 4747–28, 7 January 1775: WMA 4749–28, 6 April 1775; WMA 4751–28, 24 May 1775; WMA 3157–4, 18 May 1774; WMA 3158–4, 1 July 1774; WMA 4756–28, 19 June 1776; WMA 4757–28, 28 June 1776.

43   Wedgwood Museum, Cat. 5209. The impressed name 'Wedgwood' tells us that it was made after Bentley's death in 1780. The cameo was listed for the first time in Wedgwood's 1787 catalogue (No.271), in which it is said to be 'from Lady Templetoun'. Wedgwood received a number of 'charming groups of little figures' from Elizabeth, Lady Templetown (WMA 18958–26, JW to Lady Templetown, 27 June 1783).

44   WMA 4752–28, 5 August 1775.

45   WMA 4746–28, 2 April 1774.

46   WMA 4747–28, 7 January 1775; WMA 4749–28, 6 April 1775; WMA 4758–28, 14 September 1776.

enamel and in one respect better, as they can make the grounds any colour and finer of the kind than our enamelled grounds... He says they are obliged to colour all our cameos that have black grounds, over again with oyl or water colours, and Egginton[47] says oyl colours may be made to work as fine as any enamel, which they certainly may. B and F have connections with the Worcester people. If we refuse to let them have the cameos in white, they may set those gentry to work... I told Mr B that if we sold them plain white cameos, I knew they would cut us up, and so they will at our present prices, but then I hope the quantity will make amends, and with respect to our present stock I think we should get them framed as pictures and sell them in that and other ways as well as we can.[48]

In 1774 Boulton and Fothergill were using cameos by the dozen, and were not too particular about the subjects depicted on them. They just wanted them off-white, some of them to an exact size (presumably for the pre-made button or mount), and soon:

> We wrote you last the 13th May ordering sundry cameos which we confirm, but having since received only the 2 dozen with the impression of Hope [49] (Plate 8) we think it necessary to request herewith you would send us the others without delay as we are in great want of them and particularly of some exactly to the size inclosed to which we beg you would send us immediately 4 say 4 dozen or as many as you can of sorted but good subjects and please to observe that they must not be of a colour quite white but rather of darkish white of which colour you have sent us some before, and that they must be as flat as possible and yet the impression very distinct and clear.[50]

The ormolu-mounted vases of Plate 9 show two plain white cameos supplied by Wedgwood, made to an exact size. The subject is 'a heroic figure', chosen presumably as a 'good subject' by Wedgwood.[51] They are hand-coloured with

---

47 Francis Eginton, Boulton's modeller and japanner, who was later involved in the mechanical paintings business, was briefly a partner in the silver, plated and ormolu business and later became a painter of stained glass.

48 WMA 18504–25, JW to TB, 2 December 1773. Wedgwood suggested that they might sell plain ungrounded cameos to Boulton at half price.

49 Hope was the subject of two sizes of cameo (Wedgwood and Bentley *Catalogue*, 1777, Nos.1731 and 1732) and of an intaglio (*Catalogue*, 1774, No.206).

50 MBP, 3782/1/10, p.58, BF to JW, 6 July 1774.

51 Wedgwood and Bentley called this figure 'A Conquering Hero, probably Perseus' or 'Diomedes or Perseus' and listed a cameo under the former title in their 1773 *Catalogue*, p.14, No.1263. See Goodison, *Matthew Boulton: Ormolu*, p.110.

paint, presumably by Boulton and Fothergill. Whether Wedgwood subsequently knew that Boulton 'cut him up' by copying his cameos in metal, as he did for the other sides of these vases and for other vases of this design, I do not know. Boulton made gilt metal versions of at least nine of Wedgwood's cameos for use on the pedestals of vases, an example of plagiarism which was not uncommon in eighteenth-century decorative arts.[52]

Boulton and Fothergill showed a lively interest in the use of Wedgwood's ceramic products, including cameos, in products other than vases, boxes, buttons, and other fancy articles. It is possible that the oval frames in their earliest pattern book (Plate 10) were intended for cameos. Plate 11 illustrates a cameo, made after 1780, in a frame that might have been supplied by them. One intriguing idea was to include cameos in some way – probably as decorative borders – in decorative painted panels, presumably mechanical pictures, which Boulton was producing in the late 1770s and early 1780s.[53] Another idea put forward by Soho was to include some of Wedgwood's bas reliefs, both coloured and uncoloured, in chimney pieces, door panels, cabinets and bookcases, which Wedgwood said they were ornamenting with sharply defined tin ornaments which, when painted, simulated fine carving.[54] As with Boulton's general trade in buttons, buckles and other 'toys' these two areas of activity have not been adequately researched.

Wedgwood himself made suggestions for the use of his cameos in Boulton and Fothergill products. When he visited Soho in 1776, he noted that most of Boulton's 'time pieces and groups of figures have pyramids, or alters of white marble to lean upon,' and suggested, to Boulton's apparent pleasure, that these should be inlaid 'with our statues with blue grounds,' in other words jasperware cameos. He reckoned that appropriate subjects could be modelled for Russia or 'any other place whither his time pieces are to be sent.'[55] It wasn't a suggestion that Boulton followed. He stuck to gilt brass medallions on his ormolu-mounted ornaments.[56] Wedgwood also suggested to Boulton, and to Henry Clay, the japanner, that he should make cameos of portraits of eminent men for mounting in boxes etc. for

52   See Goodison, *Matthew Boulton: Ormolu*, pp.103–16.

53   WMA 18 684–25, JW to TB, 14 July 1776. See Robinson and Thompson 'Matthew Boulton's Mechanical Paintings', *Burlington Magazine*, August 1970. Three months later Wedgwood thought that Henry Clay, the japanner and inventor of papier mâché, who was also toying with the idea of inlaying cameos into painted cartoons to be set into cabinets, would be more successful than Boulton 'as a cabinet-maker.' But he hoped to sell a 'good many cameos' to both of them – WMA 18707–25, JW to TB, 25 October 1776.

54   WMA 18773–25, JW to TB, 24 July 1777.

55   WMA 18707–25, JW to TB, 25 October 1776.

56   See Goodison, *Matthew Boulton: Ormolu*, Plates 173–5, 301–5, 328, 331.

sale in different markets. But both men poured cold water on the idea, saying that the French were 'much superior to us' except at the cheapest end of the market.[57]

Then there was the wholesale business. Wedgwood faced tough competition in the market for intaglios, not least from James Tassie, the renowned maker of gems in hard pastes, in London.[58] Outlets that could sell in some quantity were attractive to him. In 1773 he was seeking outlets for the sale of unset intaglios, especially in Birmingham whose metal-workers dominated the trade with the jewellers' shops.[59] He reckoned that he had no chance of competing with them in the market for mounted cameos or intaglios. He approached two Birmingham firms – Boden and Smith, and Pemberton, both of whom bought intaglios from him – and offered to employ them as 'a sort of storekeepers for us. Both accepted, but Wedgwood then found that 'some of the trade' wanted 'some indifferent person as a third storekeeper.' Boulton characteristically and immediately offered himself, saying that 'everybody came without reserve to his warehouse in Birmingham.' Wedgwood had high hopes of supplying Boulton with both cameos and seals 'in the wholesale way.'[60] But he didn't want to appoint only one metal working business for fear of upsetting others. Instead, he appointed a 'good honest Presbyterian' glover, and proposed to advertise 'Wedgwood and Bentleys intaglios for seals' at his shop near the Old Cross in Birmingham.[61] Boulton accepted this. But it didn't stop him buying intaglios for sale on his own account.

There were 225 Wedgwood intaglios in Boulton and Fothergill's stock in 1782. 121 of these were 'Wedgwood's seals' in the 'Toy Room', suggesting that Boulton and Fothergill were simply retailing them. The value was 2 shillings each.[62] The other 104 were 'black Wedgwood's impressions for seals' in various sizes, mostly small and presumably waiting to be mounted. These were in one of the warehouses, along with 64 cameos, which were mostly damaged and 'out of date', some metal cameos, and some old mounts for setting cameos.[63] There were also fourteen tortoiseshell inlaid

---

57   WMA 18684–25, JW to TB, 14 July 1776.

58   WMA 18657–25, JW to TB, 24 February 1776.

59   WMA 18829–25, JW to TB, 18 April 1778.

60   WMA 18498–25, JW to TB, 14 November 1773. Wedgwood had already sent 'about 50 dozen of seals to Birmingham' – probably to Boden and Smith in May – WMA 461–25, JW to TB, 18 May 1773.

61   WMA 18504–25, JW to TB, 2 December 1773.

62   The price is interesting. In 1778 Boulton and Fothergill had ordered 500 'antique heads' at 10d each – WMA 18829–25, JW to TB, 18 April 1778.

63   MBP, 3782/2/13, Inventory 1782, pp.159, 172. The inventory was taken as a record of the stock on the death of Boulton's partner John Fothergill, the business being assumed by the new firm of Matthew Boulton.

boxes, some fitted with mounts for cameos and at least one of them fitted with a cameo.[64]

The quantities are not vast, especially in relation to Wedgwood's huge output, but they are enough to suggest that the mutual trade was in an amicable state. It remained so. In 1786 Wedgwood wrote to Boulton:

> I have left a few sets of my cameo buttons to be mounted, and I shall be glad to increase our connection in this way, as well in selling you cameos for your own trade, as in having them mounted by you for mine, both in gilt metal and steel, or in any other better way which your inventive genius may strike out. I shall likewise most probably make some farther improvements when these have had their run or are successfully imitated; though I have not much fear of the latter...

Or was he a little less confident than these words sound? Did he still have some fears of Boulton pinching his business? He continued:

> ...as I do not think them worth your notice, nor that you would run away with a little hobby horse which you saw your friend pleased with having got a stride upon; and I wish you would give your foreman in this branch a caution that they are not carried out by any of the workmen to be moulded or copied. A manufacturer in Birmingham whom you know has made a laudable attempt in this way at my warehouse in town, that is, to buy a complete set of cameos for patterns; but his intention being discovered I told him I must take care not to sell him a set of models for a few shillings, which had cost me, besides time and labor, more than twice as many guineas...[65]

By then Boulton was in partnership with John Scale in the manufacture of buttons, steel chains and sword hilts, Fothergill having died in 1782.[66] The partnership lasted to 1799. The archives record invoices from Wedgwood (Bentley having died in 1780) to Boulton and Scale for cameos to be mounted as buttons and in steel watch chains,[67] orders from Boulton and Scale for

---

64 MBP, 3782/2/13, Inventory 1782, pp.174–5.
65 MBP, 3782/12/81/65, JW to MB, 14 June 1786. Wedgwood's son subsequently wrote to Boulton (WMA 29579–49, 7 September 1786) sending some patterns of Wedgwood's own cameo buttons: 'He only wished you to see them, now he has got them ready for general sale, and that you might be informed of the price, which is 2 guineas a dozen for the coat, and 30/– for the waistcoat, with 20 percent discount. It this article should suit you, he will be glad at any time to receive your commands.'
66 John Scale had been a partner in the button business since 1777.
67 WMA 4737–28, 16 October 1786; WMA 4738–28, 7 February 1788.

cameos to be set as buttons,[68] and invoices from Boulton and Scale for supplying Wedgwood with mounted cameo buttons.[69]

Considering the size of Boulton's button and buckle business, it is surprising that so far no firm attributions can be made to his factory among the huge number of surviving gilt and cut steel mounted cameos (Plates 12 and 13). But I am sure that this will be rectified when someone makes a full study of the records of Boulton's 'toy' businesses in the surviving archives – which needs to be done. The only visual evidence in the archives is a Pattern Book which contains designs for jewellery, sword hilts, chatelaines, buttons, buckles and chains. They appear to be patterns of products from the years of Boulton's partnership with John Scale.[70] In some cases the designs are annotated with the materials used in the making – for example studs for button frames, buckles and sword hilts ('common' or 'best', 'No.1' or 'No.3', presumably made of cut and faceted steel), blue and white beads for a button, shell beads for sword hilts, enamels and glass for inserts in the frames of chatelaines. Many of the designs are clearly for plain steel, many for cut steel, and many for pierced metal, presumably steel or silver. A full analysis of this intriguing collection of designs awaits methodical study.[71] But many of the designs are marked to show that they are to hold cameos and several are specifically marked to hold Wedgwood cameos (Plates 14 and 15). There are also patterns for buttons and chatelaines that have blank spaces for decorative inserts – cameos perhaps or glass, which is specified for many others. None of these patterns has yet led to a firm attribution of a surviving object to Boulton and Scale.[72] The pattern for the seal (Plate 14, engraving No.3622) bears a strong resemblance to the seals of Venus and Cupid and Atlas illustrated in Plate 16, but the mount may have been supplied by one of Wedgwood's other Birmingham suppliers, namely Boden and Smith or their successor firm William Smith of Birmingham, who bought Atlas seals among many

68 WMA 4742–28, 3 December 1788 (cameo heads); WMA 4743–28, 10 December 1788 (a request for figures in place of heads for setting in 'good gilt buttons'); also WMA 3289–4, B&S to Wedgwood and Co, 16 April 1790, an order for 'a friend for 18 buttons with your cameos, he says 18 different sorted animals... have you 18 horses in different attitudes or have you 18 other different animals in the same size as the horse.'

69 WMA 4736–28, 24 January 1786, WMA 4741–28, 27 June 1788; WMA 4744–28, 27 November 1790.

70 MBP, 3782/21/11, Pattern Book 9.

71 Very few of Boulton's buttons, buckles, toys etc. have yet been firmly identified, let alone those with cameos. Pattern Book 9 will be a crucial part of the research when some diligent scholar sets about the task of researching the toy business. See Goodison, *Boulton: Ormolu*, pp.21–6 for the very large range of products and the variety of materials used in making them.

72 There are extensive collections of boxes, chatelaines, buttons, etc. set with Wedgwood cameos and intaglios in several museums including the British Museum, the Victoria and Albert Museum and the Wedgwood Museum. None have yet been firmly attributed to Boulton.

others from Wedgwood in 1774–5.[73] There are unfortunately no designs for boxes in the pattern book.

Design

Despite their many contacts over vases and cameos, there is little evidence of cooperation between Boulton and Wedgwood on the design of their goods.

They tapped some of the same sources, many of them well tapped also by other craftsmen of the decorative arts. Both were familiar with the source books and the plaster casts which were the common heritage of designers promoting the antique taste. Both were influenced by architects and had direct contact with them. A number of the objects produced in their factories show that they derived motifs from these common sources.[74] But of mutually shared designs there is no evidence. Even when they went 'curiosity hunting' together in London in March 1768 they were not planning to share the development of any design ideas that might result. Boulton was keen on occasions to share models. He offered to go halves on impressions that they found at a 'plaster woman' in London in 1768[75] and wrote to Wedgwood in 1770 that if he remembered correctly: 'there is another partnership model bought at Pinchbecks.[76] There are many other things of a similar nature that he [i.e. Boulton] would be glad to go partners in: when any occurs to him he will let Mr Wedgwood in, and he hopes Mr W will do the same by him'. In the same letter he wrote: 'Mr Boulton approves of Mr Wedgwood's purchasing the Triton, wishes he would take as many casts from it as he thinks proper, and then send it to Soho – after the same operation is performed there then begs to toss up or play any other game for the fee simple of the bronze or put it up to auction'.[77] This tantalising reference suggests that they may have shared the triton figure for a candlestick that they both made. But I have suggested elsewhere that William Chambers could equally have been their common source.[78]

---

73   There are many orders from Boden and Smith and William Smith for intaglios recorded in WMA in 1773–5 (WMA 18548–100 to 18569–100). At least four of the orders list the serial numbers of the intaglios – presumably the numbers in Wedgwood and Bentley's catalogue – that are required. The orders for No.68 (Atlas), are in WMA 18569D–100 (Boden and Smith, 17 February 1774), WMA 18551–100 (William Smith, 25 March 1775) and 18554–100 (William Smith, 22 June 1775).

74   See Goodison, *Matthew Boulton: Ormolu*, Chapter 3 and particularly pp.101ff. for a discussion of Boulton and Wedgwood's common sources.

75   MBP, 3782/12/2, p.4, MB to JW, 28 December 1768.

76   Christopher Pinchbeck was the son of the maker of astronomical clocks and inventor of the 'pinchbeck' alloy of copper and zinc that resembled gold. He described himself as a toyman and mechanician.

77   WMA 30392–4, MB to JW, 9 June 1770. Wedgwood had bought the models of this triton in the previous month from the London plaster moulders Hoskins and Oliver. Their invoice was dated May 1770.

78   Goodison, *Matthew Boulton: Ormolu*, pp.83–5, 102.

Nor is there much evidence of mutual loans of models and designs. Wedgwood did lend Boulton some prints in 1767 [79] and a model of a dolphin in 1771.[80] In 1770 they also both worked on the bronze tripod that James Stuart designed for the top of the 'Lanthorn of Demosthenes' at Shugborough – Wedgwood providing the bowl and Boulton the bronzework [81] – but in no sense were any of these conceived as joint designs for their mutual benefit.

The parallels between the two men in the field of design are plenty and, in the context of the fashion for the antique taste, of keen interest. But there was no methodical sharing of models, and no evidence for the joint exploitation of designs. The explanation must lie in their mutual rivalry – or at least in Wedgwood's fear of Boulton as a potential competitor. Had he shared design ideas with Boulton, the latter would surely have exploited them in some way within his diverse workshops. Wedgwood's fear of this must have lain behind his reluctance to 'unite the powers of Corinth and Etruria.'

Merchanting

If Boulton turned his back on manufacturing ceramics, he certainly remained alive to their commercial potential. He placed orders for pottery from Wedgwood for shipment to his agents overseas as early as 1769. The subsequent orders that Boulton and Fothergill sent to Wedgwood, usually written by Zacchaeus Walker, the clerk in charge of the Birmingham warehouse, give some idea of the activity of their merchanting business, about which we know too little because none of the principal accounting records have survived.

Wedgwood and Boulton shared ideas for exporting their goods, from the earliest years of their friendship. Wedgwood was keen to develop business overseas because the scale of production from his new factory demanded the development of a larger market. Boulton was intent on exporting his metalware from the beginning of his partnership with John

---

79   MBP, 3782/12/1. p.4 onwards, MB to JW, 10 July 1767.
80   MBP, 3782/12/81/37, JW to MB, 19 February 1771. The dolphin was a model for Boulton and Fothergill's silver tureen for the Admiralty, made to the design of James Stuart. See Robert Rowe, *Adam Silver* (1965), pp.81–2 and Plate 47. There is a drawing of the tureen in MBP, 3782/21/2, Boulton and Fothergill's Pattern Book 1, p.111.
81   WMA 18334-5–25, JW to TB, 24 December 1770 and many other references in both archives. Wedgwood delights in telling his partner how Boulton was making 'an immense large tripod for Mr Anson' to Stuart's design but that having cast the 5 cwt legs the workmen didn't know how to set about the bowl. He persuaded them that the bowl should be made by 'some able potter', and wrote that Stuart had said that 'Mr Anson would glory in having the arts of Soho and Etruria united in his tripod.

Fothergill, partly for the same reason but partly too because there was a well established tradition of exports in the Birmingham metal trades. The export trade was probably why he entered into the partnership with Fothergill in the first place. Fothergill brought to the partnership an acquaintance with markets in continental Europe and a network of agents, especially in the Baltic States, northern Germany, Italy and France.[82] Both Boulton and Wedgwood also used contacts with ambassadors to European courts to further their exporting ambitions.

Wedgwood picked up a useful marketing idea from Boulton soon after they first met. He wrote to Boulton in the summer of 1767:

> When I had the pleasure of seeing you last you mentioned a scheme of dispersing abroad the patterns of our manufacture, in a way which struck me then & has since engaged a good deal of my attention; which was by means of engraved prints of all the articles we make accompanying one piece of the manufacture. The thought [*torn*] me much, both as I apprehend it would be the quickest & most eligible mode of extending the knowledge of our manufactures abroad where patterns could not with any sort of convenience be sent in specie, and likewise as I am fully persuaded a *considerable*, & *proffitable* branch of commerce may be as it were created by this new mode of shewing the world what we have to dispose of.
>
> If you think the scheme worth bestowing any further thought upon, to mature it a little, I am at your service, if you can make any use of me in the prosecution of it, and shall be glad to have your thoughts upon the subject, at your leisure. I have already served some of the German Nobility with Creamcolour, besides some services which have been sent from St James's to the Court of Mecklenberg, where it is much admired. This introduction will I apprehend make it eagerly enquired after, and if the merchants can now be properly supplied with it, the consumption will certainly be great.[83]

In the following spring, Wedgwood reported on his meeting with Lord Cathcart, the newly appointed ambassador to Russia, and his wife, who were enthusiastic about taking sample wares to Russia with them and 'introducing my manufacture at the Court of Russia'. He went on:

> I must now desire you will by return of post let me know at what other courts in Germany, or Europe you should be most solicitous to have this

---

82   See Eric Robinson, 'Boulton and Fothergill 1762–82', *University of Birmingham Historical Journal*, Vol.VII, No.1, 1959, pp.67–71.

83   MBP, 3782/1/81/33, JW to MB, 19 March 1768.

manufacture introduced and I will endeavour to get it done, and at the same time it should be made known to the Introducer where the Grandees of the several States may be supplyd with the same goods.[84]

It is clear from this letter that Wedgwood saw Boulton as a potential merchant of his wares to markets in Europe. Wedgwood conducted a considerable export trade through his own contacts and agents, especially in creamware, both in Europe and beyond.[85] But he also used other firms in England as a means of enlarging his contact. The first recorded order from Boulton and Fothergill was in January 1769, but this order makes it clear that there were earlier orders. It was the first repeat order, there being 'no repetition from any other order, and all of them as well as this, are full of complaints, of the over charge of the whole sorts, this is to desire you'll put the above on the best terms.'[86]

From 1769 to 1790 there was a host of subsequent orders, many of them very extensive, containing orders for hundreds, even hundreds of dozens, of each item.[87] Most of the orders were for standard patterns of Wedgwood's creamware. In 1771, Wedgwood was concerned lest the large orders received from Boulton and Fothergill might interfere with his own orders from Russia – he didn't want his Russian orders neglected or 'the trade baulked in its first onset on any account'.[88] Boulton and Fothergill's orders were confined almost entirely to 'useful' ware. They comprised plates of all sorts, dishes and covered dishes, tureens, sugar basins, dinner and tea sets, coffee pots, coffee cups, chocolate cups, punch cups, fruit baskets, salts, chamber pots, garden pots, eye baths, and so on. Many patterns of ware were specified – gadroon on silver pattern, barley corn, mosaic and basket, feather edging and new feather edging (Plate 17), black enamelled gilt feather, purple edging, purple laurel, plain enamelled and gilt, royal patterns (Plate 17) with purple edging, purple antique border, purple laurel and grape and ivy borders, ivy, marine, blue border, blue antique border, blue porcelain figures in bas relief, etc,[89] as well as black basalt

---

84 MBP, 3782/1/81/35, JW to MB, 19 March 1768.

85 See Robin Reilly, *Wedgwood*, (1989), Vol.1, pp.80–96.

86 WMA 3121–4, B&F to JW, 21 January 1769.

87 WMA 3125–4 to 3288–4, 30386–4 to 30402–4, 1496, 4711–28 to 4724–28, 4752–28, 4755–28.

88 WMA 3151–4, a note written by one of Wedgwood's people on a letter about orders from B&F to JW, 18 January 1771. The note refers to Wedgwood's first substantial order from the Empress Catherine in 1770 for the so-called 'husk' service. Wedgwood's sale of this service to the Empress and of the subsequent 'frog' service in 1773–4, have been well summarised in Reilly, *Wedgwood*, Vol.1, pp.322–82.

89 See Reilly, *Wedgwood*, Vol.I, p.285, where many of Wedgwood's borders are illustrated from his 'First Pattern Book', including some of the borders specified in Boulton and Fothergill's orders. Reilly illustrates many plates etc. of the patterns specified in the orders.

ware. 'Ornamental' wares were few and far between. From 1783 however there seems to have been some relaxation in this distinction, perhaps reflecting the death of Thomas Bentley in 1780, and there are orders from Matthew Boulton (the successor business to Boulton and Fothergill) for busts and vases for a few agents,[90] and even one for steel-set cameos despite these normally being the business of Boulton and Scale.[91]

The orders came from Zacchaeus Walker at Boulton's Birmingham warehouse, acting for Boulton and Fothergill until 1782 and for Matthew Boulton thereafter, Boulton himself being much less involved in the metalwork and merchanting businesses now that he was preoccupied with the engine business. The vast majority were to be shipped to Isaac Broadley, or Isaac and Charles Broadley, at Hull, but a few of them were to be shipped to other Hull agents including Christopher Scott and Williamson and Waller. The role of these agents was to arrange the onward shipping by sea. It was clearly cheaper to ship the goods by canal to Hull for onward transport by sea – even to London – than using road transport. Some of the goods were to be delivered to the order of Boulton's London agent and banker William Matthews from Wedgwood's London showroom.

Each order was referenced with initials, so that the shippers could identify them, and the orders very seldom gave Wedgwood any clue about the ultimate destination of the goods. Most of these began with the letter 'A' – ACP, ACN (who seems to have been the most prolific agent of all up to 1784), ACA, ACV, AFQ, AND, ALX, ABZ, AGW, ANG, AFS (another large orderer), and so on. A few broke this mould – e.g. EH, EE, GN – but they are in a small minority. Wedgwood himself believed that most of the orders were for St Petersburg, where he shipped goods through other agents himself:[92] and there is no doubt that Boulton was supplying agents in that city. Boulton's code has so far resisted interpretation.[93] The agents were not however all in Russia. The large customer AFS, who placed orders from 1775, was at Pillaw (Pillau) or Königsberg 'up the

---

90 WMA 4711–28, MB to JW, 28 March 1783, an order for AGW for black busts of 'the King and Queen (if they are to be had)' and two vases to suit them; WMA 3196–4, B&F to JW, 3 October 1777, for ALB, black busts or heads of a number of historic figures; WMA 3229–4, MB to JW, 13 April 1784, for ACN ten vases with gilt garlands; WMA 3236–4, MB to JW, 20 October 1784, for AGW eight very handsome and large vases, 'but observe that there must always be two or two alike and one middle piece so as to make each sett of three pieces'; 3240–51, MB to Wedgwood Son and Byerley, 6 January 1791, for AKD six vases with antique ornaments, 'sorted of three pairs, of jaspis on porphire colour', etc.

91 WMA 4719–28, MB to JW, 9 January 1788.

92 WMA 18384–25, JW to TB, 5 August 1772.

93 But see Goodison, *Matthew Boulton: Ormolu*, p.179, where I identify AOQ as Charles-Raymond Grancher, a *marchand-mercier* in Paris (with thanks to Geoffrey de Bellaigue), and ALQ as William Porter, a merchant in St Petersburg. Boulton did not ship ceramics to William Porter, to whom Wedgwood shipped goods direct (WMA 18384–25, JW to TB, 5 August 1772). Porter was recommended to Wedgwood by Lord Cathcart (WMA 1442, Lord Cathcart to JW, 19 March 1771).

Baltick',[94] in what was then (and is now) Poland, and placed orders for Prince Stanislaus Poniatowski in 1780.[95] AUI and SSA, recorded from 1787, were in North Italy and Germany. AUN, from 1790, was also in Italy. But the frequent references to the need to deliver the goods to Hull in time for the ships to reach their destinations before the Baltic froze up, usually in late September, suggest that the major trade was indeed in the Baltic States.

Several letters show that agents ordered from samples or patterns, reminding us of Wedgwood's first letter to Boulton about the means of broadcasting his wares. Some may have had copies of Wedgwood's first catalogue of Queen's ware, issued in 1774, in English and French. This had a limited number of engraved illustrations but listed a wide range of 'useful' ware, with prices.[96] In 1783 Boulton asked Wedgwood to send 'a compleat book of drawings or copper plate prints containing all the antique patterns of things you make in Terra Sigilata or Black Composition' for his agent AGW.[97]

The letters include a recurrent theme of breakages, which is not surprising in view of the primitive methods of packing in casks with straw as the chief cushion against shocks, and the amount of loading and unloading that had to be done to take the goods from Etruria to Hull and then on to the destination. There were some complaints too about delays and about the quality of the ware. Perhaps in response to this it is sometimes made clear that the creamware should be 'second' or 'common' quality.

Boulton and Fothergill usually received a discount of 7½% on the orders they generated. Despite the absence of account books for the Birmingham warehouse, the merchanting business was probably profitable – unlike Boulton's luxury goods, the production of which entailed far higher fixed costs.

The commercial relationship between Boulton and Wedgwood did not develop, despite Boulton's early enthusiasm for working together on ornamental ware, beyond supplying each other with a limited quantity of goods. But Boulton was a worthwhile customer to Wedgwood, especially as a merchant of useful ware; and their admiration for each other's business achievement certainly cemented their friendship and lay behind their cooperation on the politics of trade in the 1780s.

---

94   WMA 3173–4, B&F to JW, 26 August 1775. This may have been Houssalle and Binet, with whom Fothergill had served an apprenticeship. See Robinson, 'Boulton and Fothergill 1762–82', p.66. Concealment of merchant's real names was carried over into B&F's letter books, with code names such as 'Pondicherry' (also in Königsberg), 'Senegall', etc.

95   WMA 3202–4 and 3203–4, B&F to JW, 8 April 1780 and 7 June 1780. The second order included 50 mens' chamber pots and fifty womens', all 'middle size'.

96   *A Catalogue of the different articles of Queen's Ware, which may be had either plain, gilt or embellished with Enamel Paintings, manufactured by Josiah Wedgwood, Potter to Her Majesty* (1774).

97   WMA 4712–28, MB to JW, 28 March 1783.

Chapter 11

SILVER AND ITS SUBSTITUTES

Kenneth Quickenden

Silver and a number of substitutes, especially Sheffield Plate, were used at the Soho Manufactory. The purpose of this chapter is to gauge the extent of, and the reasons for their usage there during the life of Matthew Boulton.

A key factor in the demand for silver and its cheaper substitutes was cost: how did the hierarchy of materials relate to the hierarchy of society? A mid-eighteenth century computation put the annual income of the aristocracy upwards of £10,000 and that of the gentry £8,000 at most; middle-class incomes generally ranged from £600 to less than £100; lower incomes went down to less than double figures.[1] During Boulton's lifetime those disparities hardly changed,[2] but the proportion of middle-class families rose,[3] incomes were increasingly spent on luxuries and there was a growing spirit of emulation.[4]

In part, Boulton's use of silver and its substitutes was characteristic of much industry in Birmingham. Following his inheritance of his father's firm in 1759 and the expansion of the Soho Manufactory from 1761[5] Boulton created a large firm which like many others produced 'toys' (a wide range of domestic and jewellery items), buttons and buckles. The range of materials used at Soho and Birmingham was wide, including silver and some substitutes, and others such as steel and tortoiseshell. Soho, like firms in Birmingham, innovatively used drop-stamps and fly-presses to make items economically for a wide market at home and abroad.[6]

By the mid-1760s Soho produced silver candlesticks. By the early 1770s a range of tablewares, and other artistically ambitious silver items, new to

---

1 Peter Mathias, 'The Social Structure in the Eighteenth Century: a Calculation by Joseph Massie', *Economic History Review* Second Series, X, 1, (1957), 30–45 (pp.42–43).

2 Maxine Berg, *Luxury and Pleasure in Eighteenth-Century Britain* (Oxford, 2005) p.9.

3 Berg, *op. cit.*, p.212.

4 Berg, *op. cit.*, pp.9–11.

5 H.W. Dickinson, *Matthew Boulton* (Cambridge, 1937) pp.25–45.

6 Berg, *op. cit.*, pp.166–67.

Birmingham, were also made at Soho. This, together with the production of ormolu (gilt bronze or brass mounts used chiefly on vases) was motivated by an ambition to transform his, Soho's and Birmingham's reputation. It led to the recruitment from elsewhere of silversmiths and the foundation of the Birmingham Assay Office in 1773, for which Boulton was primarily responsible.[7] Although very small articles were not required for assay (testing), larger pieces were. Sterling silver, which Boulton made, must contain at least 925 parts per thousand of pure silver.[8]

To achieve economies in production, Boulton insisted that ormolu, larger silver items and similar pieces in substitute materials were made in the same department. Similarly, with smaller items such as buttons and filigree, silver and its substitutes were used alongside other materials. This provided opportunities for flexibility in changing from one material to another and provided a basis for competition with rivals (especially London silversmiths) who specialized in one material.[9]

During the 1760s Boulton experimented with a variety of materials. Chemical amalgamation, widely used for centuries,[10] was used by Boulton by 1762.[11] Boulton bought 'silvered' candlesticks from Paris in 1765, perhaps to gain technical hints.[12] About 1770 Boulton noted a recipe: 'Silver, made into Luna Cornia [nitrate of silver], 1 Common Salt, 2 Salamoniak [ammonium chloride] 2 Glass Gall or Sandiver [a liquid saline matter found floating over glass after vitrification].[13] This was similar to recipes used elsewhere and involved mixing and grinding the materials with water, rubbing them onto the base metal, annealing, quenching in water and polishing.[14]

In 1765 Boulton was keen to learn about French-plating in London.[15] Although it had an earlier ancestry, the technique derived its popularity from eighteenth-century France. According to Denis Diderot's *Encyclopedie*, 1751–2, the process was usually carried out on copper, brass or iron. After cleaning, the object was heated to a red heat and cooled before further cleaning. The object was again heated, to a moderate temperature, and quenched to etch the surface. Cross-hatching, used especially on iron,

---

7   Kenneth Quickenden 'Boulton and Fothergill's Silversmiths', *Silver Society Journal*, 7, (1995), 342–56 (pp.342–43).

8   J. Paul de Castro, *The Law and Practice of Hall-marking Gold and Silver Wares*, 2nd ed. (London, 1935) pp.71–72.

9   Quickenden, *op. cit.* (as note 7) pp.342–44.

10   G. Bernard Hughes, *Antique Sheffield Plate* (London, 1970), p.9.

11   BAH, MS 3782/1/34, p.28.

12   BAH, MS 3782/1/35, 3 February 1765.

13   BAH, MS 3782/12/108/5, p.57.

14   Hughes, *op. cit.*, p.9.

15   BAH, MS 3782/12/108/3, p.7, 20 October 1765.

improved the adherence of squares of silver foil which were applied after the object had been heated. The first application, of two leaves, adhered with the aid of heat and burnishing. Subsequent leaves were added, four or six at a time, until as many as sixty layers were applied. The final step was to burnish the surface for a smooth finish.[16] Some silver leaf was ordered from London, in 1772, for an experiment at Soho in French-plating[17] and in 1771 some pieces were sent to John Legrix in London for French-plating:[18] he was a specialist.[19] Later there was a French-plater at the Soho Manufactory.[20]

An ancient technique, later described as close-plating but which was simply described as 'plating' or confused with French-plating[21] in the eighteenth century, was used in Birmingham. Since French-plating on steel was generally found to be unsatisfactory, close-plating was often preferred. The technique involved cleaning the article, dipping it into ammonium chloride (to act as a flux), and then into molten tin. Silver foil, cut to size, was laid over the tinned surface and pressed firmly into position. A hot iron was then drawn over the surface of the foil, thus melting the tin and forming a solder between the silver and base metal. Much burnishing was required of the lapped edges of the foil. Several patents were taken out in the second half of the eighteenth century, bringing improvements to the technique.[22]

However, these older techniques were increasingly challenged by Sheffield-plate, introduced in Sheffield about 1743,[23] which Boulton insisted on calling 'plated wares',[24] that involved fusing a thin layer of silver onto copper, on one, or from the 1760s, both sides. In Sheffield the material was first used for buttons and small articles such as knife hafts and by the 1760s for tablewares by firms which also made articles in silver often with the aid of dies. By the 1750s the material was used in Birmingham for small articles and Boulton was using it for candlesticks by 1765 and for a range of tablewares by the early 1770s.[25] Boulton placed his own 'maker's' mark and that of John

16 Tonny Beentjes and Mark Erdmann, 'French Plating', *Journal of the Antique Metalwork Society*, 13, (2005), 10–16 (pp.10–13).

17 BAH, MS 3782/1/9, p.424, AJC to WM, 12 April 1772.

18 BAH, MS 3782/1/9, pp.103–04, JW to WM, 13 May 1771.

19 Helen Clifford, *Silver in London: The Parker and Wakelin Partnership 1760–1776* (New Haven and London, 2005), p.93.

20 BAH, MS 3782, List of Workmen at Soho, c.1809.

21 Frederick Bradbury, *History of Old Sheffield Plate* (London, 1912, reprint Sheffield 1968) p.145.

22 Martin Gubbins, 'Close Plate', *Silver Society Journal*, 12 (2000), 41–43, (p.41).

23 Bradbury, *op. cit.*, p.25.

24 In 1784 Samuel Garbett informed MB that the term Sheffield-plate was widely used elsewhere (BAH, MS 3782/12/6/60, Samuel Garbett to MB, 14 July 1784).

25 Gordon Crosskey 'The early development of the plated trade', *Silver Society Journal*, 12 (2000), 27–37 (pp.27–35).

Fothergill (his partner from 1762–1782) on Sheffield-plate up to 1773, when this was prevented by Act of Parliament because of possible confusion between Sheffield-plate and silver.[26]

Boulton also experimented with non-precious metals that resembled silver. One of these was tutenague, derived from the Chinese 'pai-tung' (meaning white copper) an alloy of copper, zinc and nickel. At this time it was only available from China. Boulton's circle made efforts to understand its composition, but failed, believing the nickel to be iron. It was not until 1775 that a correct analysis was made (by the Swedish scientist Gustav Engestrom) and that was not generally known until late in the century. Boulton was familiar with the metal by the mid-1760s and decided that in its lustre and whiteness it resembled silver and (better than silver) resisted tarnish.[27] Boulton described another metal, 'white metal' as 'semi-argent' when he speculated about 1770 on its use for a range of wares.[28] The metal is an alloy of 210 parts tin, twelve of antimony and four of copper.[29] By 1762 Boulton was also aware of platina,[30] a silvery-white alloy of copper (46.5%) and zinc (53.5%).[31]

The range of materials used for buttons at Soho was wide, including pearl, steel and brass.[32] Platina [33] was used for buttons, at least on one occasion, at 12s.0d per gross, on bone bases for military uniforms.[34] Tutenague was used at least on one occasion, in 1772.[35] Buttons were also occasionally made in 'white metal'[36] but the metal only became widely used in the nineteenth century.[37] Silvering, though cheaper than other methods of adding a silver appearance, readily discolours.[38] Boulton was not enthusiastic; on one occasion when silvered buttons were made at Soho there was immediate customer dissatisfaction,[39] but normally he either factored such buttons or advised customers to go elsewhere.[40]

---

26   J.S. Forbes, *Hallmark: A History of the London Assay Office* (London, 1998), pp.222–23.

27   Keith Pinn, 'Paktong', *Silver Society Journal*, 12 (2000), 38–40 (pp.38–39).

28   BAH, MS 3782/12/108/5, pp.17–18.

29   Bradbury, *op. cit.*, pp.494–97.

30   BAH, MS 3782/1/12/2, Joshua Steele to MB, 29 October 1762.

31   G.D. Hiscox, *Formulas, Processes and Trade Secrets* (London, 1937) p.80.

32   Kenneth Quickenden,' Silver, Plated and Silvered Products from the Soho Manufactory, 1780', *Silver Society Journal*, 10 (1998), 77–95 (p.80).

33   BAH, MS 3782/1/12/2, Joshua Steele to MB, 29 October 1762.

34   BAH, MS 3782/1/9 p.52, B&F to WM, 21 February 1771.

35   Keith Pinn, *Paktong: The Chinese Alloy in Europe, 1680–1820*, Antique Collectors' Club (Woodbridge, 1999) p.55.

36   BAH, MS 3782/1/6 p.146, Order for J. Burgoyne, 29 February 1780.

37   Bradbury, *op. cit.*, pp.494–97.

38   Hughes, *op. cit.*, p.9.

39   BAH, MS 3782/2/14 p.479, MB & Scale Button Co. to Messrs Baumgartner and Hooffstetter, 6 December 1784.

40   BAH, MS 3782/1/9 pp.3–4, JW to Bustamante & Co, 3 January 1770.

Fig. 11.1. W. Humphrey, 'Coup de Boulton'. 1777.

In contrast, Sheffield-plate buttons, which Soho produced at least from 1766, were subsequently made in enormous quantities: in 1780 4000 gross against just 40 gross of silver-gilt buttons. One dozen silver-gilt breast buttons cost 24s.8d while a double gross of Sheffield-plate buttons ranged from 17s.6d to 27s.0d. Prices varied according to type (coat buttons cost more than smaller waistcoat buttons), quality of plating, the type of shank and the quality of material used for the base, such as boxwood or bone. Livery buttons in Sheffield-plate were popular. Demand was enormous: a Georgian gentleman wore as many as four dozen buttons on one set of clothes for the coat, waistcoat and breeches.[41] Buttons could be a means of conspicuous display (Fig. 11.1). In 1776 John Hodges, while only an apprentice at Soho, bought eighteen silver coat buttons at £1.1s.0½d and a further fourteen for 16s.6d,[42] an enormous outlay given his weekly wages of 7s.0d.[43]

---

41 Quickenden, *op. cit.* (as note 32) pp.78–81.

42 Kenneth Quickenden and Arthur J. Kover, 'Did Boulton Sell Silver Plate to the Middle Class? A Quantitative Study of Luxury Marketing in late Eighteenth-Century Britain', *Journal of Macromarketing*, 27, 1 (2007), 51–64 (p.58).

43 BAH, MS 3782/1/3 p.251, 31 December 1776.

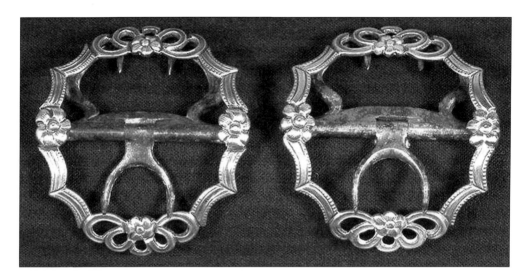

Fig. 11.2. Boulton and Fothergill, pair of silver and steel buckles, 1773-4, partial and promised gift, James C. Codell Jnr., courtesy The Speed Art Museum.

Buckles were available from Soho in a variety of materials, including gilt, steel and imitation tortoiseshell.[44] At least on one occasion, in 1772, tutenague buckles were made at Soho.[45] Silver buckles were made there in the 1760s,[46] but by 1773 Boulton was factoring silver buckles made by Thomas Mynd whose work Boulton regarded highly.[47] The silver buckles in Fig. 11.2, though with the makers' marks of Boulton and Fothergill, were therefore probably not made at Soho. However, about 1790 silver buckles were made there as were Sheffield-plate buckles.[48] Boulton had earlier refused to make the latter too [49] though he had been willing to send customers cards of plated buckles by Willmore and Alston [50] or recommended customers to go to that Birmingham firm.[51] It is not clear what kind of plating was used. Sheffield-plate presented problems in covering the copper edge [52] and French-plating on steel (which was normally used for buckles) was generally found to be unsatisfactory.[53] Close-plating was therefore often preferred and John Alston was involved with

---

44 Quickenden, *op. cit.* (as note 32), p.89.

45 Pinn, *op. cit.*, p.54.

46 BAH, MS Timmins, Collection of Original Letters, Part 1, p.11.

47 BAH, MS 3782/12/60/108, MB to JF, 28 April 1773.

48 BAH, MS 3782/12/38, MB to Mr Collins, 24 October 1793.

49 BAH, MS 3782/2/14, p.48, JH to Samuel Silver, 16 November 1782.

50 BAH, MS 3782/1/11, p.807, B&F to Andrew Grain, 3 July 1781.

51 BAH, MS 3782/2/14, p.283, JH to Samuel Silver, 26 November 1784.

52 Bradbury, *op. cit.*, p.22.

53 Bradbury, *op. cit.*, pp.6–7.

improvements to close-plating in the 1780s, though he also made improvements to French-plating, both in connection with buckles.[54] An employee, Thomas Greenhow bought a pair of 'plated' buckles for 2s.10d.[55] Boulton once bought a (probably elaborate) pair of silver shoe buckles for 27s.0d.[56] Boulton formed a partnership with James Smith in 1793, to make latchets, which pinched the two sides of a shoe together;[57] they were available (per pair), in Sheffield-plate for 3s.6d and in silver from 7s.0d to 10s.0d.[58]

Fig. 11.3. Boulton and Fothergill, pair of silver 'Lyon-faced' Candlesticks, 1768-9, partial and promised gift, James C. Codell Jnr., courtesy The Speed Art Museum.

Small filigree items were usually made in gilt base-metal or silver. Large gilt handkerchief slides (rings through which the sides of a handkerchief could be drawn together) cost 9s.0d a dozen, the same as in silver.[59] Purse runners (rings used to push coins to the ends of a fabric tube, sometimes called a 'miser' or 'stocking' purse) were made in steel at 3s.9d per dozen while those in silver filigree cost 9s.0d a dozen. Silver filigree tea-measures cost 5s.9d or 5s.0d (whereas those in Sheffield-plate cost 18s.0d a dozen).[60] Extravagant hairstyles required hat pins; those in silver filigree cost 5s.6d per dozen [61] but plated wire and pearl hat pins cost 2s.7½d for an unspecified number on a card.[62]

Boulton made candlesticks in various metals such as copper and thought about making silvered candlesticks in the 1760s but that was not pursued.[63] He dismissed as early as 1762 (for reasons which are not clear) the idea of using platina for candlesticks.[64] Early in the 1770s a number of tutenague

54   John Alston, Patent No.1511, 1785, 'Covering Buckles and Other Articles with Gold etc'.
55   BAH, MS 3782/1/5, p.78, 23 October 1781.
56   BAH, MS 3782/1/6, p.93, 12 November 1779.
57   Dickinson, *op. cit.*, p.14.
58   BAH, MS 3782/2/15 p.102, JH to E. Lock & Son, 31 January 1797.
59   BAH, MS 3782/1/6, p.305, Order for T&T Richards, 25 October 1779.
60   Quickenden, *op. cit.* (see note 32), p.89.
61   BAH, MS 3782/1/6 p.376, Order for John Wise, 10 August 1780.
62   BAH, MS 3782/1/6 p.225, Order for A.F.R. (code for an agent abroad), 26 April 1780.
63   Quickenden, *op. cit.* (as note 32), p.86.
64   BAH, MS 3782/1/12, MB to Joshua Steele, 29 October 1762.

candlesticks were sold to trade customers in London,[65] at between 25s.0d and four guineas per pair,[66] but by 1772 Boulton decided not to continue with the metal 'as our plated wares [i.e. Sheffield-plate] can be afforded as cheap and look much better'[67] though some sales subsequently were made to middle-class customers.[68] Occasionally Boulton made cast silver candlesticks: 'lyon-faced' candlesticks made for the 3rd Earl of Kerry in 1771–2 required 108 troy ozs of silver at 5s.9d per troy oz which with a fashioning charge of 2s.3d per oz., came to £43.8s.9d. That method was used in London, but through making the candlestick with a drop-stamp and dies (Fig. 11.3) only 38ozs were required and for these Boulton charged just £17.2s.0d., selling some to members of

Fig. 11.4. M. Boulton Plate Co. pair of Sheffield-plate candlesticks, c.1800. Birmingham Assay Office.

the gentry such as Sir Alexander Gilmour. The same dies were used for Sheffield-plate candlesticks at £7.17s.6d per pair.[69] Boulton was surprised that the 1st Baron Ravensworth ordered four pairs in Sheffield-plate and tried to persuade him to buy another pattern in silver; Ravensworth could not be persuaded and in 1774 bought four pairs for himself and two pairs for his friend the 2nd Marquis of Rockingham.[70] Boulton made other patterns in silver from £5 to £10 per pair and in Sheffield-plate from £1.0s.0d to £2.12s.6d.[71] In 1780, thirty in silver were sold and 2500 in Sheffield-plate.[72] There is substantial evidence for the purchase of Sheffield-plate candlesticks by the middle classes [73] (Fig. 11.4) and candlesticks remained a consistent part

65 BAH, MS 3782/1/9, p.102, B&F to Woolley and Heming, 12 May 1771 and MS 3782/1/9, p.464, AJC to William Webb, 30 May 1772.

66 Birmingham Assay Office (BAO), MS 3782/1/9 p.6, JW to John Ewer, 8 January 1770.

67 BAO, MS 3782/1/9 pp.64–5, MB to Rodney Valltravers, n.d. 1772.

68 E.g. Two pairs sold to Dr Fell, BAH, MS 3782/1/1 p.292, 11 March 1778 and four pairs sold to John Scale, a manager at Soho, BAO, MS 3782/1/7, 25 January 1774.

69 Kenneth Quickenden, "Lyon-faced' Candlesticks and Candelabra,' *Silver Society Journal*, No.11 Autumn 1999, pp.196–209 (pp.200–206).

70 Kenneth Quickenden, 'Boulton and Fothergill Silver: Business plans and miscalculations' *Art History*, 3, 3 (1980), 274–294 (p.282).

71 Quickenden, *op. cit.* (as note 69), p.206.

72 Quickenden, *op. cit.* (as note 32), pp.87–92.

73 E.g. Order for small candlesticks at £1.1s.0d per pair for Captain Packwood, 16 February 1780, BAH, MS 3782/1/6, p.134.

of production at Soho,[74] even though candlesticks of brass or iron were available from elsewhere for as little 7s.6d and 2s.0d respectively.[75]

Boulton factored snuffers, usually of steel, to provide a sharp and durable cutting edge and these sold for 4s.0d. Silver handles ('bows') could be added, in which case the cost was 15s.0d. Partially plated snuffers were sold at 8s.9d. but those described as 'entirely plated' cost 15s.6d. These may well have been Sheffield-plate, used for snuffers elsewhere, but some listed in a Soho inventory were specifically described as French-plated.[76] Another pair described as 'silvered'[77] was factored.[78]

Silver tea-urns, ranging from £27 to £100 were sold to the aristocracy and the gentry but rarely to the middle-classes (Boulton's purchase of one being an exception).[79] Even Sheffield-plate tea-urns cost £6.0s.0d. (if tinned inside) [80] or £10.10s.0d [81] if plated on both sides. There was therefore a substantial market for bronzed tea-urns with plated ornaments costing £4.10s.0d,[82] one customer, able to afford Sheffield-plate candlesticks, only bought a bronzed tea urn [83] (Fig. 11.5). Some tea-urn handles were French-plated.[84] Silver teapots, in one case charged at £9.19s.10d, were not infrequently purchased by middle-class customers, such as Mrs Ryland, wife of a local banker,[85] but Sheffield-plate teapots, cost far less (one cost £2.12.6d). In 1780 two silver teapots were sold against thirty-five in Sheffield-plate. Boulton was dismissive about making ordinary silver tankards. Although he

Fig. 11.5. Boulton designs for tea-urns. Birmingham Archives and Heritage, MS 3782/21/2, p.129.

---

74   BAO, MS PR. In 1798–99 sixty-four pairs of candlesticks were assayed and only seventy other items (apart from mounts).

75   Berg, *op. cit.*, p.185.

76   Quickenden, *op. cit.* (see note 32) p.87.

77   BAH, MS 3782/1/6 p.129, Order for Alex Baxter, 15 February 1780.

78   BAH, MS 3782/1/4 p.461, four pairs of silvered snuffers from James Wright £1.8s.0d, 23 December 1780.

79   Quickenden and Kover, *op. cit.*, p.56.

80   BAH, MS 3782/1/6 pp.382–83, Order for A.S.B. Yield, 15 August 1780.

81   BAH, MS 3782/1/6 p.305, Order for S. Ford, 27 June 1780.

82   BAH, MS 3782/1/6 p.239, Order for R. Preston, 8 May 1780.

83   BAH, MS 3782/1/2, p.333, Order for John Williams, 8 December 1781.

84   BAH, MS 3782/2/13, p.138.

85   Quickenden and Kover, *op. cit.*, p.57.

did occasionally make them in silver (expensively once at £6.17s.8d) they were produced in far larger quantities in Sheffield-plate at £1.12s.0d: in 1780 Soho sold only one silver tankard but forty-eight in Sheffield-plate.[86] Wine-labels hung from the shoulders' of bottles, were bought by the 6th Earl of Craven in Sheffield-plate at 2s.0d,[87] while the ironmaster John Wilkinson's, in silver, cost 4s.0d.[88]

Boulton factored Sheffield-plate spoons from Sheffield, observing in 1783 that few had been made at Soho resulting in 'great trouble and little profit', finding as did others, difficulty in covering the copper edge. Some French-plated spoons were recorded in 1782,[89] but the technique was time-consuming and lacked durability.[90] 'Plated' spoons were sold later,[91] but the firm continued to factor at least some of them.[92] Customers were advised to buy silver spoons since plated ones could not be made of 'proportional cheapness'[93] and from the mid-1770s Soho made silver spoons in large quantities: 512 were assayed in 1773–4.[94] An order from Richard Gore, who belonged to the gentry, consisted of a wide range of Sheffield-plate, but his tablespoons alone were silver.[95] The ironmaster John Wilkinson bought six silver teaspoons at 18s.11d each[96] while a trade customer was charged £3.12s.0d for six dozen plated teaspoons.[97]

Since Sheffield was a major place for knife manufacture, Boulton's customers were often directed there[98] or he factored knives[99] and continued to do so even after manufacture started at Soho.[100] By 1780 Soho made Sheffield-plate handles[101] and by the mid-1770s silver handles using steel blades from Sheffield.[102] Though blunting quickly, silver blades were occasionally used.[103] Sheffield-plate was unsuitable for blades because the copper edge was hard to

---

86   Quickenden, *op. cit.* (see note 32), pp.83–95.
87   BAH, MS 3782/1/6 p.610, 3 April 1780.
88   BAH, MS 3782/1/3 p.216, 20 November 1776.
89   Quickenden, *op. cit.* (see note 32), p.81.
90   Bradbury, *op. cit.*, pp.96–7.
91   BAH, MS 3782/2/15, p.221, MB to M. Richardson, 28 June 1798.
92   BAH, MS 3782/2/14, p.221, B&F to Playfair, Wilson and Co, 31 May 1784.
93   BAH, MS 3782/1/9, p.602, B&F to Dr John Turton, 14 October 1772.
94   BAO, MS PR.
95   BAH, MS 3782/1/6, p.473, 1 November 1780.
96   BAH, MS 3782/1/6, p.283, 7 June 1780.
97   BAH, MS 3782/1/6, p.575, order for James Phynn, 23 February 1781.
98   BAH, MS 3782/2/14, p.167, JH to Alex Sharp, 26 December 1783.
99   BAH, MS 3782/1/9, p.604, F. Jukes to C&L Procter, 14 October 1772.
100 BAH, MS 3782/2/15, MB to ?, 5 August 1799.
101 BAH, MS 3782/1/11, p.564, JH to Wakelyn and Taylor, 27 March 1780.
102 BAH, MS 3782/1/10, p.791, B&F to John and Robert Hinchcliffe, 24 December 1776.
103 BAH, MS 3782/2/15, p.236, MB Plate Co. to Knowill and Cador, 18 July 1797.

Fig. 11.6. Boulton and Fothergill, one of a set of silver sauce tureens for Mrs. Montagu, 1776–7, Birmingham Assay Office.

cover, and like French-plating lacked durability for such a purpose.[104] Normally Boulton followed the Sheffield practice of stamping knife handles in two halves (with the end of the blade inserted into hot pitch placed in the handle after the halves had been soldered) which replaced thicker castings traditionally used in London.[105] Exceptionally, Boulton offered to make knives with cast handles for Duke Peter Friedrich Ludwig of Holstein-Gottorp.[106]

The problems of making the prongs of forks with Sheffield-plate were considerable: silver points were sometimes added.[107] In the early 1770s customers were urged to apply direct to Sheffield for forks with Sheffield-plate handles [108] or Boulton obtained them from that source for his customers.[109] By 1780 Soho produced forks with Sheffield-plate handles and steel prongs,[110] and silver forks by 1773,[111] having previously factored them (and silver-handled knives) from Sheffield.[112]

---

104 Bradbury, *op. cit.*, pp.5–7.
105 Bradbury, *op. cit.*, p.455.
106 BAH, MS 3782/1/10, p.528, B&F to JW, 10 February 1776.
107 Bradbury, *op. cit.*, pp.335–36.
108 BAH, MS 3782/1/9, p.294, B&F to John Wace, 3 December 1771.
109 BAH, MS 3782/1/10, p.587, B&F to Benjamin Withers, 28 September 1774.
110 BAH, MS 3782/1/11, p.564, JH to Wakelyn and Taylor, 27 March 1780.
111 BAO, MS PR.
112 BAH, MS 3782/1/9, p.604, F. Jukes to C&C Procters, 14 October 1772.

Fig. 11.7. Boulton and Fothergill, set of dinner plates for Mrs. Montagu, 1776–7. Partridge Fine Arts.

In 1776–7 11,831 troy ozs of silver from Soho were passed at the Birmingham Assay Office, the highest in Boulton's lifetime.[113] In the 1770s a large proportion was for five services of plate, all for the aristocracy and gentry.[114] Elizabeth Montagu, a member of the gentry with an annual income of £7000 bought a service worth £1114.0s.11d, which she regarded in part as an investment:[115] soup tureens, plates, dishes and covers (four of which were Sheffield-plate, which could have been about one eighth the cost of covers in silver) sauceboats (Fig. 11.6) and smaller items such as ladles and asparagus tongs.[116] Boulton met her, designs were discussed with her, the design of the sauceboats was new, though probably based on designs by the leading Neo-classical architect James Wyatt who promoted the change towards a lighter and more elegant Neo-classicism. Fig. 11.6 was predominantly made with skilful traditional techniques (the base, bowl and cover were all hand-raised and the festoons of husks were shaped with specially-made punches) though

113 BAO, MS PR.

114 Quickenden, *op. cit.* (see note 42), p.56.

115 Kenneth Quickenden, 'Elizabeth Montagu's Service of Plate – Part 1, *Silver Society Journal*, 16 (2004), 131–41 (pp.134–38).

116 Kenneth Quickenden 'Elizabeth Montagu's Service of Plate – Part 2, *Silver Society Journal*, 19 (2005), 19–37 (pp.28–34).

the ribbon-and-reed border was probably die-stamped. Even with these items Boulton was competitive with London makers: he reckoned that their plates would have been heavier (20–22 troy ozs against 16 troy ozs) and his fashioning charge was 1s.2d against 1s.6d per troy oz (Fig. 11.7).[117]

Though prestigious, these orders were not profitable, largely because Boulton was operating on an overdraft and interest charges on purchases of bullion were greater than the profit margin, when, as often happened, customers paid late. Boulton declined orders from 1777 and manufacture was dramatically reduced (assay silver slumped to 263ozs in 1782–3) with the aim of increasing Sheffield-plate production.[118] External factors also militated in favour of Sheffield-plate. Apart from economic depression following the war with America from 1775 [119] platers who had been prohibited from placing their marks on pieces after 1773, were, from 1784, permitted to register marks at the Sheffield Assay Office as long as they were different from their marks on silver. The date, Birmingham Assay Office's mark (an anchor) lion passant (sterling silver) and 'maker's' initials on Boulton's silver were replaced on his Sheffield-plate by two suns.[120] This gave respectability and the new material gained further advantage from the re-introduction of a duty of 6d per troy oz (which had been dropped in 1757) on assay silver.[121]

Even by 1780, excluding buttons, 91% of the silver and Sheffield-plate items sold from Soho were Sheffield-plate.[122] Later the London agent was required to give priority to Sheffield-plate orders over silver.[123] He obtained very large orders from retailers who were given discounts for Sheffield-plate but not silver.In 1798 Rundell and Bridge of London purchased £247.15s.0d of Sheffield-plate, but only £8.0s.9d of silver. The emphasis was on making Sheffield-plate a powerful rival: in 1798 Boulton was happy to quote prices for ecclesiastical wares in Sheffield-plate, a material he had not thought appropriate for such purposes in the 1770s. In 1798 the firm offered three types of borders for Sheffield-plate dishes, two of silver with only one of Sheffield-plate, and all Sheffield-plate trays had silver borders and were double-plated.[124] An extra 14s.0d was charged for a pair of thickly-plated candlestick branches, normally costing £3.15s.0d.[125]

117 Quickenden, *op. cit.* (see note 70), pp.278–84.

118 Quickenden, *op. cit.* (as note 70), pp.287–88.

119 T.S. Ashton, *Economic Fluctuations in England*, 1700–1800 (Oxford, 1959), pp.162–4.

120 Bradbury, *op. cit.*, p.49.

121 Forbes, *op. cit.*, p.228.

122 Quickenden, *op. cit.* (as note 32), p.90.

123 BAH, MS 3782/2/15, pp.450–1, JH to RC, 20 November 1800.

124 Kenneth Quickenden 'Richard Chippindall and the Boultons', *Silver Studies. Journal of the Silver Society*, 22, 2007, p.51–65, (p.54).

125 BAH, MS 3782/1/6, p.331, Order for James Johnstone, 11 July 1780.

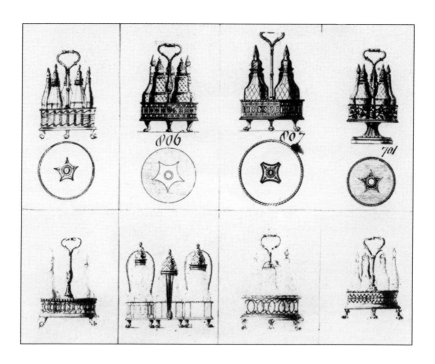

Fig. 11.8. Boulton, designs for cruets. Birmingham Archives and Heritage,
MS 3782/21/2 p.57.

Sheffield-plate ladies' toilette services, including such things as needle-cushions, looking-glasses and stands were promoted from the early 1780s.[126] Sets were increasingly bought by the middle classes.[127] In 1800 Dr H. Edgar bought three pairs of candlesticks, a pair of branches, a waiter, an epergne (a centre piece for sweetmeats) a tray, a teapot, a toast-rack, two muffineers (sugar shakers), three pairs of salts, a cream jug and three pairs of bottle stands, which, with glass dishes for the epergne and salts, came to £37.11s.6d.[128] Sets were sometimes sold to the aristocracy [129] and as far away as the West Indies.[130] Items were routinely ordered from pattern books, normally through the trade.[131] The range of goods in silver was similar to Sheffield-plate and increasingly the emphasis was, in both, on light wire work

126 BAH, MS 3782/1/11, p.641, B&F to Baumgartner and Hoffstetter, 12 October 1780.
127 BAH, MS 3782/1/6, p.437, Order by John Floud, 23 September 1780. The Sheffield-plate came to
      £46.3s.6d.
128 BAH, MS 3782/2/15, p.422, MB Co. to Dr H. Edgar, n.d.7.1800.
129 BAH, MS 3782/2/14, B&F to Lord Lucan, 14 May 1783, Sheffield-plate valued at £17.12s.0d.
130 BAH, MS 3782/2/15 MB to Robert Jones, 25 September 1799.
131 BAH, MS 3782/2/15 p.449, JH to RC, 8 November 1800.
132 BAO, MS PR, 1793–4.

for such items as bread baskets or cruet frames,[132] which often had repetitive fly-pressed bands of decoration (Fig. 11.8). There was little artistic ambition and few special items were made in Boulton's later years.[133]

Sheffield-plate increasingly dominated other substitutes. Lack of malleability confined the use of platina to buttons; nevertheless, when Boulton was offered a batch where that was less true, at the end of the century,[134] there is nothing to suggest that he took advantage of the opportunity. The use of 'white metal' seems to have been limited to buttons, but it was taken up in a major way by other manufacturers in the nineteenth century, though more as a replacement for pewter than silver.[135] Boulton made silvered buttons, and occasionally other items with this method; it was cheaper than Sheffield-plate (a pair of salts in an identical pattern cost 14s.0d as against 9s.6d)[136] but he preferred Sheffield-plate for its greater durability [137] though he also factored silvered pieces. Around 1770 there was enthusiasm at Soho for tutenague, for candlesticks and other items [138] because of its durability [139] and its cost, about the same as Sheffield-plate. However, Boulton preferred the (normally) whiter Sheffield-plate as his firm usually plated with pure silver.[140] Although he found some middle-class customers, there was little enthusiasm for tutenague in the market place [141] and supplies of the metal varied in quality [142] so that by the 1780s it was sold cheaply to clear stocks.[143] Only from the 1820s when the metal (or a close equivalent) was made in Europe to provide cheaper and more consistent supplies did the metal become widely popular.[144] The lack of durability and the tediousness of French-plating led to its decline nationally from the late 1760s as the popularity of Sheffield-plate grew.[145] It is doubtful whether French-plate ever offered a serious rival to Sheffield-plate at Soho but there were circumstances where it was useful: it could be offered to customers when required, [146]

133 Quickenden, *op. cit.* (as note 124), pp.55–56.

134 BAH, MS 3782/12/59/95, RC to MB, 2 July 1798.

135 Bradbury, *op. cit.*, p.494.

136 BAH, MS 3782/1/6 p.113, Order for Oatridge and Marindin, 21 January 1780.

137 BAH, MS 3782/1/11 p.612, JH to Mason and Lobrot, 1 July 1780.

138 E.g. dish crosses (BAH, MS 3782/1/9, JW to Woolley and Heming, 27 June 1771).

139 BAH, MS 3782/2/14 pp.126–27, JH to Benjamin Henfrey, 7 July 1783.

140 BAH, MS 3782/1/9 p.685, B&F to J.B. Rogler, 28 December 1772.

141 BAH, MS 3782/1/9 p.403, B&F to William Wilson, 19 March 1772.

142 Pinn, *op. cit.* (as note 35), p.55.

143 BAH, MS 3782/2/14, pp.126–7, JH to Benjamin Henfrey, 7 July 1783.

144 The metal was called German silver. It had a higher copper and nickel content, but less zinc than tutenague. Pinn, *op. cit.*, pp.60–71.

145 Clifford, *op. cit.*, p.93.

146 MB offered to copy covers with French-plated brass knobs BAH, MS 3782/2/14 pp.138–9, JH to J. Stuart, 21 August 1783.

small parts were sometimes French-plated [147] and it was used for repairing Sheffield-plate where silver flaked off.[148] Though not of Soho manufacture, it is likely that some of Boulton's customers were supplied with buckles finished with close-plate, though this technique was more generally used in the early nineteenth century where resilience, or the plating of a cutting edge was required, an area of difficulty with Sheffield-plate.[149] Boulton's commitment to Sheffield-plate, despite some early dependence on Sheffield for cutlery, saw Soho produce a wide range of articles so there was little need later for factoring.[150] The success of Sheffield-plate was due to its increasing resemblance to silver-plate and the greater durability of the silver surfaces and edges compared with French-plate. Moreover, although the material could not be cast (if it was to still look like silver) that scarcely mattered since silver castings could be added and the principal means of manipulation at the Soho Manufactory were hand-raising and the use of dies[151] also employed in shaping silver.

Articles were widely available in other materials at a lower rate than in Sheffield-plate but Sheffield-plate was at least half the price of silver-plate. Though the cost of making articles in the two metals was much the same, in 1780 the plated material for Sheffield-plate cost 0s.6d to 1s.0d per troy oz depending on quality,[152] but sterling cost 5s.6½d per troy oz and pure silver 6s.2d,[153] used for the finest filigree.[154] There was no tax on Sheffield-plate. Apart from the duty on newly-made silver (which increased from 6d to 1s.0d per troy oz in 1794) [155] there was a tax between 1756 and 1777 for those owning 100 troy ozs or more.[156] Moreover, silver was less valued as a means of investment than it had been, since government stocks and East India Co. shares were becoming increasingly popular.[157] Boulton did find a broad market for small silver items, medium-priced pieces sometimes sold to the middle-classes but expensive purchases of silver were generally confined to the aristocracy and gentry. But Sheffield-plate production became much larger, attracting orders from the lower classes but much more from an emulative middle-class and increasingly the aristocracy also.

---

147 BAH, MS 3782/2/13 p.137.

148 Bradbury, *op. cit.*, p.97.

149 Bradbury, *op. cit.*, pp.5–7.

150 E.g. Some Sheffield-plate candlesticks were factored from Winter, Parsons and Hall because Soho was rushed. (BAH, MS 3782/1/11, p.180, 28 February 1778).

151 Bradbury, *op. cit.*, pp.103–112.

152 BAH, MS 3782/2/13, p.137.

153 BAH, MS 3782/1/4, p.463, 14 September 1780.

154 Quickenden, *op. cit.*, p.350.

155 Forbes, *op. cit.*, p.233.

156 Clifford, *op. cit.*, p.93.

157 Clifford, *op. cit.*, p.8.

Nevertheless, the production of assay silver rose to 10,016 ozs in 1805–6 [158] in line with the increase in demand nationally.[159] In addition to candlesticks, there was demand for mainly light pieces [160] and novel items, such as wine labels.[161] Much was cheaply produced by presses, but such pieces, though of silver, were in Boulton's mind, no more than substitutes for what he had really wanted to produce when in 1771 he confided to Lord Shelburne his ambition to become a 'great silversmith'.[162] Stamped articles were not generally objects of admiration, whether in the world of silversmithing [163] or elsewhere.[164] Boulton's ambition to make services of silver-plate and large ambitious items with high levels of art and craft for the aristocracy and gentry was limited to the 1770s because such work was unprofitable. Yet this work, as James Keir wrote shortly after Boulton's death in 1809 '...greatly tended to his celebrity and admiration of his various talents, taste and enterprise.'[165]

Acknowledgements
Thanks to Gordon Crosskey and Jeremy Weston for advice during the preparation of this article.

References
Most primary source references are to the Archives of Soho, which includes The Matthew Boulton Papers, MS 3782, in Archives and Heritage, Central Library, Birmingham (BAH). *The Register of Plate and Silver Wares* (PR) is at the Birmingham Assay Office (BAO).

Abbreviations
AJC – A.J. Cabrit, clerk at Soho.
B&F – Boulton and Fothergill.
JF – John Fothergill, Boulton's partner, 1762–1782.
JH – John Hodges, an apprentice and later a manager at Soho.
MB – Matthew Boulton.
RC – Richard Chippindall, London agent.
WM – William Matthews, London agent and banker.
JW – John Wyatt, clerk at Soho.

---

158 BAO, MS PR.
159 Forbes, *op. cit.*, p.320.
160 Clifford, *op. cit.*, p.181.
161 Clifford, *op. cit.*, p.8.
162 BAO, MS 3782/1/9 p.2, MB to Lord Shelburne, 7 January 1771.
163 Goldsmiths Co, London, Court Book 17, 1767–1777, p.232, 6 May 1773. London's silversmiths contemptuously referred to silver 'stamped with dies.'
164 Berg, *op. cit.*, p.99.
165 Quickenden, *op. cit.* (as note 70), p.288.

Chapter 12

MATTHEW BOULTON
AND THE ROYAL MINT

David Symons

Matthew Boulton's relationship with the Royal Mint was complex and lasted for more than twenty years, so it is not possible to cover it in detail here. Furthermore, since this book is about Matthew Boulton and his life, the story will unapologetically be told from his side, with less emphasis on the Mint and its reactions to the upstart industrialist from Birmingham.

By the early 1770s, the Royal Mint was held in low esteem. Despite Britain's status as an economic powerhouse, its coinage in the later eighteenth century was in a deplorable condition. Coins were struck in gold, silver and copper, and there were problems with each metal. Many of the gold coins in use were old and underweight. Good coins which did exist were frequently hoarded.[1] Very few silver coins were struck by the Mint after 1750 and the silver in circulation 'had deteriorated into an assortment of worn and dilapidated genuine coins, blank discs, foreign coins and counterfeits'.[2] To be fair, this was not the Mint's fault, since it could only coin bullion brought to it either by the government or by private individuals.[3] The problem was that

---

1 Sir John Craig, *The Mint. A History of the London Mint from A.D. 287 to 1948* (Cambridge, 1953), pp.241–42; G.P. Dyer and P.P. Gaspar, 'Reform, the new technology and Tower Hill, 1700–1966', pp.398–606 in C.E. Challis (ed.), *A New History of the Royal Mint* (Cambridge, 1992), pp.431–2. Only the gold coinage really concerned the government since that is primarily what it conducted its business in, and which it recognised as being important for foreign trade. Accordingly, in 1773–7 an ambitious reform programme was put into effect. Over sixteen and a half million new coins were minted and three-quarters of the old ones in circulation were replaced (Craig, pp.242–5; Dyer/Gaspar, pp.440–1). To facilitate the introduction of the new coins, exchanges were set up across the country where the public could trade in their old coins for the new ones. Matthew Boulton was one of the agents employed to run an exchange, his first involvement in the operation of the national currency (Craig, pp.244, 263).

2 Dyer/Gaspar, p.398.

3 Dyer/Gaspar, p.431.

the price which the Mint was allowed to pay for silver bullion, which was set by the government, was too low to attract many customers.[4]

Copper coinage was also in a terrible state. The number of copper coins struck at the Royal Mint was decided by the government, which told the Mint when and how much to mint.[5] Reasonable amounts of copper coins had been struck up to 1754, but problems then arose because, while the Mint struck the coins, it did not distribute them. They could only be bought in 5s. or 10s. packets at the Mint, which was housed in the Tower of London.[6] The result was that many of the copper coins stayed in London, where they accumulated in the hands of the brewers and shopkeepers like butchers, bakers and grocers. They were stuck with large amounts of low value coin which banks would not accept and the Mint would not redeem for silver or gold coins. Understandably they complained about what they saw as a surfeit of copper, so the government had very few copper coins minted from 1755 to 1775 and none at all for more than twenty years from 1775. As a result, large parts of the country found themselves in desperate need of small change,[7] and people were forced to use a mixture of old worn regal coins, low-weight Irish coins, 'evasive' halfpennies, outright forgeries, and even blank discs.[8] In 1787 the Mint examined samples of halfpennies taken from circulation and found that just 8% had a 'tolerable resemblance' to royal coin.[9] In the same year a further element was added when the first trade tokens were issued. These were unofficial money issued by industrialists, merchants and towns to help facilitate trade. Large numbers were struck in the next ten years.

Calls for reform mounted and in February 1780 Edmund Burke introduced an unsuccessful bill in Parliament to abolish the Mint and transfer its functions to the Bank of England.[10] In his speech he pointed out that making coins was an

---

4   Craig, pp.246–8; Dyer/Gaspar, pp.433–4; G. Selgin. *Good Money. Birmingham Button Makers, the Royal Mint, and the Beginnings of Modern Coinage, 1775–1821. Private Enterprise and Popular Coinage* (Ann Arbor, 2008), pp.17–19.

5   Craig, pp.250–51; Selgin, p.20.

6   Selgin, p.22.

7   Craig, pp.251–2; Dyer/Gaspar, pp.434–7; Selgin, p.22.

8   As Craig, p.253, notes 'ordinary folk, if short of small change, cared nothing about either intrinsic value, high quality of copper, pattern or limits of legal tender'. There were thirteen Irish pence to a shilling, rather than twelve as in Britain, so Irish halfpennies were slightly lighter than their British counterparts. 'Evasive' coins were so-called because they evaded the laws on forgery by having their legends or designs changed in some way from those on genuine coins, while at the same time still looking very similar to them. Birmingham was a major centre for forgery (the term 'Brummagem halfpence' was used to describe low quality forgeries before 1750). The manufacture of forgeries became almost an open business in the town – by 1770 you could buy thirty-six forged halfpennies (with a face value of 1s.6d.) for just 1s. (Craig, pp.251–3; Selgin, pp.29–33).

9   Craig, p.253.

10   Craig, p.237; Dyer/Gaspar, p.441; Selgin, p.63.

Fig. 12.1. (Top) obverse and reverse of a 1771 halfpenny; (below, from left to right) obverses of a very worn halfpenny of George II (1727–60), a forged halfpenny, and an 'evasive' halfpenny. Birmingham Museums and Art Gallery.

industrial process and that they should be made in the best and cheapest way, which did not describe the archaic workings of the Royal Mint.[11] In 1782, the Treasury commissioned a Birmingham businessman, Samuel Garbett, and his son Francis, to investigate the Mint and its workings. Their report was submitted in March 1783, but seems to have been too thorough for the government, which thanked them, paid them £500, and then did nothing about it.[12] However, while carrying out his investigations, Garbett asked his friend Matthew Boulton for his advice. As Birmingham's leading button and 'toy' manufacturer, Boulton understood the technicalities of stamping metal and had already dipped his toes into numismatic waters, having made medals for distribution on Captain Cook's second voyage to the Pacific in 1772 and other medals in 1774 and 1781.[13] Although nothing came of the Garbetts' report, it set Boulton thinking, since William Murdock later described conversations with him in 1784 or 1785 when he mused on the idea of using a steam engine to power coin presses, and it was probably at this time that he convinced himself that he was the best man to solve the country's problems with its copper coinage.[14] Gold and silver were recognised

11   For which see Dyer/Gaspar, pp.399–424.

12   For the details, see Dyer/Gaspar, pp.441–4. See also Craig, pp.237–8; Selgin, pp.62–3.

13   D. Vice, 'A numismatic history of the Soho manufactory and mint 1772–1850', (forthcoming: to be published by the British Numismatic Society); L. Brown, *British Historical Medals 1760–1960. Volume I, The Accession of George III to the Death of William IV* (London, 1980), p.38 No.165.

14   Selgin, pp.63–4.

as being the proper concern of the Royal Mint, but copper coins were different
– the Garbetts were told by Mint officers that coining copper 'was not considered
as properly belonging to the Mint';[15] and their manufacture had been entrusted
to a consortium of private contractors as recently as 1701.[16]

These strands came together in 1786 when Boulton struck a deal with the
East India Company over the production of coins for Bencoolen (mod.
Benkulen), one of its possessions in Sumatra. Since he did not have a mint of
his own, he prepared the coin blanks at the Soho manufactory and shipped
them to London, where they were struck into coins on machines that he
installed in a warehouse owned by the Company. In this manner just over 48
tons of copper were successfully coined in 1786–7.[17] Problems that he
encountered seem to have convinced him that, if he were to get into this
business, it would be better to set up his own mint at Soho, and that it should
be powered by steam.

He was encouraged because he had high hopes of winning a contract for
a new national copper coinage. Supported by Samuel Garbett, in 1786 he
began lobbying the government.[18] However, in February 1787 he discovered
that Thomas Williams, 'the Copper King', who ran the Parys Mine Company,
also had ambitions to win the contract.[19] Both sides engaged in spoiling
operations and continued to push their own proposals throughout 1787, but
neither had clinched the contract by the time that a Committee of the Privy
Council was set up in November to look into the problems with the coinage.[20]
The Committee asked Boulton for details of his plans and samples of his
proposed coins,[21] and after he met them in January 1788 he convinced
himself that the contract had been all but promised to him:

> I was sent for to Town by Mr Pitt and the Privy Council about a new
> copper coinage which I have agreed for but at a very low price yet
> nevertheless it shall be the best Copper Coin that ever was made.[22]

---

15 Selgin, p.250.
16 Dyer/Gaspar, pp.374–7.
17 Vice; R. Doty, *The Soho Mint and the Industrialization of Money* (London, 1998), pp.299–301; B.M.
    Gould, 'Matthew Boulton's East India Company mint in London, 1786–88', *Seaby Coin and Medal
    Bulletin* No.612 (August 1969), pp.270–77.
18 Vice; Selgin, p.64. At one point Garbett and Boulton even suggested that they should be appointed
    Joint Wardens for the copper coinage and produce a new coinage at the Royal Mint, using
    machines to be supplied by Boulton (Vice).
19 Selgin, pp.64–5; Doty, pp.27–9. Williams has the distinction of being the first man to issue trade
    tokens: see Selgin, pp.40–8; they were in production by February 1787.
20 Craig, p.256; Dyer/Gaspar, p.446. For some of the underhand goings on see Vice.
21 Selgin, pp.102–3.
22 Matthew Boulton to Matthew Robinson Boulton, 8 February 1788 (MBP, MS 3782/13/36, item No.19).

*Fig. 12.2. (Top) obverse of a 1797 Cartwheel twopence, reverse of a Cartwheel
penny; (below) obverse of a 1799 halfpenny, reverse of a 1799 farthing.
Birmingham Museums and Art Gallery.*

Typically, his interest and enthusiasm got the better of his business sense
and from April 1788 he began to build himself a mint.[23] By November the
building was ready and work had begun on installing the machinery. By 1789
he had spent £7–8,000 on the mint, as well as £2,000 upgrading his rolling
mill to cope with the large amounts of copper he expected to process.[24]
Meanwhile, in late 1788, he struck a deal with his rival, Thomas Williams,
under which Williams would not go after the coinage contract, but would
supply the copper.[25]

Unfortunately for Boulton, there was still no sign of the long-expected
contract, despite his frequent lobbying of the key ministers. Late in 1789 the
Privy Council Committee enjoyed a brief flurry of activity that raised his

23   It is suggested that he started work on the mint because he was afraid that it would otherwise not
     be ready if the government suddenly placed the contract (Vice).
24   Vice. A rolling mill was needed to roll out bars of metal to the right thickness to make coins.
25   For the preceding paragraph in general, see Selgin, pp.71–3; Doty, pp.31ff. By this time Williams
     had effectively gained a monopoly position as supplier of copper in Britain.

hopes again, but the officers of the Royal Mint counter-attacked with their *Memorandum against the Proposed Alteration of the Copper Coinage*, questioning the need for a new coinage. Although it is arguable what impact this had on the Committee, once more no progress was made.[26] By June 1790 it was clear that the issue had been put off for the immediate future,[27] and Boulton was complaining about:

> the Conduct of our Government who have boy'd me up with hopes of contracting for 1500 or 2000 tons of Copper Coin & now after spending a great many Thousand pounds... I perceive that I shall be disappointed.[28]

But why was Boulton so keen to become involved in producing the nation's copper coinage? He himself was quite clear about his reasons – he saw reform of the copper coinage as necessary to put an end to counterfeiting and to stop workers being defrauded by having to accept poor substitutes for genuine coins from employers and shopkeepers. Furthermore, he saw the provision of an improved coinage as a manufacturing problem and believed he was the best person to solve it. He was also concerned to redeem the reputation of his home town, Birmingham, whose name had become synonymous with forgery; his own, and Soho's, reputation could be enhanced at the same time.[29] Boulton also had strong economic reasons for wanting the contract. George Selgin has pointed out that Boulton was facing serious financial problems. In the early 1780s most of his business interests were in poor shape and his main source of income was the premiums paid by companies that had acquired Boulton and Watt steam engines.[30] Much of that income came from engines that had been installed in Cornish copper mines, so Boulton had a keen interest in the health of the Cornish copper industry. Unfortunately, in the 1780s Cornish copper was coming under increasing pressure from Thomas Williams's Anglesey copper, which was cheaper to produce. What he needed to ensure the survival of his businesses was a new large-scale demand for copper – and a new royal copper coinage would fit the bill.[31]

Whatever his motives, in 1789 he found himself the owner of the most powerful and modern mint in the world, but lacking the main business for

---

26 Selgin, pp.110–11; Doty, p.34.
27 See Vice and Selgin, pp.103–14, for a full account of all this.
28 Matthew Boulton to Matthew Robinson Boulton, 15 June 1790 (MBP, MS 3782/13/36, item No.46).
29 Doty, pp.26–7; Selgin, pp.65–6.
30 Companies agreed to pay an annual premium equivalent to one-third of the fuel savings they made from using the new engine as against the old one it had replaced (Selgin, pp.67–8).
31 Selgin, pp.66–71.

which it had been built. To keep it functioning Boulton took on whatever work he could find, so during the 1790s the Soho mint turned out tokens, colonial coins, and medals for a variety of customers.[32] Throughout, Boulton continued to wage what Sir John Craig described as his 'guerrilla war' on the government.[33] Consummate publicist that he was he used that fact that Soho had become a tourist attraction to push the case for coinage reform with influential visitors, and samples of the Soho Mint's products were distributed wherever he thought they might aid his case.[34]

In February 1797, a financial crisis gave Boulton his great opportunity.[35] Under the economic pressures of war with France, the Bank of England's gold reserves were disappearing so quickly that on 26 February the Privy Council told the Bank to stop redeeming its banknotes for gold.[36] Faced with a potential collapse of confidence in the financial system, the government acted with speed and, in a burst of activity over the next thirteen days (26 February – 10 March), addressed the problem. First, the Bank of England and the 'country' banks in England and Wales were authorised to issue banknotes of less than £5 in value, which had hitherto been prohibited. The decision was also taken, as an emergency measure, to countermark the Bank's large stock of Spanish silver dollars with the king's head and to put them into circulation at a face value of 4s.9d.[37] The experiment was not a success. The countermarked dollars proved too easy to forge and their recall was announced on 28 September.[38]

The new banknotes and the countermarked Spanish dollars were intended to relieve problems caused by a shortage of gold coins in circulation. In addition, a new copper coinage was planned to help overcome the shortage of low-value silver coins. For this reason, copper pennies and twopences would be

---

32   Vice; Doty, pp.50–51, 302–15; D. Symons, '"Bringing to Perfection the Art of Coining": What did they make at the Soho mint?', in S. Mason (ed.), *Matthew Boulton: Selling What All the World Desires* (London, 2009), forthcoming; Selgin, pp.114–19.

33   Craig, p.264.

34   This will be clear from an examination of Vice.

35   For the events described in this paragraph, see especially G.P. Dyer, 'The currency crisis of 1797', *British Numismatic Journal (BNJ)*, 72 (2002), pp.135–42.

36   See Selgin, pp.155–6, for the background to this crisis.

37   H.E. Manville, *Tokens of the Industrial Revolution. Foreign Silver Coins Countermarked for Use in Great Britain, c.1787–1828* (London, 2001), p.3; Dyer/Gaspar, p.449.

38   Manville, *Tokens*, p.4; Craig, p.261; Selgin, pp.159–60. How did the much-reviled Royal Mint respond to this crisis? In seventeen days (5–21 March inclusive) it countermarked 1,075,250 silver dollars, not a bad performance for an institution working with man-powered screw presses (Dyer, 'The currency crisis', p.139). The old technology was perfectly capable of turning out coins in large quantities: documents about a theft from the Mint in 1798 show one moneyer operating one press, powered by four burly soldiers, striking about 4,000 guinea coins in a two-hour session (G.P. Dyer and P.P. Gaspar, 'Turning the fly', *BNJ*, 76 (2006), pp.357–9).

issued for the first time, rather than the traditional farthings and halfpennies.[39] On 3 March 1797 the Privy Council Committee on coin was reconstituted and Lord Liverpool wrote to Boulton inviting him to London to discuss the new coinage:

> There is no Man who can better judge of the Propriety of the Measure, and of the Plan that ought to be adopted, in issuing a Coinage of this Nature, than yourself: and no one will execute it with more Accuracy and Expedition.[40]

Boulton must have welcomed this letter, which is also revealing of Liverpool's low opinion of the Royal Mint. Boulton left Birmingham on 5 March, arrived in London the next day, and attended a meeting of the Committee on the 7th.[41] Although they received two rival offers, the Committee's report, submitted on 28 March, recommended that he should be awarded the contract; his mint was the only one capable of coining on the required scale.[42] The Royal Mint seems never to have been seriously considered for this work. The king gave his assent on 9 June, after terms had been agreed between Boulton and the Treasury and the coin designs had been approved.[43] The result was the famous Cartwheel coins, which were proclaimed legal tender for transactions up to 1s. by Royal Proclamation of 26 July 1797.[44]

This first government contract authorised Boulton to mint 480 tons of pennies and twenty tons of twopences. Another two contracts followed, for a further 750 tons. By the time the working dies were destroyed on 26 July 1799 the Soho Mint had produced 43,970,000 pennies and 722,000 twopences.[45] One action on the part of one of the Royal Mint officials at this time is very revealing of their attitude to Boulton. In 1799 the Mint's solicitor, John Vernon, accused Boulton of counterfeiting regal coin because, relying on verbal instructions from the Privy Council Committee, he had started minting the later batches of coins before he had received written authorisation to do so. One

---

39   There was also a fear that a new issue of halfpennies might simply drive the dross out of circulation before enough new coin was available to replace it (Dyer, 'The currency crisis', p.140; Craig, p.264–5; Dyer/Gaspar, p.446).

40   Lord Liverpool to Matthew Boulton, 3 March 1797 (MBP, MS 3782/12/General correspondence 1797/35). See Selgin, pp.162–63, for the full text of the letter.

41   Bear in mind, Boulton was already 68 at this time, having been born in September 1728.

42   Selgin, p.163.

43   Dyer/Gaspar, pp.446–7; Doty, p.315; Vice.

44   Doty, p.317; the proclamation itself is illustrated on p.316. For the coins themselves see Dyer/Gaspar, p.447; Selgin, pp.164–6; Vice.

45   Dyer/Gaspar, p.448; Selgin, pp.163–6, 178; Doty, p.318. Although all of the coins are dated 1797, they were actually struck across 1797–9.

Fig. 12.3. (Top) obverse and reverse of an 1804 Bank of England dollar token,
overstruck on a Spanish coin; (below) obverse and reverse of an 1806 penny.
Birmingham Museums and Art Gallery.

of Boulton's employees, William Cheshire, was certain that 'the Mint are endeavouring by this means to give a death blow to your coinage.' Vernon, also, apparently deliberately, ruined Boulton's attempt to prosecute a forger whom he had caught in the act in a raid on his premises in January 1799.[46]

The Cartwheel coins were intended to contain roughly their face value's worth of copper, less a small amount to cover minting costs. They were substantial coins: the penny weighing 1 ounce and the twopence 2 ounces. In fact the twopences were simply too large for convenience and appear mainly to have been used as weights or kept as souvenirs.[47] The pennies by contrast seem to have been well received,[48] although Selgin has suggested that the

---

46   Selgin, pp.176–7, 183. Boulton thought his new coins were more difficult to forge than any other
     coin ever put into circulation in Europe, but he underestimated his fellow citizens, who were
     turning out forgeries, some quite convincing, within weeks, and, as Selgin points out, they were
     doing so using traditional screw presses (Selgin, pp.174–7). See Doty, p.317, for an illustration of a
     forged Cartwheel coin, and Vice for an advertisement placed by Boulton in *Aris's Birmingham Gazette*
     offering 100 guineas for information leading to the conviction of a forger.
47   Dyer, 'The currency crisis', p.141; Selgin, p.169.
48   Dyer, 'The currency crisis', p.141; Doty, p.317.

evidence for this may be less clear-cut than has hitherto been assumed.[49] However it does seem that what the public really wanted were good quality halfpennies to replace the dross they had been forced to use for years. In any event, Cartwheel pennies remained part of the circulating currency into the middle of the nineteenth century.[50] The contracts for the Cartwheel coinage included an important innovation. For the first time an allowance was made for the cost of distributing the coins around the country. Boulton undertook to deliver them 'at every Mans Door in the two Kingdoms paper'd up in Rouleaus & pack'd in new Casks',[51] and a Soho mint ledger records the distribution of the coins, cask-load by cask-load, each barrel of pennies containing £25 worth of coins and weighing approximately 370 lbs.[52]

Following the fiasco of the countermarked dollars and the success of his Cartwheel coins, glittering prospects were opening up for Boulton. On 7 February 1798 a new Privy Council Committee was established under the chairmanship of his supporter, Lord Liverpool, 'to take into Consideration the state of the Coins of this Kingdom, and the present Establishment and Constitution of His Majesty's Mint'.[53] The Committee, which pointedly did not include the master of the Mint or any of its officers, requested advice from a number of experts, including Boulton;[54] it did not give the Mint an easy time.[55] (The Mint felt that Liverpool was openly biased in favour of Boulton.) The threat was intensified by the presence on the Committee of Sir Joseph Banks, Boulton's friend for more than twenty-five years.[56] The fact that Boulton was

---

49 Selgin, pp.168–72.

50 One survey suggests that as late as 1857 up to a quarter of the pennies in circulation were 'ring pence', very worn Cartwheels still recognisable from their rims (G.P. Dyer, 'Thomas Graham's copper survey of 1857', *BNJ* 66 (1996), pp.60–66, at p.63).

51 TNA/PRO. BT, 6/118, fos.271–2, quoted in Dyer/Gaspar, p.448. See also Doty, pp.298, 318.

52 *British Coinages 1798–1800. Consignments and Weights. Book No.1 (1797–98)* (MBP, MS 3782/3/71). Although this helped to solve the problem of distributing coins, it did not prevent them still accumulating in the hands of the brewers and others in London and other major cities. This would remain a problem after Boulton's death. It was not finally solved until a way was found to redeem these coins and put them back into circulation (Selgin, pp.172, 210).

53 Dyer/Gaspar, p.451; Craig, p.257; Selgin, pp.194–5.

54 In fact Liverpool had already written to Boulton on 30 January asking him to become involved in the process (Doty, p.149; Selgin, pp.195–6). The letter also asked him how long he thought it might take to re-equip the Royal Mint with steam-engines and machinery like his (answer: one year), and even asked him to propose terms for minting silver crowns and half-crowns. Nothing came of this last idea, but it would certainly have caused open warfare with the Mint (Dyer/Gaspar, p.452; Doty, p.149; Selgin, pp.195–6).

55 See Dyer/Gaspar, p.452, for various incidents in the late 1790s which show how worried and touchy the Mint officers were about Boulton.

56 Dyer/Gaspar, p.451. Significantly the first shipment of Cartwheel pennies to leave the Soho mint in the previous year had been a guinea's worth sent to Banks; the second was of 160 casks containing £4,000 worth of coins destined for the Treasury (MBP, MS 3782/3/71).

producing pattern silver crowns and gold guineas to demonstrate his ideas for a reformed gold and silver coinage must also have appeared ominous.[57]

The Mint community was further offended when, at Liverpool's invitation, Boulton accompanied the members of the Committee on a thorough inspection of the Mint in late April/early May 1798.[58] Boulton had himself wondered whether his visiting the Mint 'before some plan had been digested by your Lordships,... would only tend to increase envy and jealousies, which I have had some experience of within this month'.[59] His initial report following the inspection, submitted on 8 May, only offered recommendations about assaying and was uncharacteristically restrained over how to reform the coining process itself, supposedly because:

> it would extend this Report to a tedious length; and would tend only to plunge me into Disputes with Persons, whose habits & customs have establish'd Prejudices in favour of their old trades in their old ways; but whose Occupations have not allowed them to gain that Mechanical and Philosophical Experience, which more general and more extensive manufactories afford to thinking men.[60]

When pressed by the Committee, he overcame these scruples and proposed that the Mint should be re-equipped along the lines of Soho.[61] Boulton and Watt would provide and install a twenty horsepower steam engine and all the other machinery required except for the rolling mill. Boulton knew that such an arrangement could kill his own mint at Soho, so he asked that as part of any such deal he should receive a contract for the rest of the copper coinage.

The Mint officers must also have found it hard that John Rennie, an engineer and former employee of Boulton and Watt, was employed by the Committee to look at the Mint's machinery. As they probably expected, his report, submitted on 10 July 1798, criticised the current state of affairs and recommended introducing steam-powered machinery and the Soho Mint's method of working.[62] It was therefore probably a huge relief to the Mint when illness forced Lord Liverpool to step down from the Committee and retire from public life.[63] Without his leadership the question of Mint reform lapsed again and the Committee's report was never finished. Boulton blamed

---

57   Vice.
58   Dyer/Gaspar, p.451.
59   Selgin, pp.145–6, quoting TNA/PRO. BT, 6/27.
60   Doty, p.150, quoting Matthew Boulton to the Privy Council Committee on coin, 8 May 1798 (MBP, MS 3782/13/112/77).
61   Doty, p.150; Selgin, p.196.
62   Craig, p.268. See Doty, pp.149–50, for more on Rennie and his report.
63   Dyer/Gaspar, p.453; Selgin, pp.197–8.

a rearguard action by the Mint officials for the lack of action; in his opinion the moneyers 'never made the least improvement for a Centry past, they have never Coin'd ¼ of the quantity I do in equal time even in their common gothick manner'.[64]

The most useful coins for daily purchases were halfpennies and Boulton had agitated to supply these since 1797. On 17 August 1798 he was asked to make a formal proposal to coin halfpennies and farthings, which he did by 27 August. Bureaucratic delays meant that the actual order for the new coins did not arrive until 4 November 1799, but between then and July 1800 the Soho Mint was to strike 550 tons of copper into 42,480,000 halfpennies and 4,224,000 farthings.[65] Because the price of copper had risen steadily since 1797, the weight of the new coinage was lowered, so that 18d. worth of coins were struck from a lb of copper rather than 16d. as for the Cartwheels.[66] Nevertheless Boulton became concerned by rumours that the Royal Mint was going to be striking a copper coinage, and he became convinced that several Mint officers, including the deputy master, James Morrison, were in league with Thomas Williams 'to rob me of the Coinage, my Inventions, my Character & to tire me out by making everything as disagreeable to me as possible'.[67]

As the price of copper continued to rise steadily more copper coins were melted down, and they began to be in short supply again,[68] so, in the spring of 1804, discussions began about another issue of coins. On 20 November Boulton was again asked to submit proposals and an agreement was reached on 19 December of the same year for him to coin 600 tons of copper into pennies, halfpennies and farthings. The weights of the coins were once more reduced so that this time 24d. worth were struck from a lb of copper. The official order was placed on 8 April 1805, but, due to government indecision, minting did not begin until 1806. This initial order was followed by two others in September 1806 and September 1807, so that in all the Soho mint eventually turned 1,800 tons of copper into 30,645,000 pennies, a truly staggering 129,288,000 halfpennies, and a rather more modest 5,909,000 farthings.[69]

The Royal Mint tried to fight back against what they saw as the 'alienation of minting' to a private individual and had put in tenders to coin copper in

---

64 Doty, p.151, quoting Matthew Boulton to Sir Joseph Cotton, 25 November 1799 (MBP, MS 3782/12/44/385).

65 Vice; Doty, pp.319–20; Craig, p.265. Though their manufacture spread over two years, all the coins were dated to one year, 1799.

66 Selgin, pp.184–5. The rising market price of copper saw many Cartwheels vanish into the melting pots of metal dealers (Selgin, pp.172–3).

67 Matthew Boulton to Ambrose Weston, 2 December 1799 (MBP, MS 3782/12/80/154).

68 Selgin, pp.209–10.

69 Dyer/Gaspar, p.454; Selgin, pp.209–10; Doty, pp.330–31; Craig, p.265; Vice.

January 1798, October 1799 and August 1802 at rates lower than those charged by Boulton, but none were successful.[70] On the last occasion, James Morrison certainly blamed the result on 'the known bias of Lord Liverpool and Sir J. Banks in favour of Mr Boulton'.[71] The feelings of the moneyers at the Mint about the work that was being given to Boulton were again made clear in July 1806, when they pointed out that their income depended on the amount of coin they struck and that they would not have been able to support themselves on their recent earnings if they had not had some 'patrimonial property'. They requested compensation for the loss that they had undergone from the alienation of their rightful business to Soho. Neither the Privy Council Committee nor the Treasury were impressed.[72]

In between these last two copper issues, in late 1803, the government was again beset by the ongoing shortage of silver coins and tried issuing countermarked Spanish dollars, as it had in 1797. The experiment was again unsuccessful and the issue was soon bedevilled by forgeries.[73] However, Boulton had addressed the problem and, after some experimentation, suggested an alternative solution. Rather than stamp a countermark into the original coins, he proposed using the power of his steam-driven presses to strike new designs onto them, obliterating the old designs in the process.[74] Some faint elements of the old designs frequently remained visible, but typically Boulton turned this to a positive, arguing that this provided an additional security measure against forgery.[75] On the advice of Sir Joseph Banks, Boulton wrote to the directors of the Bank of England on 6 February 1804 reminding them of the problems that countermarked dollars had already caused, emphasising how hard his overstruck dollars would be to forge, and offering to carry out the work for just £100 per 400,000 coins. Convinced by his arguments they placed a contract with him on 3 March, and between 5 May and 12 July 1804 the Soho mint produced over a million of these dollars.[76] As Richard Doty has remarked, this was 'the boldest admission yet of the Royal Mint's incapacity'.[77]

The officers of the Royal Mint were incandescent. It was one thing to put up with Boulton coining copper, but another to see him nibbling away at their traditional monopoly of the coinage of silver. However, when they sent a memorandum to the Treasury on 24 February complaining that the proposed

---

70 Craig, p.266.
71 Dyer/Gaspar, p.454, quoting TNA/PRO. Mint 4/23. James Morrison to John Smyth, 18 August 1802.
72 Dyer/Gaspar, p.454.
73 Manville, *Tokens*, p.5; Craig, p.264.
74 Doty, pp.326–7; Vice.
75 Dyer/Gaspar, p.453.
76 Selgin, pp.198–9; Doty, p.327; Vice.
77 Doty, p.326.

deal would encroach on their 'ancient and exclusive rights', they were informed that the dollars were not coins of the realm, but tokens issued by the Bank of England, so their arguments did not apply.[78] Interestingly in view of their previous resistance to change, this memorandum also complained that obsolete equipment prevented the Mint from matching Soho's capabilities. This was a significant development. This admission that their equipment was out-of-date was a turning point in the battle for reform.[79] On 5 March 1804 the Privy Council Committee on coin recommended that the Mint should be fitted out with 'the most improved Engines and Machines of all kinds applicable to the fabrication of Money that can be obtained in this or any other Country'.[80] In fact there was only one source for such machines – Soho. Despite illness, which had forced him to hand over the day-to-day running of his businesses to his son, Matthew Robinson Boulton, Boulton took an active part in the discussions about the modernisation of the Mint.[81] John Rennie, now the surveyor general to the Board of Trade, was asked to report on the suitability of the existing buildings in the Tower of London for housing the new machinery, but it was not practicable to install a modern, steam-powered mint in these ramshackle buildings. A new site was identified on Little Tower Hill, where some government-owned tobacco warehouses stood. It was decided not to convert them, but to tear them down and build a purpose-built mint. On 30 July 1806 the contract was signed with Soho to supply the necessary machinery at a cost of £16,990.[82] The machinery was ready by August 1807, but building work took longer than expected. When Matthew Boulton died on 17 August 1809 not all the machinery had been installed. Only in February 1810 was building finished and the machinery ready for use.[83] Ironically, as Boulton had feared, it was clear by the first half of 1809 that the newly equipped Royal Mint was likely to shut the Soho Mint out of any share in striking the national coinage, despite the gentleman's agreement that both Matthew Boulton and Matthew Robinson Boulton thought they had that the Mint would coin gold and silver but that the copper would be left to Soho.[84] Throughout this story, Boulton's talent for innovation, his passion for finding solutions to problems, and his ability to

---

78 Selgin, p.199; Dyer/Gaspar, p.453.
79 For what follows, see generally Craig, pp.269–71; Dyer/Gaspar, pp.455–9; Doty, pp.151–9; Selgin, pp.200–1.
80 Dyer/Gaspar, pp.455–6.
81 Doty, p.152.
82 For details of what Soho was to supply, see Selgin, p.200. This was not the first complete mint that Boulton had sold; he had already supplied them to St Petersburg and Copenhagen, although neither project ran quickly or smoothly – St Petersburg took from 1796 to 1807, and Copenhagen from 1796 to 1809 (see Doty, pp.74–123 and 124–44).
83 For a description of the new Royal Mint and its machinery see Dyer/Gaspar, pp.459–67.
84 Dyer/Gaspar, p.459; Doty, pp.159, 331.

deliver those solutions shines through. Sometimes his confidence led him to plunge ahead where a more careful man would not have ventured, but fortune usually smiled upon him when he did. In the end, however, he was probably too ready to believe that a grateful government would make sure his interests would be protected after the Royal Mint had been rejuvenated.

Acknowledgements

I am grateful to David Vice for giving me a copy of his manuscript prior to publication. I would also like to thank Sue Tungate and Pamela Magrill for their assistance in the preparation of this paper.

Photographic acknowledgements

All of the items illustrated in this paper are published by permission of Birmingham Museum and Art Gallery; they are all shown at life-size.

Abbreviations

BNJ – *British Numismatic Journal*.

Craig – Sir John Craig, *The Mint. A History of the London Mint from A.D. 287 to 1948* (Cambridge, 1953).

Doty – R. Doty, *The Soho Mint and the Industrialization of Money* (London, 1998).

Dyer/Gaspar – G.P. Dyer and P.P. Gaspar, 'Reform, the new technology and Tower Hill, 1700–1966', pp.398–606 in C.E. Challis (ed.), *A New History of the Royal Mint* (Cambridge, 1992).

MBP – Matthew Boulton Papers, Archives of Soho, Birmingham Central Library.

Selgin – G. Selgin, *Good Money. Birmingham Button Makers, the Royal Mint, and the Beginnings of Modern Coinage, 1775–1821*. Private Enterprise and Popular Coinage (Ann Arbor, 2008).

Vice – D. Vice, 'A numismatic history of the Soho manufactory and mint 1772–1850' (forthcoming; to be published by the British Numismatic Society).

Chapter 13

TECHNOLOGY, ART AND DESIGN IN THE WORK OF MATTHEW BOULTON: COINS, MEDALS AND TOKENS PRODUCED AT THE SOHO MINT[1]

Sue Tungate

In 1787 Matthew Boulton set out on his third great enterprise: to solve a crisis in the nation's coinage. He had already built the most famous manufacturing business in the world at Soho, and made a practical reality of Watt's steam engine; now Boulton and his team developed the modern, high quality, fraud resistant coinage we still have today. Soho Mint combined his expertise in steam power and engineering with creative design, and possibly speeded up industrial and commercial progress by providing sufficient coin and reducing fraud. This essay focuses on the inter-relationship between art and technology in the design of Soho Mint products which were not only technically advanced, but also included some fine works of art. It will not include a full discussion of regal coinage designs or the steam powered press itself.[2]

Soho Mint produced coins, tokens and medals which are all made in a similar way but have distinct functions. A coin is a piece of metal authorized by Government to be used as money and may feature the head of the sovereign, or some design indicating authority and place and date of issue. There was a lack of small change in the late eighteenth century as the Bank

---

1 This chapter is based on a section of work for a forthcoming PhD at the University of Birmingham, and Birmingham Museums and Art Gallery funded by the Arts and Humanities Research Council.

2 Other aspects of the Soho Mint have been covered by: David Symons, *Products of the Soho Mint;* Sue Tungate, *Copper to customer: the business of the Soho Mint;* George Demidowicz, *The three Sohos: Manufactory, Mint and Foundry* in Shena Mason (ed.), *Matthew Boulton: Selling What All the World Desires* (Yale University Press, 2009); David Vice, *A Numismatic History of Soho Manufactory and Mint 1772–1850* (forthcoming British Numismatic Journal); Richard Doty, *The Soho Mint and the Industrialisation of Money,* British Numismatic Society No.2 (London, 1998).

of England was unwilling to mint low value coins. Due to the severe shortage, a large number of tokens (also known as commercial or provincial coins) were distributed by a variety of private individuals and organizations. Genuine trade tokens carried the name of the issuer and a promise of repayment in regal currency. From 1787 industrial leaders, such as Thomas Williams of Anglesey and John Wilkinson the iron master, issued heavy, well made copper penny or halfpenny tokens, with good designs, containing the real value of metal. After 1790 other smaller organisations started to issue tokens and from 1794 many pieces were made for collectors; Dalton and Hamer have identified at least seven thousand varieties.[3] In 1797 Boulton was commissioned by the Government to produce 500 tons of regal coinage, with further issues in 1799 and 1805–1807. This stopped token production for a while.

Medals have been made since antiquity to celebrate events and personalities. They are not only made for military reasons, but may reward prowess in many areas, or be presented as symbols of prestige. Collecting medals was a very popular pastime in the eighteenth century. As part of his 'toy' trade, Boulton made medals at Soho, long before he made coins or tokens, on a speculative basis as well as on commission. Medals were produced in silver, gold, brass, and bronzed or gilt copper, but were also sold as cheap versions in tin and white metal. Usually not more than five hundred copies of any given medal were struck at Soho, often less (an exception being the 14,000 Trafalgar medals made in 1806). Some commissioned medals were made in single figures over a period of years; for instance, Agriculture Society prize medals which were individually engraved. With small numbers, time and care could be taken in their production. Medal blanks may be annealed (heated) to make it easier to impart the design to the metal. However, most coin blanks are struck cold for speed and economy. This important difference must be kept in mind when considering their designs. For example, 17 million coins were made in 1791 at the Soho Mint for the East India Company. In the third regal coinage between 1806 and 1807 over 165 million coins were made in fifteen months, all struck cold.

Specially struck proof pieces were sold as collectors' items.[4] Boulton also produced pattern coins to evaluate proposed designs, and these were valued by many collectors. There are at least seventeen different varieties of regal coinage, plus coin designs for Bengal, Denmark, Russia, and Württemberg, and two token issues, for which patterns were made, but not issued. Examples of Soho Mint products can now be found in the Birmingham Museum and

---

3 R. Dalton and S.H. Hamer, *The Provincial Token-Coinage of the 18th Century Illustrated*, London 1910–1918 (in 3 volumes).

4 Proofs are struck in a special press with meticulously polished dies.

Art Gallery and Birmingham Assay Office collections.[5] Items for collectors could be made in more precious metals, but most of Boulton's coins, medals and tokens, totalling over 500 million pieces by 1809, were made in copper.

Technical aspects of design

Boulton went to great lengths to get suitable and accurate designs, and took pride in his Mint but he was working in a commercial field where the customers' views had also to be considered. Designs had to incorporate not only artistic and aesthetic concerns but also the practical needs of coining. There were limitations imposed by the lack of suitably skilled engravers, time restraints, cost, materials, and by the minting technology available.

The images on most coins, medals and tokens appear, usually in relief, on both sides. In the process of coining two hardened steel dies, each engraved with a unique design, are used, one for the obverse ('heads') and one for the reverse ('tails'). Coins were originally manufactured individually by hand, by moneyers, who struck a metal blank between the dies using a hammer. In order to form an image, the die must be struck with sufficient force to compress the metal and expand it equally in all directions. A design in high relief may need to be struck with several blows in order to make sure that the metal spreads into all the hollows of the image. A note from Boulton's pocket book in 1772 states that the 'silver Banks [Otaheite] medals took 5 blows each...... Our big hammer is 7 Score [140lbs]'.[6]

Boulton's first forays into medal making had not been particularly successful as, at this stage, he did not understand fully the complex nature of coin and medal dies, though he had experience of making button dies. The engraving for the 1772 Captain Cook 'Otaheite' medal and 1774 Regimental medals was done by an outside contractor, John Westwood Senior, who produced cracked dies and caused other delays. The 1781 Admiral Rodney medal was engraved by one of his underemployed button engravers, but did not sell well.

Prior to the Soho Mint many coins in circulation were substandard, due to cracked or worn dies, and new dies were not always identical in every detail, and would not produce identical coins. 'Hammer' dies could be used for around 17,000 strikes; and 'anvil' dies lasted for around 36,000 strikes. Since mints could make on average 10,000 coins per day, a lot of dies were

---

5   Boulton's regal coinage is described by C.W. Peck, *Copper Coins of George III* (London, 1970); many of the medals are described in Laurence Brown, *A Catalogue of British Historical Medals 1760–1960* (London, 1980). Tokens are described in various works by R.C. Bell *Commercial Coins 1787–1804* (Newcastle, 1963); *Copper Commercial Coins 1811–1819* (Newcastle, 1964) and *Tradesman's Tickets and Private Tokens* (Newcastle, 1966). There are numerous numismatic articles on Soho Mint products.

6   Birmingham Archives and Heritage (BAH), MS 3782/12/108 Item 7 1772 Matthew Boulton's Notebook.

needed, as they quickly wore out due to the forces required in striking. The rate of working at the Royal Mint had scarcely improved since medieval times despite the introduction of screw presses. These were turned manually in a process that was tiring for workers and produced uneven forces.[7] By 1787 Lewis Pingo, the Royal Mint engraver, made dies using fully lettered punches rather than individual letters, but each die still had to have fine features added separately.

Matthew Boulton used similar methods to the Royal Mint to coin for the Honourable East India Company (EIC) in 1786 and 1787 in London. After this experience he decided to set up his own mint at Soho. At first he was concerned with perfecting his coining apparatus driven by a steam engine, and preventing counterfeiting, rather than the specific design on coins. In his usual fashion he investigated and introduced a variety of technical improvements, including dies that were more easily duplicated and were made of better quality steel. He used shallow dies whose lives were extended by having concave faces.[8] As a result, coins now had designs in low relief and could be struck with one blow by Boulton's steam powered presses. By November 1789, Boulton claimed that he could make 100 million halfpence per year 'whereas the officers of the English Mint.... are very much hurried to make 3½ million of Guineas per Year'.[9] The unique thing he promised was to make every coin of a particular denomination the same appearance, size and weight, so that any imperfection immediately signified a forgery. This aspect of design played a crucial role in the modernisation of coinage. As Stebbing Shaw pointed out, 'every piece becomes perfectly round, and of equal diameter; which is not the case with any other national money ever put in circulation'.[10]

When canvassing for the regal coinage contract, Boulton wanted to employ the best artists in metal. Boulton's idea was that counterfeiting would be more difficult, if dies were made by a skilled engraver, as the quality of workmanship could not be easily copied. He was impressed by Jean-Pierre Droz, a Swiss engraver working in Paris. Droz also promised a coining press which imparted a better polish to the coin's face, and used a sexpartite collar that struck the edge inscription and the faces at the same blow. This meant

---

7   The screw press was introduced into England in around 1561. Paul H.J. Goldman, *Eloye Mestrelle and the Introduction of the Mill and screw press* Spink Numismatic Circular November 1974 Volume XXXII Number 11 p.422. The Royal Mint moved into new premises on Tower Hill by 1812, re-equipped by Soho.

8   He also experimented with annealing and rolling metal. MS 3782/12/108 Item 53 Mint Book 1788 p.56.

9   BAH, MS 3782/13/36 Item 37, 12 November 1789 MB (Soho) to MRB.

10   Stebbing Shaw, *History of Staffordshire*, Vol.II, 1801, p.118.

that the inscription would always be in the same position relative to the faces. However, this did not work efficiently, so Boulton and his workmen, including James Lawson, the supervisor at the Mint, went on to develop a functional collar, a ring-shaped piece of metal, to act as a third die and surround the metal blank as it was being struck. This produced the distinctive sharp edge of Soho products, and made clipping the edges, (to obtain valuable metal to sell) instantly detectable. The Royal Mint was unwilling or unable to introduce such an innovation. Boulton wrote in 1789:

> I have also heard of an attempt to strike crown pieces at the Tower in collers [sic], but it was found so troublesome and the coller so hazardous that I believe there never was half a dozen of them struck, and if such a thing had been proposed to the moneyers they would have concluded that it would be worth a peny [sic] at least to make a half peny'[11]

At Soho Mint the 1791 Anglesey halfpenny token and the 1791 Southampton token were the first to use Lawson's invention of the rising and falling collar. Boulton's team also appears to have mastered the multiplication of dies by this time. He employed a French mechanic Jean Baptiste Dupeyrat (1759–1834) who produced a lathe, similar to a portrait lathe, which was delivered in September 1790. Boulton wanted to keep the technical details of his minting processes secret and his use of the Dupeyrat multiplication apparatus is shrouded in mystery.[12]

Boulton also tried out other innovative technical ideas in design such as the use of a hexagonal coinage. In Bengal the cowrie shell was used instead of small value copper coins, as the cost of minting low value coins was too high. To reduce prices to the East India Company, Boulton suggested that their coins should be hexagon shaped.[13] He wrote enthusiastically to his son on 19th Sep 1792:

> By the mode I intend to make them there will be no annealing, or pickling or milling or striking or wast [sic] or remelting or scrap,... This may enable me not only to sell my Copper at £105 per ton... but may enable me to employ my Rolling Mill and sell 100 Ton at £224 per ton x by 1000 = £22,400. Hence you may see out of trifles money may be got.
>
> P.S. A Bee's Honeycomb will show you that Hexagon Money may be cut out without making any Scrap or waste.[14]

11   BAH, MS 3782/21/1, 10 September 1789 MB (Buxton) to Joseph Banks (London).
12   J.G. Pollard, *Matthew Boulton and J.P Droz* Numismatic Chronicle Vol.8 (Oxford, 1968) p.241–265.
13   David Vice, *A Pattern Cowrie for Bengal Presidency*, Format 58 (1995).
14   BAH, MS 3782/13/36 Item 88, 19 September 1792 MB (Truro) to MRB (Soho).

Unfortunately the coinage was still too expensive to replace the cowrie shell and no more than 50 trial coins were struck.

An experiment in design for a bimetal coinage (not repeated until the modern £2 coin) was tried for the Monneron Brothers of Paris in 1792 but it was found to be too costly. James Lawson wrote:

> the Copper requires two Cuttings Out and the centre piece must be accounted as waste: the silver makes a third Cutting out. No easy way of laying them in as they are in two pieces if they are fixed before and it makes another operation; also the annealing of the rings of copper, as even in tubes the quantity will be considerable.... It seems likely to make a beautiful money provided there is enough allowed for the making, which will be much more expensive than any other.[15]

By 1802 Matthew Boulton was worried that his methods were being claimed by the French. He designed a medal to counteract these assertions. He wrote:

> I have some thought on striking a piece.... of the size of my peny [sic] piece, provided Mr Dumarest would engrave *my head* expeditiously in the Reverse. I purpose to make 4 Aides expressive as to Size of pence, ½ pence, farthings & ½ farthings. My distributing this piece at 1d each all over the world will defeat all the Parisian Spies & show the perfection of ye Coining better than writing a Book. 12 of them may be wrapped up in a Roulow [sic] that may be wraped in a printed Explanation. Round the Edge in indented Letters neater that any that has yet been done, I would put the inscription.[16]

This inscription is in French and translated it reads:

> (400) Matthew Boulton erected at Soho, England in 1788, a steam powered machine to strike coins (480). In 1798 he set up a much better one with eight new presses (560) These circles and numbers indicate the diameter and number of pieces struck per minute (640) by eight children without fatigue, of the smallest or greatest volume (720), With 8 combinations one can (800) increase efficiency to the necessary degree.[17]

This medal stands as a record of Boulton's technical achievements, and each numbered circle indicated how many coins of that diameter could be struck in one minute by Soho's steam-powered presses.

---

15   BAH, MS 3782/12/66 Item 30, 14 April 1792 James Lawson (Soho) to MB (London).
16   BAH, MS 3782/12/75, 1 November 1802 MB (Soho) to Zaccheus Walker Jr. (Paris).
17   Translated by the author.

Fig. 13.1. Techniques Medallic scale medal with Matthew Boulton Portrait.
Birmingham Assay Office.

Artistic design

A design for a coin, medal or token needs to have some sense of order to please
the aesthetic sense but it must also be useful, and be practical for mass
production. There are two faces and an edge, all of which may be engraved.
The principle design on the face (field) is usually a pictorial representation of
some authoritative figure or activity. The rim, where the face meets the edge,
may be ornamental, with a toothed or beaded border or can be lettered. In
1794 Noel-Alexandre Ponthon, Boulton's engraver at Soho, came up with a
new concept in design, using a raised border with incused lettering which
protected the designs on the face (Fig. 13.1).[18] This feature became famous in
the 1797 'cartwheel' penny, but was later removed due to the difficulty in
striking great quantities of large coins with borders. The third side, the edge,
could be decorated with vertically or diagonal stripes, or with more complicated
patterns, or may be lettered; many of the earlier tokens have edge inscriptions
saying where the token could be redeemed. Medals usually have plain edges,
but a special dedication is found on the edge of the Trafalgar medal.

Inscriptions were an important functional part of the design, to give the
value, or the identity of the issuer; or to instill some message, such as MAIL
&/POST COACHES/TO ALL PARTS OF/ENGLAND as in the 1795 token made
for Christopher Ibberson.[19] Often a main legend or inscription is located in an
arc around the field of the design. Another inscription or the date may be placed

18   This raised border was first used for the 1794 Copper Company of Canada halfpenny, and the 1794
     Lancaster halfpenny token and on the EIC issues of the 1794 and 1797 Madras coinages.
19   Ibberson was the proprietor of the George and Blue Boar in London, a stage coach terminus.

*Fig. 13.2. Inscriptions in Arabic, English, Welsh, Latin and Persian.
Birmingham Assay Office.*

in the exergue; an area banded by a straight line under the field. Some simple Soho products, like the truck tokens for Pen-y-darran Works run by the Homfrey family, have only inscriptions on both sides. There are also inscriptions on the reverses of various tokens and medals, sometimes surrounded by a wreath.

The challenge of providing Soho Mint's products for diverse markets in over twenty different countries meant that designs had to include inscriptions in at least ten languages. The East India Company (EIC) was a very important customer of the Soho Mint, and their resident specialist, Dr Charles Wilkins provided most of the translations for coins sent out to India and Sumatra, plus the relevant weights. The 1786 Sumatra coinage used antique Persian script in the Malay language, and the 1791 and 1794 coinages for Bombay have simple Arabic inscriptions. In contrast, the 1794 Madras coins and later Sumatra coins show a coat of arms with a Latin inscription. The projected Bengal coinage of 1809 proved the most complex, with the value of the coin in three languages: Urdu in the middle, Hindi to the right and Bengali on the left. The EIC College medals were inscribed in Sanskrit or Arabic to award as prizes for learning the specified language. All these inscriptions became part of the artistic design. (Fig. 13.2).

Boulton resorted to a variety of experts for the inscriptions, but also suggested several himself. Most of his early medals had inscriptions in Latin but he also used English, for example, on medals given to the officers, seamen and marines who had remained loyal at the time of the Nore Mutiny.[20] Medals in other languages were produced; in Italian featuring Ferdinand of Naples, and for the Monneron Brothers in French. More unusual were the 1798 medals in Welsh for the Hafod Friendly Society, and inscriptions in Gaelic for Inverness tokens.

The team at the Soho Mint issued at least one hundred and fifty different designs up to 1809, for customers all over the world. Boulton did not have one dominant style for his Mint products but was interested in the evolution of both modern and neoclassical designs, down to great detail. He was influenced by political and artistic ideas from around the globe, via his agents, who gathered information on taste and fashion.[21] Boulton also had a large collection of coins and medals, books, prints and engravings to use as design sources. Design decisions made at Soho were influenced by perceived marketing prospects, and models were often purchased from fashionable sculptors such as John Flaxman. Successful motifs were sometimes repeated in different Mint productions.

Coins, medals and tokens are 'capsules of history' and the designs chosen by Boulton cover virtually all aspects of eighteenth-century life, with images representing individuals, organizations and even nations. The dies were made by at least twelve different engravers, and show both portraits and allegorical figures, events and views of buildings, and designs relating to agriculture, industry, commerce, mining and transport. Medals were produced depicting events such as the expedition of Captain Cook to the Pacific, and battles from the American War of Independence, the Third Mysore war and the French Revolution. They have images of royal occasions such as the marriage of the Prince of Wales or the execution of Louis XVI, and scenes of domestic life as on the 'Seasons' Medals made for George Washington. A poignant design, fifteen years before the abolition of the slave trade, is seen in the clasped hands of the ex-slave and the white man on the Sierra Leone coins for the colony set up in 1791.

Sometimes the design was entirely determined by the customer, and innovation was not welcomed. The design for the Sumatran (Bencoolen) coinages, incorporating the balemark of the East India Company, was established without Soho having any input.[22] When Boulton made several

---

20 The medal made for Earl St Vincent has his portrait. The reverse shows a seaman shaking hands with a naval officer with the legend LOYAL AND TRUE.

21 The context of 'antique taste' and the sources of Boulton's designs have been discussed by Sir Nicholas Goodison, *The context of Neo-classicism* (forthcoming in S. Mason (ed.), *op. cit.*)

22 The design of the Sumatra copper coins was by John Marsden in 1783, the elder brother of the orientalist William Marsden, who supplied the inscriptions to Boulton. F. Pridmore, *The Coins of the British Commonwealth of Nations Part 4 India* (1975) p.220.

trial strikes in 1787 with new innovations in design, John Motteux of the EIC wrote: 'The new Impressions [of Sumatran coins] for the Copper are not so well approved as the old were; the old dies being liked, why change?'[23]

None of the enormous issues of Soho-produced EIC coins involved portraits, but were simple designs. However Boulton needed an engraver skilled in producing portraits for the British regal coinage and found this initially in Jean-Pierre Droz. George III's bust was engraved by three of Boulton's workers; Droz, Conrad Heinrich Küchler and Thomas Wyon, and he is depicted in various styles from antique to modern in at least seven different versions. He appears on the regal coinage facing right, but several medals have him facing left. Küchler's portrait of George III was the one finally used on the 1797 regal coinage. Boulton's other main engravers, Noel-Alexandre Ponthon and Rambert Dumarest, also produced skilled portraits. More than twenty five individuals were portrayed on Soho Mint products, including the Duke of Bridgewater, Horatio Nelson, Lord Howe, Lord Cornwallis and Alexander Suvarow. Rousseau and Lafayette were depicted by Dumarest on medals made for the Monneron brothers during the French Revolution. Ponthon portrayed merchants such as Isaac Swainson and Daniel Eccleston on tokens.[24] Monarchs from other countries also feature, such as Ferdinand of Naples and Sicily, Gustav III of Sweden, Christian of Denmark, Alexander of Russia, Frederick of Württemberg and John of Portugal, which shows a wide range of customers for the Soho Mint. Boulton did not forget women; as well as Catherine the Great, his engravers made representations of Queen Charlotte, Marie Antoinette and the Princess of Wales. The portraits were intended to be as realistic as possible. Goodison recounts the trouble taken with Nelson's likeness for the Trafalgar medal, and similar care was taken with other individuals.[25]

One of the more controversial figures, portrayed by the freelance engraver John Gregory Hancock, was John Wilkinson, an industrialist and a colleague of Boulton. He supplied the castings for parts of the Soho Mint press, as well as steam engine cylinders, He was also involved with Boulton in copper contracts. His Soho produced 'Forge' tokens show his bust in profile,

23   B.M. Gould, 'Matthew Boulton's East India Mint in London 1786–88', *Seaby's Coin and Medal Bulletin* No.612, (1969) p.270–277.

24   Swainson carried on business at Velno's Vegetable Syrup Warehouse. Due to a spelling mistake on the die, the order was countermanded and only 18 impressions were struck. Eccleston spent several years in Antigua and Barbados and was a liquor merchant, insurance broker and a coin collector.

25   Nicholas Goodison, *Matthew Boulton's Trafalgar Medal* (Birmingham City Council, 2007).

*Fig. 13.3. Portraits of John Wilkinson and Alexander Suvarow.
Birmingham Assay Office.*

reminiscent of regal coinage (Fig. 13.3), with the legend JOHN WILKINSON
IRON MASTER. The edge is inscribed WILLEY SNEDSHILL BERSHAM
BRADLEY, the places where Wilkinson had his main works. This use of his
portrait on a token was parodied in a poem.[26]

EPIGRAM ON MR WILKINSON'S COPPER MONEY
In Greece and Rome your men of parts,
Renown'd in arms or form'd in arts
On splendid coins and medals shown,
To make their deeds and persons known;
So Wilkinson, from this example,
Gives of himself a matchless sample!
And bids the **Iron** monarch pass
Like his own metal wrapt in **Brass**!
Which shows his modesty and sense,
And how, and where, he made his pence.
As iron when 'tis brought in taction,
Collects the copper by attraction,
So, thus, in him 'twas very proper,
To stamp his brazen face on **Copper**

---

26   Desmond King-Hele, *Erasmus Darwin* (London, 1999) p.244.

The design on the reverse of the Wilkinson token shows the interior of a smithy showing a large drop hammer and a workman holding a piece of metal on an anvil. This may be one of the first images of a working man available to the poorer classes. Other designs show the tools used in industry, such as on the arms of the Associated Irish Mine Company featured on Boulton's first steam struck token in 1789 for the Cronebane Mine. These show a crest in the form of a windlass, and two shovels and three pickaxes. These images of industry were important to the growing industrial workforce.

Industrial buildings depicted include a view of Soho Manufactory on the reverse of a rare 1792 medal featuring Boulton's portrait. The 1793 Leeds token made for Birchall and Brownbill shows a view of the Leeds Cloth Hall where cloth was displayed for sale.[27] The obverse showing a bishop was copied by Ponthon from Hancock's Cronebane design. Boulton wrote to his son in January 1793: 'take St Patrick from the Chronebane dye [sic], may Serve for Bishop Blazes head, of which you may consult with Ponthon & Lawson'.[28] St Patrick's crozier was removed and replaced with a wool comb.

Boulton was not averse to recycling ideas. Dumarest used the same shield shape on the 1791 Cornish token, the 1791 Southampton token and the 1791 Glasgow token showing their respective coat of arms. Coats of arms were used to indicate the respectability of the issuer, and were a feature on several other tokens and on foreign coinage, including that for the Gold Coast, on later issues for the East India Company and projected coinages for Denmark and Württemberg. Very complex coats of arms are seen on Ponthon's 1796 Penryn token. This detailed design was meant to enhance Lord Dunstanville's reputation as well as to be used as money. 19,173 tokens were made including one gold, sixty silver and forty bronzed proofs.

The 1789 Anglesey token made for the Parys Mine Company does not indicate anything about the issuer, Thomas Williams, 'the Copper King'. Perhaps he was sufficiently self confident not to need self advertisement. The token shows the cipher PMCo. in boldly flourished script, and the bust of a Druid with a flowing beard. The Druid motif is repeated in the 1791 halfpenny made for the Cornish Metal Company. The design, initially engraved by Hancock, was reused partly because the dies, already made by Dumarest for the Anglesey token, had been rejected by Williams, but perhaps also as a symbol of the Celtic peoples, connecting the copper mining communities of Wales and Cornwall. The legend CORNISH COPPER HALF AN OUNCE tells the truth. The coins weigh 13g (the equivalent to ½oz).

---

27   Samuel Birchall was author of one of the earliest books on the 18th century tokens, published in 1796.

28   BAH, MS 3782/13/36 Item 94 London, 18 January 1793 MB to MRB (Soho).

Many medals have a reverse with a design portraying an event important to the life (or death!) of the person involved. The 1794 Cornwallis medal has his portrait on the obverse, and on the reverse, an emotional scene, taken from life, of his encounter with the sons of Tipoo Sahib who were being given as hostages in the Third Mysore war.[29] This design, with a Latin inscription, was for sale in Britain. A second medal featuring Cornwallis' actions in 1799 was intended for the native troops of the EIC. The obverse design has the 'Tiger of Mysore' being subdued by the 'Lion of Britain' with an Arabic inscription on a flag, the reverse showing the battle field, with a Persian inscription underneath. Since the late eighteenth century was a time of many battles, Boulton made at least fifteen medals featuring military themes. Some were commissioned by various Volunteers Associations or by individuals (such as the Davison Nile Medal), but others were made on a speculative basis. The 1805 Nelson medal was made at Boulton's own expense for presentation to those involved in the Battle of Trafalgar.

Designs for celebrations of events such as the Recovery of Health of George III in 1789, Victory of the Glorious Fourth of June 1794, or the Union of Great Britain and Ireland in 1802 needed to be available near to the event for a speculative market interested in contemporary news. Sometimes the designs were beautiful, but arrived too late, such as the one for the Marriage of the Prince and Princess of Wales, which also had an error in the date. However, three different versions of medals in silver, ordered by George III to celebrate Queen Charlotte's birthday at Frogmore in 1795, were made in a very short space of time, using a simple inscription for the reverses and two previously engraved dies. The whole order was completed and dispatched within six days.

Another dramatic set of medals was designed to commemorate the Executions of Louis XVI and Marie Antoinette (Fig. 13.4). Two have the conjoined busts of Louis and Marie Antoinette on the obverse and the third has the Queen alone. Three scenes in Paris are depicted on the reverses. One shows the King saying farewell to his family. Through the window can be seen the Place Louis XV (by then renamed Place de la Republique and now known as the Place de la Concorde) where Louis was executed. Another medal depicts a large crowd surrounding the guillotine and the executioner is showing Louis XVI's head to the crowd. The third illustrates Marie Antoinette being transported to her execution in October 1793. She is in a horse drawn cart in front of a large crowd. These medals were intended for sale in Britain to those sympathetic to the fate of the French Royal family. The lively and vivid scenes served as

---

29   Cornwallis defeated Tipoo Sahib and made him surrender half of his possessions. A painting of the
     surrender was made by Henry Singleton and a mezzotint engraving by J. Grozer was available by
     15 August 1793. J.G. Pollard, *Matthew Boulton and Conrad Heinrich Kuchler,* Numismatic Chronicle
     Vol.X (London, 1970) p.259–318.

Fig. 13.4. Events. 1794 (dated 1793). Execution of Marie Antoinette. 1794 Lord Howe (The Battle of the Glorious 4th June). Birmingham Assay Office.

reportage of the events and sold in tin, copper, copper gilt and silver, with around 1400 produced between 1793 and 1800.[30] Different medals had been ordered by the Monneron brothers and sold in France, earlier in the Revolution. These included designs with Louis XVI accepting the constitution, and one with the seated figure of 'Liberty', holding a spear with the cap of liberty on its end. However, revolutionary symbols were not used frequently in Soho designs, the only other example was the token made for Arnold Works in 1802.[31]

Most of the medals produced at Soho Mint feature a portrait in profile on the obverse, but tokens more commonly have allegorical figures in their design. These include druids, or saints as previously mentioned; also Hygeia, the Goddess of Health, on Swainson's token; and a semi-nude river god on the Glasgow token, and on a pattern coin for Canada. Hymen, the god of marriage, holding a flaming torch, appears on the medal to celebrate the Marriage of the Prince and Princess of Wales in 1795, with a panoramic view of London in the background. A female figure, 'Peace', appears on the 1798 Davison Nile medal and on the 1802 medal to celebrate the Peace of Amiens. On the medal of 1802 presented to the Birmingham Loyal Association, she is depicted actually giving a medal to a soldier in Roman dress. The design to celebrate Suvarow's 1799 victories features him as Mars, raising the seated female figure of Italy; with a fallen French soldier on the left. Most of these images would have been understood by the purchasers of medals or commissioners of tokens who were generally of the more educated classes.

Symbols of nationality are seen in many of the Soho Mint's designs. A significant figure was Britannia, representing Britain since Roman times.

---

30   BAH, MS 3782/12/108 Item 69 Medal ledger 1793–1816.
31   The reverse shows the Roman fasces with an axe, spear and cap of liberty.

Fig. 13.5. Agriculture and Manufacturing. 1794 Lancaster-Eccleston Token. 1798 George Washington medal. Birmingham Assay Office.

Britannia was used on the reverse of the 1797 regal coinage. She holds a trident, symbolising Britain's domination of the sea, along with ships in the background. She also appears on the British Victories medal of 1798 where she is surrounded by a pile of arms. On the 1801 Union of Britain and Ireland medal she is shaking hands with Hibernia. Boulton, when designing dies for the British regenerated dollar in 1804, was horrified to find that the Bank of England had no coat of arms and used their seal which depicted Britannia as she was an important symbol of British identity.[32] Other national symbols, such as the lion of Mysore and the elephant of Ceylon (Sri Lanka), are used in designs, and the Russian double eagle is used both on the medal for Catherine the Great in 1796, and on the pattern coins for Alexander of Russia made in 1804.

Both British naval power and the ability to feed the nation were important in times of war. Britannia, with a shield, cornucopia or a lion, appears on Agricultural Society medals from 1793 on, and she appears with agricultural implements in 1797. Agriculture is also an important feature on the 1798 George Washington 'Seasons' medals. One design features a man sowing seed while another shows a man with cows and sheep, and a small hut in the background (Fig. 13.5).[33] Another recurrent theme on Soho products were ships representing their importance to the economy, in trade and defense. Several medals feature battleships; coins for the colonies of Bermuda and Bahamas have similar designs of ships in full sail. The combination of symbols

---

32 Regenerated dollars were Spanish reales over-stamped with the portrait of George III and used to increase the supply of silver coins.

33 The third design has women spinning and weaving, with a baby being rocked in a cradle in the foreground. These were intended as gifts to give a peaceful message to native Indian chiefs.

to represent agriculture, manufacturing and commerce is seen on Eccleston's 1794 Lancaster token, which used the sails, masts and rigging of a ship in conjunction with a plough and a flying shuttle.[34]

Conclusion

The designs for Soho Mint coins, medals and tokens are numerous and varied, and their manufacture depended on the efforts of many individuals with a wide range of skills. Boulton obviously took great care with artistic input but his main concern was the design of the Mint equipment itself, and producing coinage for general use rather than medals for a restricted audience. He wrote in 1802 that:

> 'we do not pretend to excel in Engraving but in Coining, ... The most important improvement to be desired in ye art of Moneying is not in making beautiful specimens but in making such Money as cannot be counterfeited with Profit to the Culprit, by such means as will produce a million of pieces per day if necessary, at a small expense'.[35]

Nevertheless some of the products of the Soho Mint are not only excellent examples of improved coining technology, but are beautiful works of art in themselves. They offer an interesting insight into many aspects of life in the eighteenth century. His steam powered mint machinery and new techniques of producing dies made it possible to generate images on a mass scale and distribute them around the world.

Acknowledgments

Thanks to the staff of the Birmingham Libraries and Archives Services, and to Dr David Symons, Dr Malcolm Dick, Dr Richard Clay, Professor Peter Jones, and Val Loggie.

Abbreviations

MB – Matthew Boulton.
MRB – Matthew Robinson Boulton.
EIC – Honourable East India Company.
BMAG – Birmingham Museum and Art Gallery
All MS references are to the Matthew Boulton Papers in the Archives and Heritage, Central Library, Birmingham.

---

34   The design of the plough may have been drawn by John Phillp, who came to work for Boulton in 1793 at the age of fourteen. Phillp was later employed as an engraver but also made many sketches of the coining apparatus and mint designs. Phillp Album BMAG 2003/0031/14 1794 Pencil drawing (70 x 140mm).
35   BAH, MS 3782/12/75, 1 November 1802 MB (Soho) to Zaccheus Walker Jr. (Paris).

Chapter 14

'REAL KNOWLEDGE AND OCCULT MISTERIES': MATTHEW BOULTON AND THE BIRMINGHAM ASSAY OFFICE

Sally Baggott

'I am very desirous of becoming a great Silversmith, yet I am now determined never to take up that branch in the Large Way I intended, unless powers can be obtained for a Marking Hall at Birmingham.'

Matthew Boulton to the Earl of Shelburne, 7 January 1771.[1]

Established by an Act of Parliament in 1773, the Birmingham Assay Office has continued to carry out its statutory duty of assaying and hallmarking precious metals for over 230 years, and it is now the largest assay office in the world. Yet, without Matthew Boulton, it is arguable that the Birmingham Assay Office would never have been established at all. It is the sole surviving enterprise in which Boulton had a hand, and it serves as a lasting testament to his legacy in Birmingham and beyond. Boulton began producing silver at the Soho Manufactory in partnership with John Fothergill in 1766, but from the beginning, their venture met with serious obstruction, and five years later in a letter to the Earl of Shelburne, Boulton expressed the concern that his ambition to become a 'great Silversmith' would be impossible without the establishment of an assay office in Birmingham.[2] Indeed, it has been a legal requirement since 1300 that if precious metal articles are to be offered for sale, they must be assayed (tested) to determine their precious metal content, and hallmarked to guarantee that

---

1   Birmingham Archives and Heritage (BAH), Matthew Boulton Papers (MBP), MS 3782/1/9.

2   BAH, MBP, MS 3782/12/89/13. This date has been arrived at using evidence given before the Parliamentary Committee of 1773 by Samuel Garbett, a manufacturer and refiner of precious metals in Birmingham who supplied Boulton and Fothergill with silver. Garbett stated that he had been supplying the partners with silver for the 7 years previous to 1773.

the metal is of a legal standard or fineness. In order to comply with the law, therefore, like every other silver manufacturer in Birmingham, Boulton and Fothergill were required to send their goods for assay and hallmarking to an assay office, the nearest being Chester. The round trip of 144 miles from Birmingham to Chester increased costs, and brought with it other problems, such as the risk of damage or robbery, considerable delays or the danger of designs being copied which Boulton was not prepared tolerate. Having travelled to London in January 1773 to begin his campaign, by May that same year, Boulton had skilfully overcome objections from some powerful quarters, and succeeded in gaining the 'Act for appointing Wardens and Assay Masters for assaying Wrought Plate in the Towns of Sheffield and Birmingham.'[3]

In just under five months, then, Boulton had achieved his objective. There are various accounts of how he did so, each one drawing substantially on material in the Matthew Boulton Papers. Arthur Westwood's from 1936, written whilst he was junior Assay Master at Birmingham, remains the most comprehensive to date.[4] In his biography of Boulton, published the following year, H.W. Dickinson recounts the events of the 1773 campaign whilst acknowledging his debt to Westwood; in an article from 1964, Eric Robinson argues that 1773 was Boulton's first experience of leading a parliamentary campaign; and in her history of the Birmingham Assay Office, published in 1993, Jennifer Tann begins with Boulton's part in its establishment.[5] Boulton emerges from these accounts as a remarkably modern figure, a shrewd business man, exceptionally skilled in argument, rhetoric and public relations, but his part in the establishment of the Birmingham Assay Office has been, to an extent, eclipsed by more obvious aspects of his life, such as his partnership with James Watt or his association with the Lunar Society. Furthermore, the documents relating to the establishment of the Birmingham Assay Office bring to light a great deal regarding the wider cultural context of the late eighteenth century. The story of Boulton and the Birmingham Assay Office is also one of intense rivalry between London and the provinces, of conflict between the craftsmen and industrialists, and of tension between the old and the new.

It is clear that when Boulton began producing silver at Soho, he was aware that if the silver business was to succeed, an assay office in Birmingham was

---

3   Plate Assay (Sheffield and Birmingham) Act (13 Geo.3.c.52) The term 'plate' requires some clarification; it is used to describe objects made of solid precious metal, not articles that are made of base metal with a thin covering of silver or gold.

4   Arthur Westwood, *The Assay Office at Birmingham. Part 1: Its Foundation* (Birmingham: 1936).

5   H.W. Dickinson, *Matthew Boulton* (Cambridge: Cambridge University Press, 1937) pp.63–70; Eric Robinson, 'Matthew Boulton and the Art of Parliamentary Lobbying' in *The Historical Journal*, VII, 2 (Cambridge: 1964) pp.217–220; Jennifer Tann, *Birmingham Assay Office 1773–1993* (Birmingham: The Birmingham Assay Office, 1993) pp.13–26.

necessary. In 1766, after his second visit to Soho, the Earl of Shelburne wrote 'Another thing they are in great way of is an assay-master, which is allowed at Chester and York; but it is very hard on a manufacturer to be obliged to send every piece of plate to Chester to be marked, without which no one will purchase it.'[6] In the light of the relationship between Boulton and the Earl and their correspondence at the time, Kenneth Quickenden has noted that these remarks were the result of Boulton pressing the Earl on the matter of an assay office for Birmingham.[7] Five years later, Boulton was again raising the issue; at length, he apologised in a letter to the Earl for the delay in meeting an order for two candlesticks which he attributed to 'the wilful or careless bad packing of them at Chester,' and he stressed the point that he could not become a 'great Silversmith' without an assay office in Birmingham.[8] It is surely too much of a coincidence that the candlesticks were a commission for the Earl whose support Boulton had previously enlisted. In his efforts to cover up the length of time taken at Soho to produce articles in silver, Boulton would sometimes overstate the delays caused by sending work to Chester for assay and hallmarking, and, furthermore, there is not any correspondence from Boulton to his agent in Chester, James Folliot regarding any damage caused at the Chester Assay Office.[9] The letter, then, is Boulton making use of an opportunity to explain away his inability to meet orders on time, whilst stressing to his influential acquaintance the need for an assay office in Birmingham.

By 1772, Boulton was intent on petitioning Parliament; in a letter to the Duke of Richmond, he wrote,

> I am now manufacturing plate with a degree of Elegance..., I think I should push that article into a cheaper and more elegant style than 'tis now in, and that for purpose I expect the Town of Birmingham will present a petition to Parliament this session praying for the establishment of an Office here, for assaying and marking of wrought plate.[10]

Evidently aware that the campaign would come to nothing if he delayed any longer, by January 1773, Boulton was in London and fully absorbed in lobbying Parliament.[11] Exposure in the press had drawn his activities to the

---

6   Lord Edmund Fitzmaurice, *Life of William, Earl of Shelburne*, Vol.1 1737–1766 (1875) quoted in Westwood, p.4.

7   Kenneth Quickenden, *Boulton and Fothergill Silver*. Unpublished thesis submitted for the degree of Doctor of Philosophy, Westfield College, 1989, p.26.

8   BAH, MBP, MS 3782/1/9.

9   Quickenden (1989), p.27.

10   Quoted in Westwood, p.8.

11   See reply from Soho to Mr Gilbert Dixon, Clerk to the Sheffield Cutlers' Company, dated 24 December 1772, quoted in Westwood, p.9. On Boulton's activities early in 1773, see Quickenden (1989), p.29.

attention of the Sheffield Cutlers' Company, and Gilbert Dixon, Clerk to the Cutlers had contacted Boulton, asking if there might be a similar petition put before Parliament for an assay office in Sheffield.[12] Concerned that it might weaken the Birmingham case, Boulton was apprehensive at first, but events progressed rapidly, and the Sheffield petition was presented on 1 February, with the Birmingham petition following the next day.[13] The petition from Birmingham focussed on the inconvenience and expense of sending silver to Chester, in addition to the lack of growth in the Birmingham silver trade as a result. Boulton also distributed a carefully prepared document, entitled *Memorial relative to Assaying and marking wrought plate at Birmingham*.[14] Here, demonstrating sound knowledge of the legislation, he repeated the arguments put forward in the petition, adding that any innovation in design was liable to be copied whilst goods were at Chester, and stating that the expansion of silver manufacture in Birmingham would contribute ultimately to the national economy.[15] In support of Boulton's petition, several Birmingham manufacturers and merchants presented a petition on 25 February in which they accused the London Goldsmiths' Company of passing silver that was 2 pennyweights below the legally required standard.[16]

The press had provided the London Goldsmiths' Company with knowledge of Boulton's campaign, and a means to express their protest against it, and their considerable objections were formalised in a succession of six petitions in opposition to the Birmingham and Sheffield Bill.[17] Presented in the name of the Wardens and Assistants of the Company or Mistery of Goldsmiths of the City of London, the first of these was submitted on 17 February, and it asserted that the duty of assaying and hallmarking was too great to be assigned to towns such as Birmingham and Sheffield where there was little skill in gold and silversmithing. If Birmingham and Sheffield were allowed assay offices, it argued, the outcome would be an increase in fraud and deceit, in addition to increased difficulties in detection, leading to the debasement of the standard and the ruin of the country.[18] The second London petition was presented the next day by the 'Goldsmiths, Silversmiths and Plateworkers, of the City of London, and places adjacent', who stated that

---

12 BAH, MBP, MS 3782/12/88/5.

13 See Tann, p.18.

14 BAH, MBP, MS 3782/12/89/21, 23.

15 BAH, MBP, MS 3782/12/89/23.

16 See Quickenden (1989), p.30. The legal standard for silver at this time was sterling which equates to 11 ounces and 2 pennyweights of pure silver in the Troy pound. 18 pennyweights of copper were added to make up the alloy. Sterling has remained a legally recognised standard of silver, and it now most usually expressed as 925 parts pure silver per thousand.

17 BAH, MBP, MS 3782/12/88/10,11; cited in Westwood, pp.15–18.

18 BAH, MBP, MS 3782/12/88/10.

the granting of assay offices in Birmingham and Sheffield would bring the entire trade into disrepute, which would again be detrimental to the economy on a national scale.[19] In the petition of 25 February, it was alleged by the London workers that Sheffield and Birmingham manufacturers were applying marks that closely resembled the hallmark to base metal articles plated with silver, and that there was little enough work in London to employ trained hands without opening the market up to provincial competition.[20] On March 8, the London workers presented a further petition in which they brought the charge that Birmingham and Sheffield silver wares contained more iron than was legally permissible, and both London factions presented their final petitions on 6 May, repeating their earlier attacks on Birmingham and Sheffield, just twelve days short of Boulton's victory in the Commons.[21]

Boulton had cast himself in the role of spokesman and defender of the Birmingham trade, and he was not likely to suffer the insults of the London opposition. In answer to their case, he distributed his *Reply of the Petitioners from Birmingham and Sheffield to the Case of the Goldsmiths, Silversmiths and Plateworkers of London and Places Adjacent* and a second document entitled, *Observations Relative to The Standard of Wrought Plate*.[22] Taking the Londoners to task for their derogation of the silver trade in Birmingham and Sheffield, he eloquently undermined each of the arguments they had brought against the establishment of assay offices in the two towns. In a letter to Boulton, dated March 11, Joseph Wilkinson had rightly praised his careful and effective strategy; '...[I] am happy to find that your Manoeuvres in Turning their own Batterys upon themselves – May that ever be the case where such mean and dishonourable Arts are adopted!'[23]

Indeed, Boulton's intellectual abilities proved productive during the campaign, but his case was also helped by his connections in both the Commons and the Lords. On 11 May, he wrote to Fothergill 'I do not despair, and as to the House of Lords, I have twice the interest in that House than in the lower House.'[24] He had friends in the Commons too, and arguably in exactly the right places. When the Parliamentary Committee, appointed for the reading of the Birmingham and Sheffield petitions met for the first time on 17 February, Thomas Skipwith, M.P. for Warwickshire, with whom Boulton was well-acquainted, was in the chair.[25] Another committee was

---

19   BAH, MBP, MS 3782/12/88/11.
20   Cited in Westwood, pp.15–16.
21   Cited in Westwood, pp.17–18.
22   BAH, MBP, MS 3782/12/89/13 and 6.
23   BAH, MBP, MS 3782/12/88/21.
24   Quoted in Westwood, p.25.
25   Kenneth Crisp Jones ed, *The Silversmiths of Birmingham and Their Marks: 1750–1980* (National Association of Goldsmiths Press, 1981) p.28.

appointed to investigate the charges relating to irregularities in the manufacture and assay of silver, and at their first formal meeting on March 8, the chair was occupied by Thomas Gilbert, M.P. for Lichfield, who was equally well-known to Boulton.[26] From reports in the Birmingham press, it appears that Gilbert spoke strongly in support of the Bill when it was debated in the House of Commons.[27] After March 8, the two committees appear to have sat concurrently, but the outcome of their enquiries proved more damaging to the London opposition than Boulton could have anticipated.[28]

The joint Parliamentary Committee spent days questioning witnesses regarding statements in the various petitions, but the allegations of irregularity in the manufacture and assaying of silver had clearly caught their attention. The charge that Birmingham silver contained more iron than was legally permissible was found to relate to some candle-snuffers manufactured by Benjamin May and sold to London retailers; it was the sole instance of this allegation that was proven.[29] The matter of the Birmingham and Sheffield manufacturers applying marks to plated wares that closely resembled the hallmark was more or less overlooked; it took up little of the Committee's time with witnesses. On 16 March, Abraham Portal, a London goldsmith was questioned on this matter, but when asked if he knew of any Birmingham or Sheffield manufacturer attempting to pass plated articles as solid silver, he replied that he did not. However, this is arguably the one charge of which Birmingham and Sheffield were guilty. Boulton and Fothergill applied a maker's mark to their Sheffield plate that consisted of the initials 'B&F' with a crown either side. It was exactly the mark they registered at Chester Assay Office, and which was applied to the silver they had assayed and hallmarked there. The absence of any preventative measure in the 1773 Act, or any subsequent legislation allowed the practice to continue, and through the nineteenth into the

---

26 Quickenden (1989) pp.30–31. The terms of reference of this Committee were 'to enquire into the Manner of conducting the several assay offices in London, York, Exeter, Bristol, Chester, Norwich and Newcastle-upon-Tyne, and the manner in which Wrought Plate is assayed and marked, and also into the Frauds and Abuses that have been committed, and attempted to be committed, by the Manufacturers or vendors of Gold and Silver Plate, and Plated Work.' Quoted in Westwood, p.16.

27 *Birmingham Gazette*, 24 May 1773 quoted in Westwood, p.26.

28 Westwood, p.16. It is clear that after 8 March that the two Committees combined their roles as the Matthew Boulton Papers contain only one set of reports from successive sittings.

29 BAH, MBP, MS 3782/12/88/16, 36 and 36b Joseph Wilkinson wrote first to Boulton on this subject on February 1773, defending May's ingenuity rather than decrying his attempt at fraud. May wrote to Boulton in April apologising for any embarrassment or trouble caused by his manufacture of these candle-snuffers, and stating that silver buckles often contained more iron than the offending articles due to the chape being made of steel. The chape is the part of the buckle to which the strap or ribbon is attached.

Fig. 14.1. Sign from the King's Head Inn, New Street, the site of the Birmingham Assay Office's first premises. Birmingham Assay Office.

twentieth century, manufacturers of plated wares continued to apply marks to plated wares that often closely resembled a hallmark.[30]

The Committee, however, went to great lengths to investigate the allegation that London had been passing sub-standard silver. Witnesses included many senior officials, such as the Prime Warden and the deputy Warden to the Goldsmiths Company, and the Assay Masters of Chester and Exeter, and the Committee were at great pains to understand exactly the processes involved in assaying.[31] On the day before they reported their findings, the Committee had

---

30   BAH, MBP, MS 3782/12/88/24.

31   BAH, MBP, MS 3782/12/88 See documents relating to the establishment of the Birmingham Assay Office where the proceedings of the Parliamentary Committee are detailed.

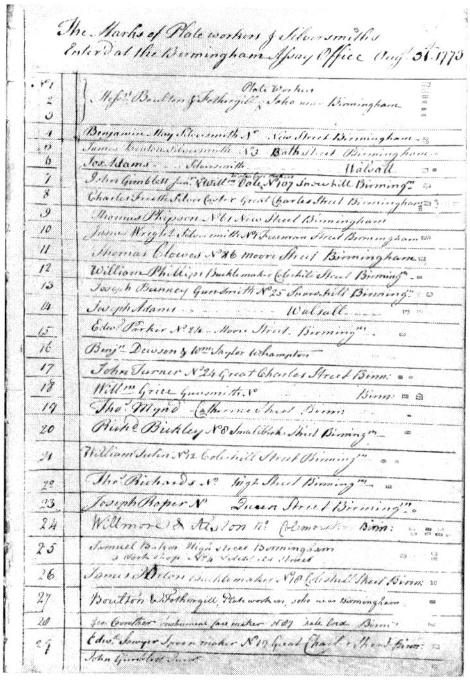

Fig. 14.2. First page of the Plate Register of sponsors' mark (1773–1858),
Birmingham Assay Office, Boulton and Fothergill's entry is the first.

obtained 22 pieces of silver bearing the London hallmark; these were assayed independently, and of the 22 articles, 21 were found to be below the legally required standard.[32] Amendments were subsequently made to the Bill to introduce more rigorous checks and regulations in order to reduce abuses of the system and fraud.[33]

The Bill passed through the Commons on 18 May, and was given Royal Assent in the House of Lords on 28 May. Three months later, the Birmingham Assay Office opened for business on 31 August in three rooms above the King's Head Inn on New Street, rented from the Landlord. (Fig. 14.1). Not only were Boulton and Fothergill the first to register their sponsor mark and to submit work for assay and hallmarking, the partners also contributed financially to the setting up of the Office.[34] (Figs. 14.2, 14.3, 14.4). Whilst Boulton was in London during the campaign, business was generally conducted in the Crown and Anchor Tavern in the Strand. When the Bill met

---

32   Westwood, p.24.

33   See J.S. Forbes, *Hallmark: A History of the London Assay Office* (London: Unicorn Press, 1999) p.223.

34   BAO, Register of Sponsor's Marks, Book A (1773–1858), p.1; Plate Register, 1773–1792. On Boulton and Fothergill's contribution, see Westwood, pp.30–31.

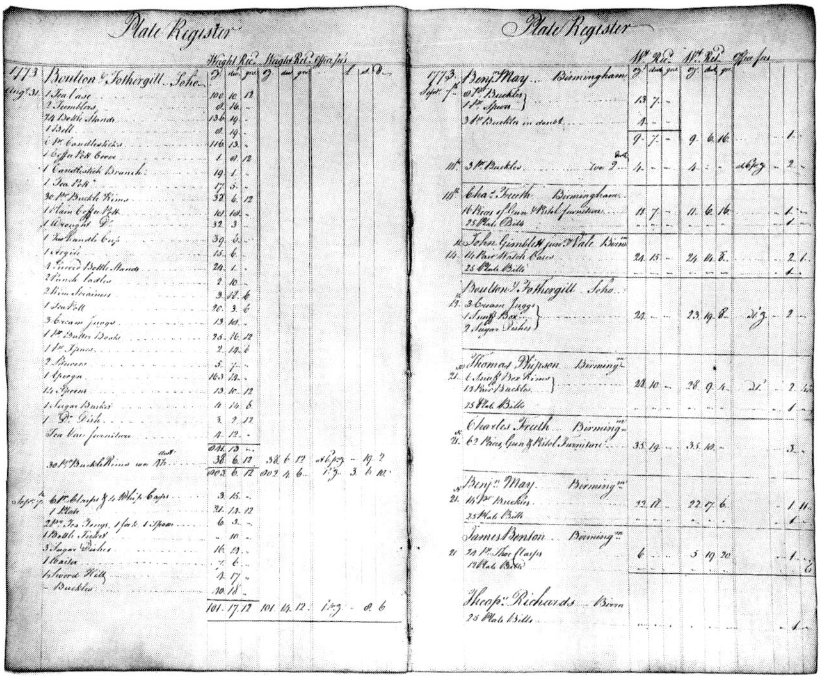

Fig. 14.3. First page of the Plate Register (1773–1792), Birmingham Assay Office, showing the first consignment submitted to the Birmingham Assay Office on August 31 1773 by Boulton and Fothergill.

with success, it seems that the Birmingham and Sheffield contingents chose to adopt their respective marks from the sign of tavern. It was written into the Act that Sheffield's mark was to be the crown, whilst Birmingham's would be the anchor, but quite how the two marks were decided upon is not known. The story of a decision being made on the toss of a coin seems to have originated with Westwood in 1936.[35] In 1904, Sheffield adopted the mark of the Yorkshire Rose on gold, and since 1975, they have also used this mark on silver, but the Birmingham Assay Office still use the anchor, and for 236 years it has stood as a symbol of integrity and independence; exactly the values on which Boulton had based his campaign.

The story of how the Birmingham Assay Office came to be established, then, is exciting if only for the very speed with which events progressed, with the acumen Boulton brought to his campaign surely driving things forward. The sources, however, reveal another story, a subtext that evidences the wider cultural context in which Boulton's battle with London took place. The cut

35 Westwood, p.31.

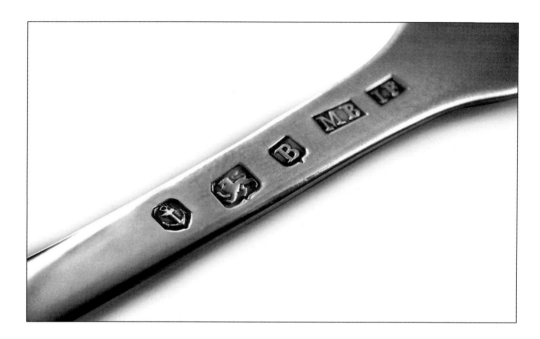

Fig. 14.4. Hallmark from a tablespoon, Boulton and Fothergill, Birmingham, 1774. Birmingham Assay Office.

and thrust of business in the late eighteenth century certainly comes to light, with arguments over markets, disagreements about quality and charges of dishonesty. Heightened tension between the old and the new, however, is a defining feature of periods of rapid cultural and economic change, and, on a more fundamental level, the campaign of 1773 represented a struggle between the traditional culture inhabited by the London Goldsmiths' Company and the burgeoning industrial character of Birmingham.

In their successive petitions, the London contingent persistently elevated their own position whilst simultaneously derogating the abilities of the silversmiths of Birmingham and Sheffield. The London workers argued that silver production was 'carried on in the City of London by the most exquisite and skilful Artists in all its variety of useful and curious Branches in much greater perfection than in any other place in these Kingdoms,' that London silver possessed 'Elegance [and] Utility' whereas in Sheffield and Birmingham there were '...few persons at all conversant with or skilled in the Gold and Silver Manufactory.'[36] What few there were, they said, were '...confined to some of the least important Branches of the said Manufactory, which are wrought and done there in a specious but very slight and unserviceable

---

36　BAH, MBP, MS 3782/12/88/11.

manner.'[37] London silver, then, was all that silver should be, and everything that Birmingham and Sheffield were incapable of producing. William Bingley had worked for Boulton at Soho, and when he came before the Parliamentary Committee, he defended the Birmingham trade well, stating that Boulton's patterns were more handsome than any he had seen in London.[38] Likewise, when Samuel Garbett – the only witness to be called for Birmingham, but a highly dependable ally to Boulton – was questioned by the Parliamentary Committee, he stated that not one in five hundred of the buckle patterns made in Birmingham were available in London.[39] Furthermore, innovation in design and a greater number of individuals entering the trade, he responded, would be significant advantages of an assay office in Birmingham.[40] According to Garbett, the Birmingham trade was not narrow, as London had suggested, and neither was Birmingham silver inferior in design or utility; Boulton was manufacturing a wide range of articles, including 'Tureens, Candlesticks, Vases, Coffee Pots', all 'Ornamental Utensils'.[41]

Further into the investigations of the Parliamentary Committee, the fundamental reason for London's disparaging statements about Birmingham silver comes to light. A great deal of attention was focussed on whether the manufacturers in Birmingham or Sheffield were producing 'heavy' or 'slight' candlesticks.[42] The term 'heavy' referred to candlesticks manufactured by casting, an older technique still widely used in London at the time that was much more expensive due to the amount of metal involved whilst the term 'slight' referred to candlesticks produced by die-stamping, a newer, significantly cheaper method developed and used by Boulton at Soho.[43] Inigo Wakelin, a silversmith in the Haymarket could not have stated the difference between cast and stamped candlesticks more clearly when he told the Committee that '[candlesticks] of 30 ounces would cost more than those stamped on account of Workmanship.'[44] Though it was shrouded in issues of aesthetics and use-value, the real argument here was about old and new

---

37   BAH, MBP, MS 3782/12/88/11.

38   BAH, MBP, MS 3782/12/88/18.

39   BAH, MBP, MS 3782/12/89/13.

40   BAH, MBP, MS 3782/12/89/13.

41   BAH, MBP, MS 3782/12/89/13.

42   See accounts of the Committee's meetings MBP, BAH, MS 3782/12/88.

43   I do not mean to imply here that the manufacture of silver at Soho was an entirely industrialised process, using die-stamping as the only technique. Undoubtedly, this was the method favoured at Soho for the manufacture of candlesticks, but many examples of the articles Boulton produced were made by a combination of more industrial and older craft techniques. Quickenden provides a comprehensive account of Boulton's methods of manufacture in 'Boulton and Fothergill Silver: Business Plans and Miscalculations' in *Art History*, Volume 3, Number 3, September 1980, p.283.

44   BAH, MBP, MS 3782/12/88/15.

methods of manufacturing, and the fact that the silver produced using the new method of die-stamping by Boulton and other Birmingham manufacturers was cheaper and would, therefore, threaten the market for the more expensive silver made in London. In his *Memorial*, Boulton's admonition to London was logical and succinct:

> But as Birmingham is not near to any Market for Plate, it can deprive the other Towns of no Part of their Trade, except by working better than they do and cheaper; and against Losses of Business by these Means the proper Securities are not Privileges, but Excellence in Design and Workmanship, and moderate Prices.[45]

Nevertheless, the London workers argued that their trade could not withstand such competition; it was carried on, they said, to '...an extent sufficient to supply the greatest demands,' and that the decrease they were already experiencing in their business would be worsened further by an increase in the Birmingham and Sheffield trades to the point where many more skilled hands would '...experience in their turns Distresses of the same kind with which so many poor honest or discarded workmen and their Miserable Families are now sinking under.'[46] For the London contingent, in a declining market, they could meet the current levels of demand, and they already had surplus labour. They could ill-afford, therefore, to loose market share to Birmingham or Sheffield, and had to protect themselves from competition. Suggesting that London itself, not competition from any other quarter, had caused the decline, in their reply to the London case, the Birmingham and Sheffield petitioners stated that the decline of the London market was due to '...*exhorbitant Prices*, in spite of the *very Prevailing Taste for Plate*...' which made London silver '...unsaleable to all but *a few rich* People.'[47] Later in the same document, the point was stressed again:

> It does not follow that that if the 'Goldsmiths Manufactory in Sheffield and Birmingham should be *increased*, that of London must suffer a *proportionable Decrease*.' Should they all Three make better and cheaper Plate than London now does, most infallibly every one of them would make and sell more; ...*exhorbitant Prices*, by *diminishing* the *Demand*, deprive Workmen of Bread.[48]

45   BAH, MBP, MS 3782/12/89/23.
46   BAH, MBP, MS 3782/12/88/11.
47   BAH, MBP, MS 3782/12/89/13.
48   BAH, MBP, MS 3782/12/89/13.

Boulton's influence in the *Reply* is unmistakeable; competition not monopoly would benefit the trade by bringing prices down and improving quality, thus driving up demand and increasing employment in the trade. In a market they perceived to be declining, London's attitude was understandable, but the conservative turn of their argument represented an older order of economic thinking when set against Boulton's more progressive perception of the market.

In order to protect their market, the London trade had to prevent their authority to assay and hallmark precious metals being weakened by the establishment of assay offices in Birmingham and Sheffield, and they drew on all they could in making their case. Using their full title of the 'Wardens and Commonalty of the Mistery of Goldsmiths of the City of London', in their first petition, the Goldsmiths' Company argued that '...the power of trying touching assaying and marking of Gold and Silver plate is a very great and important trust,' that they had executed their duty, which was of national significance and with which they were charged by the Crown, with 'the utmost care and fidelity,' and that they had been 'a Guild or Corporation time out of Mind.'[49] The privilege to which Boulton objected so strongly inhered in their royal and national associations, and in their historical provenance. The London plateworkers, in the petition presented the following day, took things a step further; the power of assaying gold and silver, they said, was 'sacred'.[50] Despite their assertions, the actual practice at Goldsmiths' Hall had been shown to be inept as they had been passing and hallmarking silver that was below the required standard. What emerged during the Parliamentary enquiry was that the processes of preparing samples of silver for assay were open to abuse by manufacturers due to the absence of any checks on the individuals responsible at Goldsmiths' Hall.[51] In addition, the lack of scientific understanding in relation to the refining of silver during assay had interfered with the Chief Assayer's ability to uphold the legally required standard.[52] No witnesses from Sheffield or Birmingham were questioned as to their understanding of refining or assaying, but from private letters written by Garbett to Boulton, the two men evidently had considerable understanding of the processes involved.

Armed with what appears to be Garbett's substantial knowledge of refining, they were confident that they would be much better placed to conduct the business of an assay office. Throughout Garbett's letters to

---

49   BAH, MBP, MS 3782/12/88/10.
50   BAH, MBP, MS 3782/12/88/11.
51   See accounts of the Committee's meetings where sampling and assaying techniques are discussed. BAH, MBP, MS 3782/12/88/19, 26, 32, 33, 34, 35.
52   See Forbes, pp.219–223 for an account of the problems encountered by London.

Boulton during this time, the Birmingham trade is privileged above London by expertise and knowledge in science of metals; 'the London Refiners,' he wrote to Boulton, 'have Lost the Art of making silver quite fine.'[53] Birmingham, however, quite clearly had the advantage; in a letter dated 3 May, Garbett wrote that he was about to dispatch 50 ounces of silver by fly to Boulton, which he said 'shall be as fine as we can make it and I don't doubt that 11oz 2dwt. of it and 18dwt. of copper will be better than the Standard of 11oz which is allowed to pass at Goldsmiths' Hall.'[54] Mindful of the need to protect what he knew, he continued '...I expect it will be better than the Standard Plate of the Kingdom for Reasons not prudent to put on Paper even to you.'[55] Still urging secrecy, he concluded, '...when you have obtained the Law I suppose you and I shall be made acquainted with their most sacred Art and Mistery – but don't let Us give any of them our Real knowledge in exchange for their Shabby Occult Misteries.'[56] Science, then, was the 'Real knowledge', and the 'sacred Mistery' which the London Goldsmiths used to bolster their case was now 'Shabby' and 'Occult'. Completely reversing the charges of audacity, ineptitude, dishonesty and provincial backwardness implicit in the London case, Garbett asked 'What must we Country Folks think of the Insolence of such Pretenders to Accuracy.'[57]

What was an argument about the rights and wrongs of allowing assay offices to be established in Birmingham and Sheffield was also a conflict between the old and the new in which each side sought to prove its case against the other. Indeed, 'other' is an appropriate term, since each side privileged their own position by direct oppositional reference to its 'other'. So, where London could draw on its metropolitan, national, historical and traditional significance, Birmingham by definition was provincial, new and lacking in the historical provenance of craft guilds or incorporations. The Goldsmiths' Company had discharged their important duty with 'care and fidelity', the Birmingham trade by turns was careless, dishonest and likely to abuse the privilege of being granted an assay office.[58] If London possessed 'the most exquisite and skilful Artists' who could manufacture silver 'in all its variety of useful and curious Branches in much greater perfection than in any other place in these Kingdoms,' then Birmingham's output was produced by unskilled workers, it was unattractive, of no use value, and of poor quality.[59]

---

53   BAH, MBP, MS 3782/12/88/40.
54   BAH, MBP, MS 3782/12/88/37.
55   BAH, MBP, MS 3782/12/88/37.
56   BAH, MBP, MS 3782/12/88/37.
57   BAH, MBP, MS 3782/12/88/37.
58   BAH, MBP, MS 3782/12/88/10.
59   BAH, MBP, MS 3782/12/88/11.

Conversely, in Birmingham's perception, London silver was 'not of *uncommonly intrinsic* value,' the workmanship was not 'so *masterly*', the designs were not 'so *elegant* or *convenient*', and London prices were not 'so *reasonable*'.[60] Therefore, Birmingham silver displayed all the qualities of good workmanship, and economic, aesthetic and use-value that its 'other' did not. Moreover, Birmingham silver was cheap by comparison. Finally, where London was involved in 'Shabby Occult Misteries', Birmingham men, like Boulton and Garbett were in possession of new, scientific 'Real knowledge'.[61]

Shrouded though it was in powerful rhetoric, the conflict between London and Birmingham was essentially about the market for silver and the ways in which the assay offices functioned in relation to its protection or its expansion. The Parliamentary enquiry was eventually persuaded by Boulton's rigorous argument, and without close analysis of the records of all three Assay Offices concerned, it is difficult to tell exactly how much of an impact the establishment of the Birmingham and Sheffield Offices had on the trade in London. The existence of an assay office in Birmingham undoubtedly contributed to the enormous expansion of the Jewellery Quarter in the years after 1773, leading up to the early twentieth century. As a result the Birmingham trade spawned some of the leading silversmiths of the period who enjoyed international status in their own time, and whose work is now held in historic collections of regional, national and international significance.[62] Boulton's own venture in silver, however, was not particularly successful in an economic sense. He arguably over-estimated the reduction in cost that die-stamping would bring about, often having to resort to older, more expensive techniques, and having to pay wages at London rates to workers that he brought from London to Soho for their skills. Likewise, he miscalculated the extent to which he could expand the market and found himself competing in the London market at London prices.[63] In addition, Boulton and Garbett's knowledge of refining metals most surely depended upon the earlier practices developed by the London trade. Despite the dispute about 'sacred Misteries' and 'Real knowledge' between the guardians of a time-honoured craft and innovative industrial entrepreneurs like

---

60   BAH, MBP, MS 3782/12/89/13.

61   BAH, MBP, MS 3782/12/88/37.

62   In addition to the collections at the Birmingham Assay Office, Boulton silver features in the collections at Birmingham Museums and Art Gallery, the Victoria and Albert Museum, Windsor Castle, and at the Speed Museum in Louisville, Kentucky, U.S.A. The Birmingham Assay Office Silver Collection holds 140 items in metal produced at Soho, the majority of which are in silver, with a few in other metals, such as steel and Sheffield Plate.

63   On the economic failure of the Boulton and Fothergill silver business, see Quickenden, 'Boulton and Fothergill Silver: Business Plans and Miscalculations' in *Art History*, Vol.3, No.3, September 1980, pp.274–294.

Boulton, the new clearly involved a good deal of reference back to the old. Nevertheless, Boulton does emerge as an advocate for modern business interests with abilities that would serve him well throughout his career; skilled in rhetoric and public relations, and practised at making use of friends in high places. The attributes that enabled him to establish the Birmingham Assay Office successfully are exactly those that that render Boulton such a fascinating and charismatic figure to us in the present.

NOTES ON CONTRIBUTORS

Dr Jim Andrew is an engineer who worked in Birmingham industry and public health before joining the Birmingham Museum of Science and Industry in 1974. He researched many aspects of the exhibits and in 1991 he was awarded his PhD by Birmingham University for research on Boulton and Watt's water supply engines. Following partial retirement he continues as Collections Advisor to Birmingham Science Museum.

Olga Baird was born and studied in Leningrad (St Petersburg, Russia). She worked at the National A.S. Pushkin Museum in St Petersburg from 1976–2000. From 2001, she has worked on projects for West Midlands museums and is developing a new display of Victorian artworks at Wolverhampton Art Gallery. Her main interests are Museum Studies, and Art and Culture in the Enlightenment. She has published papers in England, Russia and internationally.

Dr Sally Baggott is Curator of the Birmingham Assay Office and Assistant Director of the Centre for Birmingham and Midlands History at the University of Birmingham. Sally read English Literature and Cultural Studies as an undergraduate at Birmingham, before going on to study for her PhD. in late nineteenth century literature.

Dr David Brown has been a teacher in secondary, further and higher education. He has published over a dozen articles on eighteenth and nineteenth century British social and economic history and is completing a book with Ashgate on the history of peddling. He is a Fellow of the Royal Historical Society. He is currently Course Leader for Sixteenth Century History at Cadbury College, Birmingham.

George Demidowicz is head of Conservation and Archaeology for Coventry City Council. He has researched Birmingham's landscape, topography and industrial archaeology, including water mills and the Soho Manufactory, Mint and Foundry. A volume on the origins and development of the Soho complex is forthcoming. He recently completed a study of medieval Birmingham, based on hitherto unknown records, which has transformed our knowledge of the town before the Black Death.

Dr Malcolm Dick is Acting Director of the Centre for Birmingham and Midlands History at the University of Birmingham. He was manager of the Revolutionary Players Project between 2002 and 2004, which created a website of the history of the West Midlands www.revolutionaryplayers.org.uk. In 2005 he edited and contributed to *Joseph Priestley and Birmingham* and wrote *Birmingham: a History of the City and its People*.

Sir Nicholas Goodison is the author of *Matthew Boulton: Ormolu* (2002), a revised edition of his *Ormolu: the Work of Matthew Boulton* (1974). He has published other papers and articles about Boulton, including *Matthew Boulton's Trafalgar Medal* (Birmingham Museum, 2007). He was formerly Chairman of the London Stock Exchange, the Courtauld Institute of Art, the Burlington Magazine and the National Art Collections Fund, and is President of the Furniture History Society.

Peter Jones is Professor of French History at the University of Birmingham. He has written books on the French Revolution and his study, *The French Revolution, 1787–1804* was published in 2003. Recently, he has been researching the history of Birmingham and the West Midlands in the eighteenth and early nineteenth centuries. His book *Industrial Enlightenment: Science, Technology and Culture in Birmingham and the West Midlands, 1760–1820* was published in 2008.

Val Loggie was formerly curator of Soho House, Birmingham: the former home of Matthew Boulton. She has worked in a number of museums and historic houses in the Midlands and is now following an AHRC funded collaborative PhD on works on paper related to Matthew Boulton at the University of Birmingham and Birmingham Museums and Art Gallery.

Shena Mason is a writer with a long-standing interest in the life of Matthew Boulton. From 1993–1995 she ran Birmingham Museum and Art Gallery's

Soho House and Archives Appeal, and subsequently wrote the guidebook to Soho House. Her book on Miss Anne Boulton, *The Hardware Man's Daughter*, was published in 2005, and she is the editor of BM&AG's exhibition publication for the Matthew Boulton Bicentenary Exhibition in 2009.

Kenneth Quickenden is the Heritage Jewellery Professor at Birmingham City University where he was previously Head of the School of Theoretical and Historical Studies in Art and Design. He is a graduate of the Courtauld Institute at London University and wrote a doctoral thesis on the silver of Matthew Boulton at Westfield College, London University. His main publications have been on Boulton and contemporary jewellery and metalwork.

Dr David Symons has a BA in Ancient History and Archaeology and a PhD on Anglo-Saxon numismatics from the University of Birmingham. He has worked at Birmingham Museum and Art Gallery since 1977 and is now Curator of Antiquities and Numismatics. David has served on the council of the British Numismatic Society and was editor of the society's journal, the *British Numismatic Journal* from 2002 to 2007.

Fiona Tait has worked as an archivist in Birmingham Archives and Heritage for over twenty years. She was seconded to catalogue the papers of James Watt & family for the Archives of Soho project, 1999–2004, and continues to enjoy assisting researchers using the Archives of Soho.

Sue Tungate graduated with BSc in Biological Sciences, taught science in England and worked outside teaching in Germany and the USA. She obtained a MA in English Local History at the University of Birmingham in 2003 and is now working towards an AHRC funded collaborative PhD on the coins, medals and tokens of Matthew Boulton's mints at the University of Birmingham and Birmingham Museums and Art Gallery.

Jenny Uglow, OBE, FRS, is a publisher and writer, with a particular interest in the eighteenth century. Her book, *The Lunar Men, the Friends who made the Future* (2002) won the James Tait Black Memorial Prize for Biography, and the PEN Hessel-Tiltman prize for History. She is particularly proud to have received honorary degrees from the universities of Birmingham, Aston and Central England.

INDEX

Index Notes: AB = Ann Boulton; JW = James Watt; MB = Matthew Boulton; MRB = Matthew Robinson Boulton. Page references appearing in *italic* print refer to Plates and Figures.

A

Abbott, Lemuel Francis, *V,* 74-5
agriculture, 90
  as design motif, 199
Albion Mill, London, 80-1
Alexander I, Emperor of Russia, 100, 101, 103
allegorical depictions, *VI,* 198-9
Alston, John, 158-9
America, 29
Andrew, Dr Jim, 7-8, 217
Anglesey *see* Parys Mine Company
Angerstein, Juliana, 103
Anglo-American war (1812-15), 29
Archives of Soho, 2, 75
Aris's Birmingham Gazette, 53
Aris, Thomas, 53, 79
Arkwright, Richard, 67
artisans' houses, 51, 54
  building clubs, 52-3
Assay Office *see* Birmingham Assay Office
Aston Hall, 74
Attwood, Thomas, 26
Aubert, Alexander, 36

B

Babington, Mary, 31
Babington, Revd. Zachary, 31
Babington, Zachariah (shoemaker), 34-5
Bacounin, Pavel, 102-3
Baggott, Dr Sally, 10-11, 217
Bagot, Lord, 57

Baird, Olga, 7, 217
balloon, MB's notes on, *87*
Bank of England, 176, 199
Banks, Sir Joseph, 40, 65, 73
Baskerville, John, 66
Battle of Trafalgar, 105
beam engine, 110-11, 127, 128
beamless engine, 125
Beechey, Sir William, *IV,* 6, 72, 73-4
Bentley, John, 32
Bentley, Thomas, 27
  letters from JW, 133, 134, 137-8, 139; on cameos, 140, 141-2
Berg, Maxine, 3
Bicknell, John, 24
Billington, Elizabeth, 41
Bilston, 17, 18-19
bimetal coins, 190
Bingley, William, 211
Birch, Wyrley, of Hamstead Hall, 47-8, 49, 51
Birmingham, 13-29
  'birth' and development, 20-9; building expansion, 20-2, 51-2; industrial economy, 4, 26-7; natural resources, 14-15; population figures, 20; regional context and location, 14-19
  Brass House, *XIV*
  during wars with France and America, 28-9
  fashion ('toy') goods production, 25-6, 27, 31
  Jewellery Quarter, 215
  metal-goods production, 20, 22-4, 27; plating, 155

(Birmingham continued...)
modern conceptions of, 13-14
poor of, 55-6
riots (1791), 40, 59; (1800), 101
silversmithing, 206; evidence to
    Committee on Assay Bill, 210-13, 214-
    15; maker's mark, 209
theatre, 60, 95-6, 99
transport to London and Cornwall, 37
wholesalers, 144
Birmingham Assay Office, 10-11, 164
archives, 78, 79
establishment of, 154, 208-16
lobbying for, 201-8
maker's marks, 165, 209
Birmingham Canal, 16, 17
Birmingham Canal Company, 18
Birmingham Commercial Committee, 46
Birmingham Gazette, 53
Birmingham Heath enclosures, 47, 54-6, 57
Birmingham Memorial on [Russian] Mint,
    80
Birmingham-Fazeley canal, 16
Bishton, John, 54
Black Country, 4, 13, 15-16, 18-19
Bloye statue, *XV*
Boden and Smith, 146
boilers, 87
Bolton, John, 31
Boswell, James, 12
Boulton, Ann (MB's second wife), 33
    death, 41
    dress style, 37-8
    Packington estate, 47
    portrait, 63, 64, 70
Boulton, Anne (MB's daughter), 2, 34, 41, 43
    dental work, 38-9
    letter to MB, 68
    portrait, 74
Boulton, Christiana (MB's mother), 31, 34
Boulton, John and Elizabeth (MB's paternal
    grandparents), 31
Boulton, Mary (MB's first wife), 32-3
Boulton, Matthew
    biographical events: birth, 30; ancestral lines,
        4, 31-2; childhood and education, 4-5,
        32; first marriage, 5, 32-3, 45; second
        marriage to AB, 5, 33-4, 45, 47; leases
        land at Soho, Handsworth, 5, 34, 118;

(Boulton, Matthew continued...)
    friendship with Josiah Wedgwood, 132-
        5; campaigns on assay law, 202-9; visits
        Holland, 81; visits Ireland and France,
        82-3; friendship with Alexander
        Woronzow, 94-106; appointed sheriff
        of Staffordshire, 50; awarded Royal
        Mint contract, 126, 176-7; visits Royal
        Mint, 179-80; accused of forgery, 177-
        8; death, 29, 60, 74, 106, 183
    business activities: breadth of, 78; factoring,
        161-2; fashion, 'toy' business, 118, 145-
        7, 153-4, 172; financial problems, 175;
        merchanting, 88, 148-52; minting, 88-
        9, 122-4, 126-7, 173-84, 185;
        partnership with James Watt *see*
        Boulton and Watt; partnership with
        John Fothergill *see* Boulton and
        Fothergill; partnership with John
        Scale, 145-6, 151; printing process, 70-
        1; silver and substitutes, 9, 153-69, 215
    character and attitudes: circumspection, 12;
        competitiveness, 135, 141; dress style,
        37-8, 75; love of learning, 32, 91-2;
        political and social views, 44, 50-1, 53-
        4, 58-9; pragmatism, 40; problem
        solving, 183-4; sociability, 40, 133;
        social ambitions, 30-1, 61-2
    experiments: recorded in notebook, 87-8;
        silver plating and substitutes, 154, 156;
        sun and planet gear link, *111,* 112
    illnesses, 37, 90, 105, 183
    interests, 37: astronomy, 84; civic activities,
        41, 59-60; early reading, 32; garden
        design, 42-3; lobbying activities, 40,
        58-9: *Memorial Relative to Assaying and
        marking wrought plate in Birmingham,*
        204, 212; *Reply from the Petitioners of
        Birmingham and Sheffield,* 205, 213
    landownership, 5, 45-52, 54, 56, 57-8: and
        attitude to artisans' housing, 50-1, 52-3
    letters: on ceramics, 133, 134-5, 136, 147;
        on class distinctions, 44; on coining,
        173, 175, 181, 189, 200; on education,
        95; on enclosures, 54, 58; on fate of the
        poor, 50-1, (ascribed to MB, 53); on
        food riot (1800), 101; on portraits of
        himself, 67, 101; on purchase of piano,
        35; on Russian connections, 92, 96-7;

(Boulton, Matthew continued...)
   on silversmithing, 201, 203, 205; on
   Soho, 52; on steam engine technology,
   110, 115; on trade embargo, 28; on
   triton figure, 147; to AB, 37, 38, 70; to
   MRB on notebook, 77
notebooks, 6-7, 37, 77-91: breadth of
   content, 78-9; on agriculture, 90; on
   all things used at the Mines, 80; on
   Boulton & Fothergill, 79-80; on
   business interests and products, 85-7;
   on coining and related items, 88-9,
   187; on eggs, 90; on experiments, 87-
   8; on ideal home retreat, 36, 83-4; on
   journey to Ireland, 82; on journey to
   Warwick, 37; on medicine, 90; on
   Memorial on Russian Mint, 80; on
   property ownership, 85; on Soho
   House and grounds, 43-4, 83-5; on
   visit to Carnmath, 81-2; on visit to
   Paris, 82-3
portraits, 6, 63-75: and other likenesses,
   75-6; by C.F. von Breda (1792), *III*,
   67-8; by J.S.C. Schaak (1770), *II*, 64;
   by L.F. Abbott (1797-1801), *V*, 74-5; by
   Sir William Beechey (1798), *IV*, 63-4;
   first exhibited, 66; reflecting MB's rise
   in society, 72, 73-4
statue, *XV*
studies on, 1-3, 11
Boulton, Matthew (MB's father), 4, 31-2, 33
Boulton, Matthew Piers Watt (MB's
   grandson), 129
Boulton, Matthew Robinson (MB's son), 34,
   41, 73
   control at Soho, 60, 125, 128, 129-31
   Great Tew estate, 46, 61
   letter to MB, 67
   letters from MB, 43, 77, 95, 189
   marriage, 61
   notebooks, 77, 90
   upbringing and inheritance, 60-1
Boulton, Watt and Company, 8, 125
   engines manufactured by, 128
   see also Boulton and Watt
Boulton and Fothergill, 79-80
   assay law and, 201-2, 208; maker's mark,
   206-7
   cameos, 140-5

(Boulton and Fothergill continued...)
   purchases and exports, 148-52
   vases, 135-9
Boulton and Scale, 145-6, 151
Boulton and Watt, 81, 86, 180
   steam engine technology, 107-15, 117,
   120-1; manufacturing of engines, 124-
   5; pumping engine (1777), *109*
   see also Boulton, Watt and Company
Boulton Plate Company, 128
Brass House, Broad Street, Birmingham, *XIV*
Breda, Carl Frederick von, *III*, 67-8
   letters to MB, 69, 71
British Association for the Advancement of
   Science in Birmingham, 22
Broadley, Isaac (Hull agents), 151
Brown, Dr David, 5-6, 217
Brown, Mather, 66-7
Bruland, K, 2
buckle making, 22, 24, 25, 86
   at Soho, *158*, 158-9
   see also button making; fashion ('toy')
      goods production
Burke, Edmund, 25, 171-2
button making, 25, 31-2
   at Soho Manufactory, 118-19, 145-6, 156-
   7, 167
   see also buckle making; fashion ('toy')
      goods production
Buxton, 88

C
cameos and intaglios, 139-47
   box mounted, 140-1
   buttons, *IX*
   candle vases, *VII*
   gilt metal versions, 143
   jasper cameo, 'Socrates,' *VIII*, 143
   jasper double sided, *X*
   ormolu frames, *VIII*, 143
canals, 3, 15-16, 17, 133n
   accommodating Soho Manufactory, 56
   Birmingham Canal, 16, 17
   Birmingham-Fazeley, 16
   effect of, 18
   Staffordshire and Worcestershire, 16
   Trent and Mersey (Grand Trunk), 16, 133
candlesticks, *159*, 159-61, *160*, 203
   'heavy' and 'slight,' 211

cannon ('Carronades'), 88
carbonated water, 39
Castelcicala, Prince Fabrizio Ruffo, 98
catalogues, 152
Cathcart, Charles Schaw, 9th Lord, 149
Catherine II, Empress of Russia, 93, 150n
Chacewater engine, 110
Chalklin, C.W., 20, 22, 52
Chambers, William, 65, 147
  letter to MB, 67-8
Charlotte, Queen of Great Britain, 65
Chelsea factory, 138
Cheshire, William, 178
Cheslyn Hay enclosures, 46, 53-4
Chester Assay Office, 202, 203, 207
Chippendall, Richard, 73
Clay, Henry, 25, 143
Clay, Richard, 11
close plating, 158-9, 168
coats of arms, 196
coin pressing
  countermarking, 176, 182
  design, 186-200; bimetal coins, 190;
    Cartwheel, *173*, 177, 178-9, 191;
    Druid motif, 196; hexagon coins, 189-
    90; inscriptions, 191-2, *192*; national
    symbols, 198-9; portraits, 194-5;
    technical aspects, 187-90
  issued by Royal Mint, 170-2
  issued during financial crisis (of 1797),
    176-7
  Soho Mint production, 177, 181, 182,
    186, 188-9; machinery, 122, 126-7,
    130; MB's notebook entries, 88-9, 187
Colmore, Lionel, 54, 56
Cook's second voyage, 65
copper coinage *see* coin pressing
copy press, 113
corn mill, Blackfriars Bridge, 124
Cornwall
  Cornish Metal Company, 196
  mining, 28, 81, 86, 175
  travel to, from Birmingham, 37
county towns, 19
Court, W.H.B., 14
Coventry, 14
Cox (jeweller) of Shoe Lane, 137, 138
Crescent Building at Soho, 125-6, *126*, 130
Cronebane mine, 196

Cross, A.G., 93
cruets, *166*
Cumberland, Richard, 40

D
Dalton, R. and Hamer, S.H., 186
Darwin, Erasmus, 1, 4, 39, 57
Day, Thomas, 39
Demidowicz, George, 8, 218
dentistry, 38-9
Deritend, 20-1
Deritend school, 32
design
  for cruets, *166*
  of coins, 186-200; bimetal coins, 190;
    Cartwheel, *173*, 177, 178-9, 191;
    Druid motif, 196; hexagon coins, 189-
    90; national symbols, 198-9; portraits,
    194-5
  of medals, 186, 191, 193; allegorical
    depictions, 198; commemorating MB's
    achievements, 190; commemorating
    royal events, 197-8, *198*; industrial
    depictions, 196
  of tokens, 186; Anglesey token, 196; coats
    of arms, 196; technical aspects to, 187,
    189; Wilkinson token, *195*, 195-6
  of vases and cameos, 147-8, *166*
  technical aspects, 186-90
  see also pattern books
Dick, Dr Malcolm, 3, 218
Dickinson, H.W. and Jenkins, R., 108
Dickinson, H.W., *Matthew Boulton*, 75, 202
dies, 187-9, 193-6
diner services *see* tableware
Dixon, Cornelius, 41
Dixon, Gilbert, 204
Doty, Richard, 2, 182
drive shaft tunnel, Soho Mint, 130-1, *131*
Droz, Jean-Pierre, 188, 194
Dudley, 17, 19
Dudley Cave, 97
Dumarest, Rambert, 194, 196
Dumergue, Charles, 38-9, 40
Dupeyrat, Jean Baptiste, 189
Dupin, Charles-Pierre, 18
dyes, 88
Dyott, Matthew, 31
Dyott, Sir Richard, 31

E

East India Company, 173, 186, 188, 189
  coin inscriptions, 192, *192*
  design decisions, 193-4
Eaves, John, 118
Edgeworth, Maria, 74
Edgeworth, Richard Lovell, 39
educational programmes, 94-5
eggs, 90
Eginton, Francis, 66, 70-1, 142
elites, interests of, 46, 51, 61
  annual incomes, 153, 164
enclosures
  at Barton under Needwood, 46, 47
  at Birmingham Heath, 47, 54-5, *55*, 55-6
  at Cheslyn Hay, 46, 53-4
  at Handsworth, 46, *48*, 48-52, *83*, 85
  at Needworth Forest, 46, 57-8
  at Perry Common, 55
  at Sutton Coldfield, 54
  at Tettenhall, 52
  at West Bromwich, 52
encroachers on common land, 51
Engestrom, Gustav, 156
Engine Works at Soho, 124, 128
Engine Yard at Soho, 124-5
engravers, 71, 73
  designs for dies, 187-9, 193-6
Equiano, Olaudah, 12
Enlightenment, *viii-ix*, 46
  educational programmes, 94-5
  Russian idea of noble upbringing, 98
Etruria factory, 16, 27, 133
  transportation from, 151-2
Etruscan (black basalt) ware, 139-40
experiments recorded in MB's notebooks,
  87-8
exports
  MB's and JW's merchanting activities, 27,
    88, 148-52
  of Birmingham manufacture, 26-7, 88
  to America, 29
  to Europe, 26-8
  to St Petersburg and the Baltic States, 151-2
  trade embargoes, 27

F

Falmouth, 81-2
Farey, John, 114

fashion ('toy') goods production, 25-6, 27, 31
  MB's production of, 118, 145-6, 153-4, 172
  see also buckle making; button making;
    medals
filigree, 159
financial crisis (of 1797), 176
Fisher, Jabez, 21
Folliot, James, 203
Fordyce, Dr, 90
forks and knives, 162-3
Foster, Andy, *XIV*
Fothergill, John, 26-7, 34, 64, 138, 149
  Albion Mill, MB's notebook entry on, 79-
    80
  debts, MB's notebook entry on, 79-80
  letter from MB, 205
France, 82-3
Franklin, Benjamin, 40
French Revolution, 21-2, 96
  effect on trade, 28
  medals commemorating, 197-8, *198*
French-plating, 154-5, 158-9, 162, 167-8

G

Galton, Mary Anne, 68
Galton, Samuel, 39
Garbett, Francis, 172-3
Garbett, Samuel, 15-16, 23, 27, 28
  investigates the Royal Mint, 172-3
  Parliamentary Committee on Assay Bill
    and, 211; letter to MB, 213-14
Garbett, Samuel jnr, 82
General Chamber of Manufacturers, 46
George III, King of Great Britain, 197
  engraved depictions, 194
Gilbert, Thomas, 206
Gilliberg, Francis, 69
Gilmour, Sir Alexander, 160
glass-works, 29
Gooch, Sir Thomas, 54, 56-7
Goodison, Nicholas, 2, 8-9, 194, 218
Gough, John, of Perry Barr, 54-6
Great Hockley Pool, 8
Great Saredon, 47
Great Tew estate, Oxfordshire, 46, 61
Green, Benjamin, 63-4, 71
Green, Valentine, 74
Greig, Samuel and Mary, 104
Grimaldi, William, 72-3

H

hallmarks, 165, 206-7, 209
Hancock, John Gregory, 194-5, 196
Handsworth enclosures, 48-52
   artisans cottages, 51
   Birmingham Heath, 47, 54-6, 57
   Handsworth Common, *83, 85*
Hardy, Julius, 22, 27
Harris, J.R., 3
Hausted, Revd. John (schoolmaster), 4, 32
Herschel, Sir William, 40, 41-2, 74
hexagon coins, 189-90
Hills, Richard, 108, 110
House of Lord Committee book on
      Handsworth messuages, 49-50
Hull agents, 151
Hunter, John (London surgeon), 36
Hutton, William, 24
   History of Birmingham, An, 16, 20, 21, 30

I

incomes of social elites, 153
industrialisation
   depictions on coinage and medals, 196,
      199
   division of labour, 23-4
   gentrification process, 30, 62; portraiture,
      63-76
   incomes, 153
   resistance from the old order, 210-15
inscriptions, 191-2, *192*
intaglios and seals, *XIII,* 144-5

J

James Toy and Son, 128-9
James Watt and Co, 128
Jardine, Miss (Ekaterina Woronzow's
      governess), 94
Jars, Antoine-Gabriel, the younger, 23
jasper ware
   cameo buttons, *IX,* 146
   cameos, *VI;* double sided cameos, *X;*
      'Socrates' cameo, *VIII*
Jenks, Frederick, 129
'Job Nott' (anonymous pamphleteer), 53
Johnson, Rev. Robert Augustus, 39
Johnson, Samuel, 30
Jones, Peter, 3-4, 5, 218

K

Keir, James, 2, 18, 39-40
Kemble, John Philip, 96
Kerry, Francis Thomas FitzMaurice, 3rd
      Earl of, 160
Kettle, Tilly, 63-4
knife-cases, 134-5
knives and forks, 162-3
Kretoff, Major General, 103-4
Küchler, Conrad Heinrich, 194

L

La Rochefoucauld brothers, 18
laminating, 118-19
'Lanthorn of Demosthenes' tripod, 9, 148
Lap Engine House at Soho, 122-3, 128, 129
Latchet Company, 125, 128-9, 159
Lawrence, Thomas, 67
Lawson, James, 123, 189, 190
Leeds token, 196
Leith Battery, 88
Letouche, Mr, 82
Lewis, Paul, 23
Lichfield, 4, 19
line engraving, 73
Lichtenberg, Georg Christoph, 24
Liverpool, Robert Banks Jenkinson, 2nd
      Earl of, 177, 179-80, 182
Loggie, Val, 6, 218
London Goldsmiths' Company, 204-8, 210-15
   statement on Birmingham and Sheffield
      production, 210-11, 212, 213
Lotman, Yury, 98
Lunar Society, 1, 39-40, 59

M

makers' marks, 165, 206-7, 209
Malesherbes, Chrétien de, 24
manufacturer-merchants, rise of, 30
Marxist philosophy, 46, 62
Mason, Shena, 2, 4-5, 11, 94, 97, 218-19
Matthews, Charlotte, 38, 73, 95
Matthews, William, 151
Maudslay, Henry, 125
May, Benjamin, 206
medallion of MB, *XVI*
medals, 172
   commemorating MB's achievements, 190;
      after his death, *XVI*

(medals continued...)
commemorating royal events, 197-8, *198*
design, 186, 191, 193; allegorical
     depictions, 198-9; industrial
     depictions, 196
Executions of Louis XVI and Marie
     Antoinette, 197-8, *198*
Lord Howe medal, *198*
see also fashion ('toy') goods production
medicines, 90
*Memorial Relative to Assaying and marking
     wrought plate in Birmingham,* 204, 212
merchanting, 148-52
Millar, James, 6, 66
Miller, David, 1, 2
mines
     Ireland, 82
     Parys Mine Company, 82, 122, 173, 174;
          Anglesey token, 196
     referred to in MB's notebooks, 80, 86
minting coins, 88-9
Money, J.D., 45
Monneron Brothers, 190, 193, 194, 198
Montagu, Elizabeth, 40, 164
Morrison, James, 182
Motteux, John, 194
Moussin-Pushkin, Alexei Semyonovich, 92
Muirhead, J.P., 107-8
Muirhead, Lionel, 65
Murdock, William, 11, 125, 172, *XV*
     table top engines, 128
Mynd, Thomas, 158

N
nailers, 51
Napoleonic campaigns, 105
national symbols, 198-9
Needworth Forest enclosures, 57-8
New Birmingham Directory, The, 20
Newcomen engines, 108, 111-12, 120
notebooks belonging to MB
     appearance of, 78
     archive, 77-8
     breadth of content, 78-9
     on business interests and products, 85-7;
          coinage and related items, 88-9;
          experiments, 87-8
     on food, medicines and agriculture, 90
     on making a balloon, *87*

(notebooks belonging to MB continued...)
     on Soho House, garden and property, 83-5
     recording thoughts, 79-81
     recording travels, 81-3
Nottingham, 52

O
Orders-in-Council crisis, 29
ormolu, 138, 143, 154

P
painted panels, 143
Palmer, William, 70
panels, painted, 143
Papps, Harry, 82
Paris, MB's visit to, 82-3
Parliamentary Committee on Assay Bill
     (1773), 205
     evidence given to, 210-13
     investigation into irregularities of
          manufacture, 206-8
Parys Mine Company, 82, 122, 173, 174
     Anglesey token, 196
patents, 23-4, 123
pattern books, 27, 146-7
     Boulton and Scale, *XI, XII*
     jasper cameo 'Socrates,' *VIII*
     ormolu frames, *VIII*
     Wedgwood 'Shape Drawing Book,' *XIII*
     see also design
Paul I, Emperor of Russia, 96, 100
Peel, Sir Robert, 59
Pemberton, Birmingham wholesalers, 144
Penryn token, 196
Perry Common, 49, 55
petitions relating to assaying, 204-5
Phillp, John, 42
Piers, Daniel (MB's maternal grandfather),
     31
Plated and Button Works at Soho, 128-9
platers' marks, 165, 206-7
plates, shapes and borders, *XIII*, 150, 164,
     164
platina, 156, 167
plating *see* silver and its substitutes
Pointon, Marcia, 69
Ponthon, Noel-Alexandre, 191, 194, 196
poor rates, 51
Portal, Abraham, 206

portraits, 63-76
  exhibitions, 65, 69, 72, 73, 74
  on coins, 194-5
  prints of, 70-1, 73
  replica miniatures, 69-70, 72-3
Price, Stephen, 116
Priestley, Joseph, 1, 39, 66
Priestley, Mary, 68
printing process, 70-1
printmakers, 70-1
  line engraving, 73
Privy Council Committee on coin, 173-4,
    176-7, 183
  under Lord Liverpool, 179-80, 182
Prosser, Richard, 23, 24
pumping engines, 108, *109*, 120-1, *121*, 127-8
purse runners, 159
Pushkin, Alexei Semyonovich, Moussin-, 92

Q
Quickenden, Kenneth, 9, 203, 219

R
Raspe, R.E., 67
Rees' Cyclopaedia, 114
Rennie, John, 66, 70, 122, 180
*Reply from the Petitioners of Birmingham and
    Sheffield,* 205, 213
Reynolds, S.W., 71
Rhodes, William, 74
Richmond, Duke of, 203
Riddell, Isaac, 56-7
Robinson, Ann *see* Boulton, Ann
Robinson, Dorothy, 33
Robinson, Eric, 2, 45, 61, 202
Robinson, Luke (MB's brother-in-law), 33
Robinson, Luke (MB's father-in-law), 32-3,
    47
Robinson, Mary (MB's first wife), 32-3
Roebuck, John, 108
roller spinning machine, 23
Rolling Mill at Soho, 129
Rooker, Edward, 118
rotary engine ("steam wheel"), 28, 108-10,
    111, 111-12
  at Soho, 123, 124, 127
  sun and planet gear, *111*, 112, 124
Rousseau, Jean-Jacques, 95
Royal Academy exhibitions, 65, 69, 72, 73

Royal Mint, 9-10
  attitude to MB's interests, 175, 177-8,
    179-80, 181-3
  calls for reform of, 171-2; and
    modernisation, 183
  condition and distribution of coinage,
    170-1; tokens and, 185-6
  financial crisis and countermarking, 176
Rundell and Bridge, London, 165
Russian contacts at St Petersburg, 101-2, 151
Russian Embassy, 92-3, 106
Russian mint, 80, 88-9
Russian visitors to Soho, 7, 94-8, 100-1, 102,
    106
Ruston, Edward, 118

S
Sablukov, Ekaterina and Nikolai, 102-3
Saint-Fond, Barthélemy Faujas de, 14-15
Samoilov, Count Alexander, 102
sauce tureen, *163*, 164-5
Savery steam pumps, 108
Scale, John, 78, 124, 145
Schaak, J.S.C., *II*, 64
Schlatter, Felix, 102
Schofield, Robert, 2
Schweppe, Jacob, 39
seals, 144-5
sets of plated items, 166
Sharp, William, 73
Sheffield, 4, 20, 204-5
  campaign for Assay Office, 204-9
Sheffield Cutlers' Company, 204
Sheffield plate, 153, 155, 157, 158, 160,
    161-2, 166
  increase in production, 165, 167-8
  knives and forks, 162-3
  ladies' toilette services, 166
Shelburne, William Petty, 2nd Earl of, 201,
    203
shippers' identity codes, 151-2
Siddons, Sarah, 41
silver and its substitutes, 153-69
  buckles, 158, *158*
  candlesticks, 159, 159-61, *160*
  close plating, 158-9, 168
  coinage, 170, 182
  cutlery, 162-3
  diner services, *XIII*, 150, *163*, *164*, 164-5, *166*

(silver and its substitutes continued...)
filigree items, 159
increase in Sheffield plate production,
    165, 167-8
investigation into irregularities, 206-8
ladies' toilette services, 166
medals, 197
platers' marks, 165
platina, 167
purse runners, 159
snuffers, 161
tea-urns and teapots, 161
tutenague, 156, 159-60, 167
Simond, Louis, 29
Skipwith, Thomas, 205
Small, William, 8, 39, 66, 87, 108-9
Smeaton, John, 67
Smethwick *see* Soho Foundry, Smethwick
Smiles, Samuel, 2, 32, 50
Smirnov, Yakov (James Smirnove), 93
letters to MB, 94, 95, 98, 100
Smith, James and Benjamin, 78, 125
Snow Hill, MB's family home
preparations at MB's marriage to AB, 34
servants, 34-5
Snow Hill manufactory and warehouse, 31-
    2, 85, 118
snuffers, 161
Soho archives, *ix*, 2
Soho Foundry, Smethwick, *viii*
exports, 88
opening, 18, 116-17
under James Watt and Co, 128
Soho House
building of, *1*, 34
buildings: contents and decoration, 35,
    134; fossilry, 36; museum plans, 36;
    observatory, 84; re-design and
    refurbishment, 41-2; study and
    library, 35-6
garden, 42, 84-5
Handsworth enclosure act and, 48-9, 52,
    83, 85
household: family coach, 37; menus, 38,
    39; records of, 78-9; servants, 35
Wedgwood's visits to, 133
Woronzow's visits to, 7, 94-8, 102; and his
    son, Mikhail, 100-1; correspondence
    relating to, 98-100

Soho Manufactory, *viii*, 34, 108
copper coinage, 173
enclosures act and, 56, 57, *83*
end of manufacture, 128-9
Engine Works, 124, 128
Engine Yard (1801-1804), 124-5
MB acquires freehold, 47-8
MB leases land, 5, 34, 47, 118
MB's notebook entries, 85-6
Plated and Button Works, 128-9; button
    making, 118-19, 145-6, 156-7, 167;
    laminating, 118-19; silver and its
    substitutes, 153-69
power (in 1805), 127-8
views of, *117, 119, 126*; and Watt's
    pumping engine, *121*
water mill, 8, 117-20; pumping engine,
    120-1, *121*, 129; rebuilding (1785-86),
    121-2; steam power, 122-3
Soho Mint, 122
construction, 123-4, 174; axonometric
    view of, *117*
Crescent Building, 125-6, *126*
demolition of, 131
design and technology, 183-200; technical
    aspects, 187-90
distribution from, 179
power systems, 116-31, 123-4, 126-7, 129;
    at the New Mint, 126-7, 129-31; Lap
    Engine House, 122-3, 128, 129;
    Rolling Mill, 129
production, 177, 181, 182, 186, 188-9;
    machinery, 122, 126-7, 130
Russian visitors to, 94, 96-7, 102, 106
under the Latchet Company (1798-9), 125-7
Soho Plate Company, 128
Soho Volunteer Corps, 59
Somerville, Mary Fairfax, 104
Southern, John, 123, 126
spoons, 162
St Petersburg, 97, 101-2, 151
Staffordshire and Worcestershire canal, 16
Staffordshire enclosures, 46-7
stationers, 79
steam power technology, *viii*, 18, 81, 86
beam engine, 110-11, 127, 128
Boulton and Watt, 107-15, 117, 120-1;
    manufacture of engines, 124-5;
    pumping engine (1777), *109*

(steam power technology continued...)
  design characteristics, 114-15
  pumping engines, 108, *109*, 120-1, *121*, 127-8
  rotary engine ("steam wheel"), 108-10, *111*, 111-12; at Soho, 123, 124, 127; sun and planet gear, *111*, 112, 124
  used at Soho, 120-5, *121*, 127-9; coinage pressing, 126-7, 129-31
  straight line motion, 112
Stobart, John, 17
Stokes, Dr. Robert, 39, 40
Stourbridge, 17, 19
Stroganov, Count Pavel Alexandrovich, 105
Stuart, James, 148
Sutton Coldfield enclosures, 54
Suworow, Field-Marshal Alexander, 96
  medal, 99, *195*
Symons, Dr David, 9-10, 219

T
table top engine, 128
tableware
  cruet designs, *166*
  knives and forks, 162-3
  plates, shapes and borders, *XIII*, 150, 164, *164*
  sauce tureen, *163*, 164-5
  spoons, 162
Tait, Fiona, 6-7, 219
Talbot, Lord, 57
tankards, 161-2
Tann, Jennifer, 2, 3, 107, 202
Tassie, James, 144
Taylor, John (snuff box manufacturer), 25, 26
tea-urns and teapots, 161
Techniques Medallic scale medal, *191*
technology, art and design, 185-200
Telford, Thomas, 65
Tettenhall enclosures, 52
Theatre Royal, Birmingham, 95-6, 99
Thomason, Edward, 24, 25
Thompson, F.M.L., 61
Time Team (tv programme), 131
Timmins, Samuel, 22-3
Tipton, 18-19
Tipton Green chemical works, 18
token production, 186, 196
  Lancaster-Eccleston token, 199, 200

(token production continued...)
  technical aspects to, 187, 189
  Wilkinson token, *195*, 195-6
Tonson, Jacob, 47
tortoiseshell boxes, *VI*, 140-1
'toy' goods *see* fashion ('toy') goods production
transportation
  discomforts, 37
  innovations, 18th and 19th centuries, 15-18
  of exports goods from Etruria, 151-2
  recorded in MB's notebooks, 81-3
Treasury of England, 172
Trent and Mersey (Grand Trunk) canal, 16, 133
Tungate, Sue, 10, 219
tunnel, Soho Mint, 130-1, *131*
turn-pikes, 15
Turner, Michael, *English Parliamentary Enclosure*, 46
tutenague, 156, 159-60, 167

U
Uglow, Jenny, *ix*, 2, 219

V
van Marum, Martinus, 22
vases
  candle vases, ormolu and white marble, *VII*, 142-3
  MB's interest in, 135-9
  metal mounts, 136-7, 138
Vernon, Lord, 57
Victoria County History, 117-18
Volta, Alessandro, 15
von Breda, Carl Frederick, *III*, 67-8
  letters to MB, 69, 71

W
Wakelin, Inigo, 211-12
Wales, 82
Walker, Adam, 22
Walker, Zaccheus, 66, 74, 148, 151
Walsall, 17, 19
Walsall turnpike, 52
water mill at Soho Manufactory
  construction and running, 117-20
  rebuilding, 121-2
  steam power at, 122-3
  Watt pumping engine, 120-1

water power, 116-31
Watt, Ann (JW's wife)
  on MB, 31
Watt, Annie, 37
Watt, James, 1, 2, 7-8, 17, 28, 39, 49, 86
  copy press, 113
  on first visit to Soho, 118
  on MB, 30
  portraits, 67, 68-9, 70, 74
  start of partnership with MB, 110, 120
  statue, *XV*
  steam engine development, 107-15, 120-1
Watt, James Jr, 78, 125
Wedgwood, Josiah, 1, 8-9, 22
  canal construction and, 15-16
  letters on MB and production, 133, 134,
    137, 140, 141-2
  letters to MB, 134, 138-9, 145, 149-50
  Lunar Society and, 39
  relationship with MB, 132-52; business
    rivalry, 135, 137-9, 145; design
    influences, 147-8; intaglios and seals,
    144-5; merchanting, 27, 148-52;
    purchases from MB, 134-5; supply of
    cameos to MB, 139-40
  'Shape Drawing Book,' *XIII*
Wedgwood and Bentley, 132-52
Wednesbury pit, 16
Wesley, John, 82
West Bromwich, 19
  enclosures, 52
West Midlands region, 17, 23, 45
  interests of the elite, 46, 61
Westwood, Arthur, 202
Westwood, John Senior, 187
Whitehurst, John
  letter to MB, 39
Wilkins, Dr Charles, 192

Wilkinson token, *195*, 195-6
Wilkinson, John, 74, 123, 186, 194-5, *195*
Wilkinson, Joseph, 205
Wilkinson, William, 61, 123
Willenhall, 19
Williams, Thomas, 173, 174, 186, 196
Willmore and Alston, 158-9
Withering, William, 39, 43, 68, 70
Wolverhampton, 17-18, 19
Worcester, 19
Woronzow, Count Alexander, 7, 41, 92-106
  letters to MB, 99, 100, 103, 105
  on Pavel and Madame Bacounin, 102-3
  on Russia at turn of 19th century, 101
Woronzow, Count Semyon Romanovich, 92,
  93, *93*
Woronzow, Countess Ekaterina, 93, 99, 103-4
  letter to MB on Battle of Trafalgar, 105
  marriage, 106
Woronzow, Mikhail, 93, 94-5, 100-1
Wrigley, E.A., 14, 15
Wyatt, James, 41, 164
Wyatt, John, 23-4, 118
  on MB, 42-3
Wyatt, Samuel, 41, 74
Wyon, Thomas, 194

Y
Yardley property bought by MB, 47
Young, Arthur, 4, 22
  *Farmer's Tour through the East of England,
    The*, 30
  on enclosures, 50, 51

Z
Zamoyski, Stanislaw Kostka, 103
Zoffany, Johan, 65
Zumpe (piano manufacturer), 35